SNAPPY SAYINGS

Wit & wisdom from the world's greatest minds

Bradford G. Wheler

BookCollaborative.com

Cazenovia, New York

SNAPPY SAYINGS

By Bradford G. Wheler

Wit & wisdom from the world's greatest minds

BookCollaborative.com
P.O. Box 403
Cazenovia, NY 13035
Editor@www.BookCollaborative.com

ISBN-13 978-0-9822538-0-9

Library of Congress Control Number: 2008911856
Humor & Wit, Quotations, History & Criticism

Cover and Interior Design by AuthorSupport.com

Printed in the United States of America

CONTENTS

Acknowledgments

This book is the result of years of love and enjoyment of and with history, art, humor, and the English language. I'm not sure how to thank all the people in my life who helped with this process. My parents and relatives for sure, many fine teachers and professors, also my interesting and engaging friends, I need to thank them all.

A few people deserve special thank for their direct involvement in this book. My wife Julie for encouraging me to do something with the thousands of quotations I collected and had collecting dust in the closet. My niece Anne Redmond for not only encouraging me to produce this book but agreeing to give up much of her January break from Cornell to work on the book with me. Without her artist's eye and computer skills I never would have gotten off dead center. She made the work fun and helped form the vision of what I hope is a somewhat insightful but mostly fun book.

Also a very special thank you to my dear friend Jay Walker for his thoughtful foreward. Jay is a true lover of books and has one of the finest private libraries in the country. I've known Jay since the mid 1970's when we lived together as members of the Sigma Phi Society at Cornell University. His genius, audacity, and energy are only exceeded by his generous giving of himself to his family and friends.

I owe a great deal to several professionals without whom I could never have completed the book. Nancy Kelner who took my hand written quotations and my cut and paste biographies and turned them into working documents. Michelle and Jerry Dorris at AuthorSupport.com for interior and cover design and layout. I also want to thank them for all the hand holding they did. There were so many things I didn't know about producing a book. Simom, Ethan, and their co-worker on the one to one training team at the Apple Store for patiently working on my computer skills. Thank you to my web designer Brian Hoke at Bentley & Hoke LLC. Your work is just beginning. I also want to thank the support staff at Lightning Source Inc.

Thank you all for not only helping me with this book but opening my eyes to several new and fun projects.

Foreword

Pithy quotations, much like jokes, play an unusual role in our lives. Though we are hard pressed to remember more than a few of them, their impact runs much deeper. As they are consumed, they seem to bypass our memory pathways and go directly to some special place in the brain that allows us to feel the words, like a kind of music. The sentences, like notes, disappear, and an emotion is called forth as if reading were not involved. This is the "magic" of a written communication that reaches us at a very different level.

Much as we do not have to think about laughing, to instantly laugh at a humorous anecdote or saying, the same is true to feel the essential truth of a quotation — a few short words that we intuitively recognize as revealing an insight, a confirmation, or a connection to our rich patterns of experience.

A collected book of quotations presents us with an unusual challenge. It is not a book to be read in the classic sense of a sequential story. Though it can be used as reference book for speechwriters, that is not the intent with this volume. There are far larger and more weighty volumes filled with every imaginable quote. And, of course, the Internet, opens a world of a billion saying and quotations to endlessly browse.

Instead, the author has taken the hard task of culling and selecting from a world of infinite possibilities and combinations, much like a master distiller must carefully select and blend his ingredients to offer up a sensation both pleasant and stimulating. His goal is simple. If successful, we might sit back and simply enjoy the sensation of a thought that has stood the test of time.

The result is a book to be tasted or sipped, much like one might pour oneself a small after-dinner drink from a bar stocked with hundreds of exotic liqueurs. Drink too much or mix them together, and the effect is lost. Select and savor just the right one, and a meal becomes a memory.

As you open a page at random and choose your elixir, you are transported to another place and time. Whether it is the smile of irony, the nod of recognition, or the slight shake of the head that reminds us, "oh, how true that is," the joy of a wonderful quotation is not in the remembering or repeating of it, but in the simple act of allowing it to melt into the fabric of the mind, like some cotton candy of thought, sweet, ephemeral, and yet deeply satisfying in a wonderful and human way.

Jay Walker

Mr. Walker is the founder of Priceline.com and Walker Digital. He is the recipient of Cornell University's 2009 Entrepreneur of the Year Award.

Introduction

This book didn't start as a book. It certainly didn't start as a part of a new business publishing venture (BookCollaborative.com) that marries the internet, outsourcing, social networks, and on demand printing. My original idea was to collect fun "Snappy" quotations you could enjoy reading and maybe actually use in a speech, or toast, or at a party. I envisioned an indexable card system. The cards would fit in your pocket for quick reference and re-file themselves for future retrieval by topic. It was a variation on the old library card file system, for those of us old enough to remember that.

Thus started my decades long collection of hand written 3'' by 5" index cards of "Snappy Sayings". As the number approached 3,000 and the topic indexed file boxes became yards long, I realized I was facing a time when I would actually have to do something with these wonderful words.

I decided to prefect my indexable, auto-re-filing, pocket fitting card system. Thus Joke Box/Quote Box was, if not born, at least conceived. I determined the practical size of the cards to fit in your pocket. How many easy to read lines per card. How many cards per Joke Box/Quote Box. How many index topics per box, and on and on. On paper, I had it figured out. Of course manufacturing, distributing and marketing an unknown product that looked sort of like a book and by 2000 was outperformed by the simplest of computer databases was somewhat problematic.

Deciding to leave these practical problems for later, I plowed ahead based on my calculations. Eighteen topics per Joke Box/ Quote Box, about twelve cards per topic and about three "Snappy Saying" per card. Now I had the parameters to produce the content for the first Joke Box/Quote Box. Just pick the best 700 – 800 quotations out of my 3,000 index cards of "Snappy Sayings", organize them into 18 topics of about 12 sheets in a way that would be really fun, no… GREAT FUN to read and use.

I poured over my index card collection, selecting about 1600 – 1700 "Snappy Sayings" organizing them into twenty-two groups. Then I reduced it to 800 or so organized in page order for the twenty-two topics. I carefully placed each page group of index cards on the face of the photocopier and I had my hand written draft of "Snappy Sayings".

That's where the project stalled for about five years. In December 2007, my wife asked if I was ever going to do anything with that book stuff in the cabinet? It's not really a book. It's, it's well, it's sort of hard to explain. Her comment was "maybe it should be a book".

Around Christmas I was visiting with my niece Anne who was home from Cornell. Somehow the topic came up. Anne said "why not do a book, you can always do your box thing later". That, along with her offer of help, persuaded me to knock the five years of dust off my draft and produce this book.

During this period I was reading several interesting books

(Wikinomics, Groundswell, The Innovator's Solution, Microtrends, Predictably Irrational, Seeing What's Next, Strategic Intuition, Outliers, Buy-ology, and others) and thinking there had to be better business models than my last business. As the book progressed the idea for a business venture took shape. The book became a vehicle to develop a collaborative publishing venture using twenty first century technical developments and focusing on two areas of personal enjoyment, Wit & Wisdom and Art & Artists. For a detailed explanation go to www.BookCollaborative.com.

With BookCollaborative.com's first publication what you get is about 800 "Snappy Sayings" illustrated and organized into twenty-two chapters. These "Snappy Sayings" are distilled from many thousands of quotations I have read. They have been filtered through my unique and ___________ (you fill in the blank) worldview and sense of humor.

My hope is you will find it funny, insightful and enjoyable. Really what I want is for you to have GREAT FUN with "Snappy Sayings" from some of the brightest and wittiest minds of all times. It is also my hope that the second edition of Snappy Sayings will replace most of the current illustrations with original art and photos from collaborating artists. As you read through the book, if any of your drawings, photos, or paintings better fits the spirit of the quotations on that page go to www.BookCollabortive.com and suggest that they be included in the second edition of Snappy Sayings.

Bradford G. Wheler
Cazenovia, N.Y. 2009

Chapter 1

Money

Honesty is the best policy – when there is money in it.

- Mark Twain (1835 – 1910)

Creditors have better memories than debtors.

- Benjamin Franklin (1706 – 1790)

I'm a rich man as long as I don't pay my creditors.

- Titus Maccius Plautus (255– 184 BC)

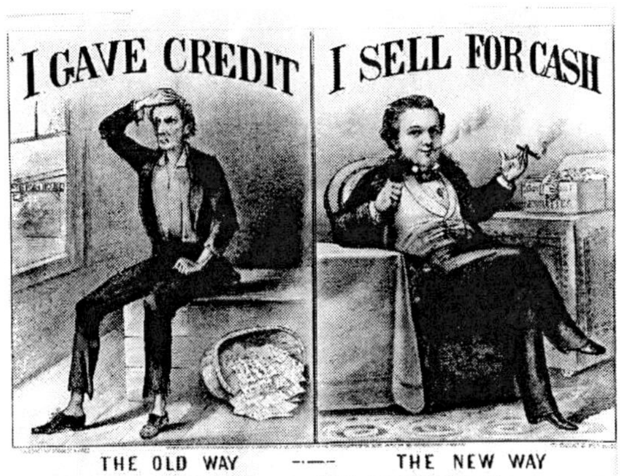

Nothing is so well fortified that money cannot capture it.

- CICERO (106 – 43 BC)

In this world nothing is certain but death and taxes.

- BENJAMIN FRANKLIN (1706 – 1790)

Money-getters are the benefactors of our race, to them .... are we indebted for our institutions of learning, and of art, our academies, colleges and churches.

- P. T. BARNUM (1810 – 1891)

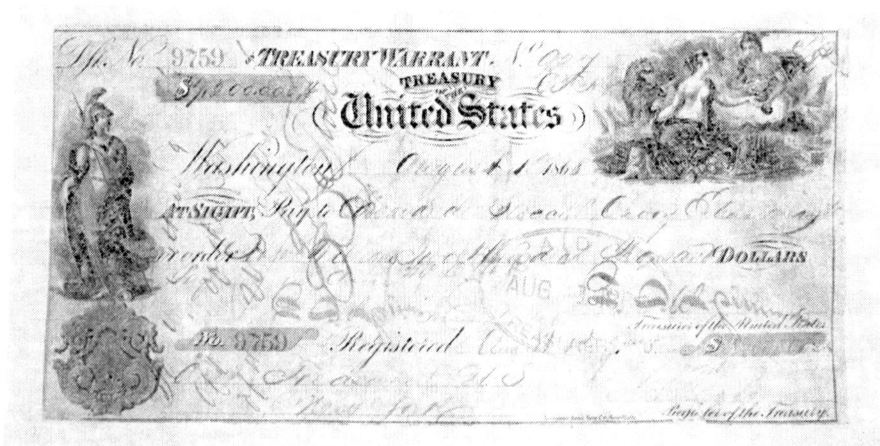

Cancelled Check From the Alaska Purchase

I've been rich and I've been poor – and believe me, rich is better.

- Sophie Tucker (1884 – 1966)

By the time we've made it, we've had it.

- Malcolm Forbes (1919 – 1990)

The two most beautiful words in the English language are "check enclosed".

- Dorothy Parker (1893 – 1967)

I enjoy being a highly overpaid actor.

- ROGER MOORE (1927 –)

Cocaine is God's way of telling you you've got too much money.

- ROBIN WILLIAMS (1951 –)

I hope you'll accept my personal IOU. It's worth its weight in gold.

- W. C. FIELDS (1880 – 1946)

I believe that the power to make money is a gift from God.

- John D. Rockefeller (1839 – 1937)

Lack of money is the root of all evil.

- George Bernard Shaw (1856 – 1950)

I'd like to live like a poor man with lots of money.

- Pablo Picasso (1881 – 1973)

Money often costs too much.

- RALPH WALDO EMERSON (1803 – 1882)

After a certain point, money is meaningless.
It ceases to be the goal.
The game is what counts.

- ARISTOTLE ONASSIS (1906 – 882)

Money is better then poverty, if only for financial reasons.

- WOODY ALLEN (1935 –)

The trouble with being poor is that it takes up all of your time.

- Willem De Kooning (1904 – 1997)

Gentility is what is left over from rich ancestors after the money is gone.

- John Ciardi (1916 – 1986)

Virtue has never been as respectable as money.

- Mark Twain (1835 – 1910)

While you're saving your face, you're losing your ass.

- LYNDON B. JOHNSON (1908 – 1973)

A billion here, a billion there – pretty soon it adds up to real money.

- SENATOR EVERETT DIRKSEN (1896 – 1969)

A nickel ain't worth a dime anymore.

- YOGI BERRA (1925 –)

When it is a question of money, everybody is of the same religion.

- VOLTAIRE (1694 – 1778)

It is only by not paying one's bills that one can hope to live in the memory of the commercial classes.

- OSCAR WILDE (1694 – 1900)

Saving is a very fine thing. Especially when your parents have done it for you.

- WINSTON CHURCHILL (1874 – 1965)

Make money and the whole nation will conspire to call you a gentleman.

- George Bernard Shaw (1856 – 1950)

The chief value of money lies in the fact that one lives in a world in which it is overestimated.

- H. L. Mencken (1880 – 1956)

Money doesn't satisfy greed; it stimulates it.

- Publilius Syrus (85 – 43 BC)

They say that money talks, but the only thing it ever said to me was goodbye.

- Joe Louis (1914 – 1981)

Nobody works as hard for his money as the man who marries it.

- Frank Mckinney "Kin" Hubbard (1868 – 1930)

My problem lies in reconciling my gross habits with my net income.

- Errol Flynn (1909 – 1959)

Income-tax returns are the most imaginative fiction being written today.

- HERMAN WOUK (1915 –)

The income tax has made liars out of more Americans than golf.

- WILL ROGERS (1879 – 1935)

The hardest thing in the world to understand is income tax.

- ALBERT EINSTEIN (1879 – 1955)

Chapter 2

Advice

Whoever fights a monster should see to it that in the process he does not become a monster.

- Friedrich Wilhelm Nietzsche (1844 – 1900)

No man can think clearly when his fists are clenched.

- George Jean Nathan (1882 – 1958)

He is more likely to contribute heat than light to discussion.

- Woodrow Wilson (1858 – 1924)

It is better to debate a question without settling it than to settle a question without debating it.

- JOSEPH JOUBERT (1754 – 1854)

Plato

Wise men talk because they have something to say, fools because they have to say something.

- PLATO (428 – 348 BC)

Wisdom comes by disillusionment.

- GEORGE SANTAYANA (1863 – 1952)

To receive a favor is to sell your liberty.

- PUBLILIUS SYRUS (85 – 43 BC)

'Tis an ill cook that cannot lick his own fingers.

- William Shakespeare (1564 – 1616)

He that lies down with dogs shall rise up with fleas.

- Benjamin Franklin (1706 – 1790)

Every man who will not have softening of the heart must at last have softening of the brain.

- G. K. Chesterson (1874 – 1936)

Neville Chamberlain & Adolf Hitler

The one sure way to conciliate a tiger is to allow oneself to be devoured.

- Konrad Adenauer (1876 – 1967)

May God defend me from my friends; I can defend myself from my enemies.

- Voltaire (1694 – 1778)

The word friend is common, the fact is rare.

- Phaedrus (15 BC – 50 AD)

Franklin D. Roosevelt, 1931

When you get to the end of your rope, tie the knot and hang on.

- Franklin D. Roosevelt (1882 – 1945)

Genius is 1 percent inspiration and 99 percent perspiration.

- Thomas Alva Edison (1847 – 1931)

You may have genius. The contrary is, of course, probable.

- Oliver Wendell Holmes (1841 – 1935)

There's always something about your success that displeases even your best friends.

- Mark Twain (1835 – 1910)

Even a paranoid can have enemies.

- Henry Kissinger (1923 –)

Failure has no friends.

- John F. Kennedy (1917 – 1963)

A great many people think they are thinking when they are merely rearranging their prejudices.

- William James (1842 – 1910)

Minds are like parachutes: They only function when open.

- Thomas Robert Dewar (1864 – 1930)

Nothing in the world is more dangerous than sincere ignorance and conscientious stupidity.

- Martin Luther King, Jr. (1929 – 1968)

There is only one good – knowledge; and only one evil – ignorance.

- Socrates (470 – 399 BC)

An idea isn't responsible for the people who believe in it.

- DON MARQUIS (1878 – 1937)

Greater than the tread of mighty armies is an idea whose time has come.

- VICTOR HUGO (1802 – 1885)

Consistency requires you to be as ignorant today as you were a year ago.

- BERNARD BERENSON (1865 – 1959)

Character is much easier kept than recovered.

- Thomas Paine (1737 – 1809)

Thomas Paine

Consider yourself a great orator if you can talk yourself into unpleasant duties.

- Publilius Syrus (85 – 43 BC)

Experience is not what happens to a man. It is what a man does with what happens to him.

- Aldous Huxley (1894 – 1963)

The measure of a man's real character is what he would do if he knows he would never be found out.

- Thomas Babington MaCaulay (1800 – 1859)

He can compress the most words into the smallest idea of any man I have ever met.

- Abraham Lincoln (1809 – 1865)

There is no expedient to which a man will not go to avoid the labor of thinking.

- Thomas Edison (1874 – 1931)

No one ever went broke underestimating the taste of the American public.

- H. L. Mencken (1880 – 1956) / P. T. Barnum / (1810 – 1891)

When a man seeks your advice,
he generally wants your praise.

- LORD CHESTERFIELD (1694 – 1773)

He that is good for making excuses
is seldom good for anything else.

- BENJAMIN FRANKLIN (1706 – 1790)

There is nothing so absurd
but some philosopher has said it.

- CICERO (106 – 43 BC)

LAGONDA AGRICULTURAL WORKS
SPRINGFIELD
OHIO
CLARK COUNTY
HARDER, BROKAW, & CHILD

CHAPTER 3

Work

The reason worry kills more people than work is that more people worry than work.

- ROBERT FROST (1878 – 1963)

If you have a job without aggravations, you don't have a job.

- MALCOLM FORBES (1919 – 1990)

Work is much more fun than fun.

- NOEL COWARD (1899 – 1973)

There's no such thing as a free lunch.

- Milton Friedman (1912 – 2006)

Moderation is a fatal thing. Nothing succeeds like excess.

- Oscar Wilde (1854 – 1900)

Take a chance. Remember; Lady Godiva put everything she had on a horse.

- W. C. Fields (1880 – 1946)

Necessity never made a good bargain.

- Benjamin Franklin (1706 – 1790)

There are three kinds of lies: lies, damned lies, and statistics.

- Mark Twain (1835 – 1910)

Every crowd has a silver lining.

- P. T. Barnum (1810 – 1891)

If you make money quickly you must economize quickly or you'll quickly go hungry.

- Titus Maccius Plautus (255 – 184 BC)

Some folks can keep so busy doing nothing that they seem indispensable.

- FRANK MCKINNEY "KIN" HUBBARD (1868 – 1930)

Thunder is good, thunder is impressive; but it is lighting that does the work.

- MARK TWAIN (1835 – 1910)

Always be smarter than the people who hire you.

- LENA HORNE (1917 –)

False becomes true when the boss decides it is.

- PUBLILIUS SYRUS (85 – 43 BC)

Meetings are indispensable when you don't want to do anything.

- John Kenneth Galbraith (1908 – 2006)

A conference is a gathering of important people who singly can do nothing, but together can decide that nothing can be done.

- Fred Allen (1894 – 1956)

Meetings are an addictive, highly self-indulgent activity that corporations and other large organizations habitually engage in only because they cannot actually masturbate.

- Dave Barry (1947 –)

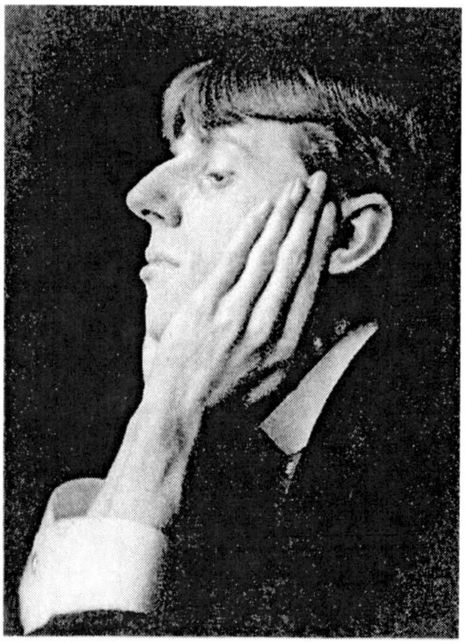

Idealism is fine, but as it approaches reality the cost become prohibitive.

- WILLIAM F. BUCKLEY, JR. *(1925 – 2008)*

Idealism increases in direct proportion to one's distance from the problem.

- JOHN GALSWORTHY (1867 – 1933)

The worst form of inequality is to try to make unequal things equal.

- ARISTOTLE (384 – 322 BC)

By working faithfully eight hours a day, you may eventually get to be a boss and work twelve hours a day.

- Robert Frost (1878 – 1963)

If ants are so busy, why do they attend so many picnics?

- W. C. Fields (1880 – 1946)

I do not like work even when someone else does it.

- Mark Twain (1835 – 1910)

Housework can kill you if done right.

- Erma Bombeck (1927 – 1996)

My father taught me to work; he did not teach me to love it.

- Abraham Lincoln (1809 – 1865)

Hard work is damn near as overrated as monogamy.

- Huey P. Long (1893 – 1935)

The world is full of willing people; some willing to work, the rest willing to let them.

- Robert Frost (1878 – 1963)

The brain is a wonderful organ. It starts working the moment you get up in the morning and doesn't stop until you get into the office.

- Robert Frost (1878 – 1963)

The trouble with the rat race is that even if you win you're still a rat.

- Lily Tomlin (1939 –)

Work is of two kinds; first altering the position of matter at or near the earth's surface relatively to other matter; second telling other people to do so. The first kind is unpleasant and ill paid – the second is pleasant and highly paid.

- Bertrand Russell (1872 – 1970)

Charles Lindbergh

Choose a job you love and you will never have to work a day in your life.

- Confucius (551 – 479 BC)

I don't know the key to success, but the key to failure is trying to please everybody.

- Bill Cosby (1937 –)

Luck is a matter of preparation meeting opportunity.

- Oprah Winfrey (1954 –)

I couldn't wait for success so I went ahead without it.

- JONATHAN WINTERS (1925 –)

It takes twenty years to make an overnight success.

- EDDIE CANTOR (1892 – 1964)

When down in the mouth, remember Jonah. He came out all right.

- THOMAS EDISON (1847 – 1931)

Chapter 4

The Professions

Being a hero is about the shortest lived profession on earth.

- Will Rogers (1879 – 1935)

Every profession has its secrets .... If it hadn't, it wouldn't be a profession.

- Hector Hugh Munro "Saki" (1870 – 1916)

The physician can bury his mistakes, but the architect can only advise his client to plant vines.

- Frank Lloyd Wright (1867 – 1959)

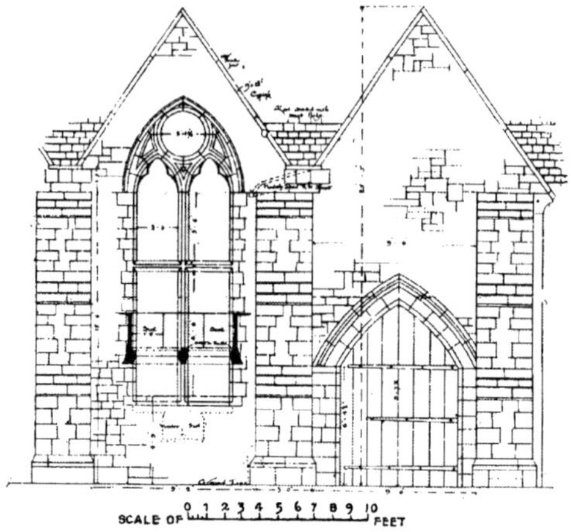

Architecture is frozen music.

- JOHANN WOLFGANG GOETHE (1749 – 1832)

If all economists were laid end to end, they would not reach a conclusion.

- GEORGE BERNARD SHAW (1856 – 1950)

An economist is a man who couldn't tell the difference between chicken salad and chicken shit.

- LYNDON B. JOHNSON (1908 – 1973)

A doctor's reputation is made by the number of eminent men who die under his care.

- George Bernard Shaw (1856 – 1950)

God heals and the doctor takes the fee.

- Benjamin Franklin (1706 – 1790)

He had had much experience of physicians, and said "the only way to keep your health is to eat what you don't want, drink what you don't like and do what you'd druther not."

- Mark Twain (1835 – 1910)

The best doctors in the world are Doctor Diet, Doctor Quiet and Doctor Merryman.

- JONATHAN SWIFT (1667 – 1745)

It's amazing the little harm they do when one considers the opportunities they have.

- MARK TWAIN (1835 – 1910)

Doctors and lawyers must go to school for years and years often with little sleep and with great sacrifice to their first wives.

- ROY G. BLOUNT, JR. (1941 –)

A lawyer with his briefcase can steal more than a thousand men with guns.

- Mario Puzo (1920 – 1999)

Lawyers are the only persons in whom ignorance of the law is not punished.

- Jeremy Bentham (1748 – 1832)

.... as scarce as lawyers in heaven.

- Mark Twain (1835 – 1910)

A successful law suit is the one worn by a policeman.

- ROBERT FROST (1870 – 1963)

Agree, for the law is costly.

- WILLIAM CAMDEN (1551 – 1623)

Lawyers spend a great deal of time shoveling smoke.

- OLIVER WENDELL HOLMES, JR. (1841 – 1935)

Homer has taught all other poets the art of telling lies skillfully.

- Aristotle (384 – 322 BC)

There is no money in poetry; but then there is no poetry in money, either.

- Robert Graves (1895 – 1985)

T. S. Eliot

In the case of many poets, the most important thing for them to do is to write as little as possible.

- T. S. Eliot (1888 – 1965)

Free verse is like free love; it is a contradiction in terms.

- G. K. CHESTERTON (1874 – 1935)

All bad poetry springs from genuine feelings.

- OSCAR WILDE (1854 – 1900)

William Shakespeare

A poet more than thirty years old is simply an overgrown child.

- H. L. MENCKEN (1880 – 1956)

There are no dull subjects, there are only dull writers.

- H. L. Mencken (1880 – 1956)

After writing for fifteen years, it struck me I had no talent for writing. I couldn't give it up. By that time, I was already famous.

- Mark Twain (1835 – 1910)

Never let a domestic quarrel ruin a day's writing. If you can't start the next day fresh, get rid of your wife.

- Mario Puzo (1920 – 1999)

The covers of this book are too far apart.

- AMBROSE BIERCE (1842 – 1914)

This is not a novel to be tossed aside lightly. It should be thrown with great force.

- DOROTHY PARKER (1893 – 1967)

A well-written life is almost as rare as a well-spent one.

- THOMAS CARLYLE (1795 – 1881)

Without music, life would be a mistake.

- FRIEDRICH WILHELM NIETZCHE (1844 – 1900)

Wagner's music is better than it sounds.

- MARK TWAIN (1835 – 1910)

I don't know anything about music.
In my line, you don't have to.

- ELVIS PRESLEY (1935 – 1977)

Anything that is too stupid to be spoken is sung.

- VOLTAIRE (1694 – 1778)

Of all noises, I think music is the least disagreeable.

- SAMUEL JOHNSON (1709 – 1784)

Only sick music makes money today.

- FRIEDRICH WILHELM NIETZCHE (1844 – 1900)

CHAPTER 5

The Arts

There are moments when art attains almost the dignity of manual labor.

- OSCAR WILDE (1854 – 1900)

Art is a jealous mistress.

- RALPH WALDO EMERSON (1803 – 1882)

If you could say it in words, there would be no reason to paint.

- EDWARD HOPPER (1882 – 1967)

**Every time I paint
a portrait,
I lose a friend.**

- JOHN SINGER SARGENT (1856 – 1925)

A work of art is useless. So is a flower.

- OSCAR WILDE (1854 – 1900)

Everyone wants to understand painting. Why don't they try to understand the singing of the birds? People love the night, a flower, everything which surrounds them, without trying to understand them. But painting – that they must understand.

- PABLO PICASSO (1881 – 1973)

If that's art, I'm a Hottentot!

- Harry S. Truman (1884 – 1972)

Modern art is what happens when painters stop looking at girls and persuade themselves that they have a better idea.

- John Ciardi (1916 – 1986)

Abstract art is a product of the untalented, sold by the unprincipled, to the utterly bewildered.

- Al Capp (1909 – 1979)

Art, like morality, consists of drawing the line somewhere.

- G. K. CHESTERTON (1874 – 1936)

I'm glad the old masters are all dead and I only wish they had died sooner.

- MARK TWAIN (1835 – 1910)

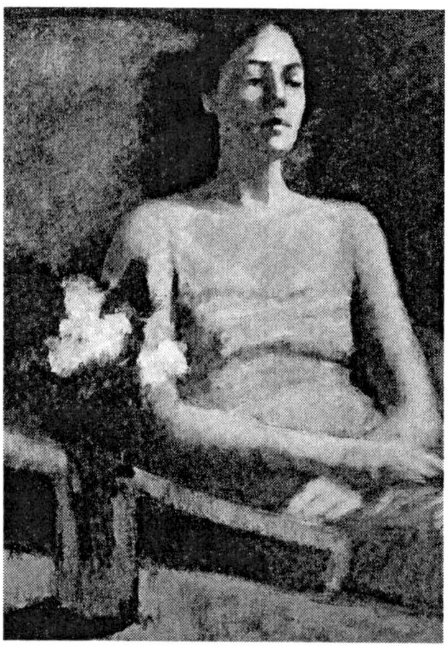

The great tragedy of the artistic temperament is that it cannot produce any art.

- G. K. CHESTERTON (1874 – 1936)

A dramatic critic is a man who leaves no turn unstoned.

- George Bernard Shaw (1856 – 1950)

Critics are eunuchs at a gang-bang.

- George Burns (1896 – 1996)

A good review from the critics is just another stay of execution.

- Dustin Hoffman (1937 –)

The play was a great success but the audience was a total failure.

- OSCAR WILDE (1854 – 1900)

There's less in this then meets the eye.

- TALLULAH BANKHEAD (1902 – 1968)

I didn't like the play, but then I saw it under adverse conditions – the curtain was up.

- GEORGE S. KAUFMAN (1889 – 1961)

I don't understand anything about the ballet; all I know is that during the intervals the ballerinas stink like horses.

- Anton Chekhov (1860 – 1904)

I love acting. It is so much more real than life.

- Oscar Wilde (1854 – 1900)

Acting: It is the most minor of gifts and not a very high class way to earn a living. After all, Shirley Temple could do it at the age of four.

- Katharine Hepburn (1907 – 2003)

Actresses will happen in the best regulated families.

- OLIVER HERFORD (1863 – 1935)

Always remember before going on stage, wipe your nose and check your flies.

- SIR ALEC GUINNESS (1914 – 2000)

Modesty in an actor is as fake as passion in a call girl.

- JACKIE GLEASON (1916 – 1987)

An actor's a guy who, if you ain't talking about him ain't listening.

- MARLON BRANDO (1924 – 2004)

A celebrity is a person who works hard all his life to become well known, then wears dark glasses to avoid being recognized.

- FRED ALLEN (1894 – 1956)

Scratch an actor and you'll find an actress.

- DOROTHY PARKER (1893 – 1967)

A sign of celebrity is that his name is often worth more than his service.

- DANIEL J. BOORSTIN (1914 – 2004)

A celebrity is one who is known to many persons he is glad he doesn't know.

- H. L. MENCKEN (1880 – 1956)

You'd be surprised how much it costs to look this cheap.

- DOLLY PARTON (1946 –)

Dorothy Parker

Hollywood is a place where they place you under contract instead of under observation.

- WALTER WINCHELL (1897 – 1972)

The only "ism" Hollywood believes in is plagiarism.

- DOROTHY PARKER (1893 – 1967)

I didn't release that movie, it escaped.

- SAMUEL GOLDWYN (1882 – 1974)

The Hollywood tradition I like best is called "sucking up to the stars".

- Johnny Carson (1925 – 2005)

Producers shouldn't get ulcers; they should give them.

- Samuel Goldwyn (1882 – 1974)

Hollywood is the only place in the world where an amicable divorce means each one gets 50 percent of the publicity.

- Lauren Bacall (1924 –)

Chapter 6

Education

Education is the best provision for old age.

- Aristotle (384 – 322 BC)

A little learning is a dangerous thing.

- Alexander Pope (1688 – 1744)

**The roots of education are bitter,
but the fruit is sweet.**

- Aristotle (384 – 322 BC)

The school of hard knocks is an accelerated curriculum.

- MENANDER (342 – 292 BC)

Two things reduce prejudice: education and laughter.

- LAURENCE J. PETER (1919 – 1988)

Education: That which reveals to the wise, and conceals from the stupid, the vast limits of their knowledge.

- MARK TWAIN (1835 – 1910)

Soap and education are not as sudden as massacre but they are more deadly in the long run.

- Mark Twain (1835 – 1910)

I must say I find television very educational. The minute somebody turns it on, I go to the library and read a good book.

- Groucho Marx (1890 – 1977)

I took a course in speed reading and was able to read "War and Peace" in twenty minutes. It's about Russia.

- Woody Allen (1935 –)

It doesn't make much difference what you study, as long as you don't like it.

- FINLEY PETER DUNNE (1867 – 1936)

Education: The path from cocky ignorance to miserable uncertainty.

- MARK TWAIN (1835 – 1910)

Education: The inculcation of the incomprehensible into the indifferent by the incompetent.

- JOHN MAYNARD KEYNES (1883 – 1946)

Is sloppiness in speech caused by ignorance or apathy? I don't know and I don't care.

- WILLIAM SAFIRE (1929 –)

Men are born ignorant, not stupid; they are made stupid by education.

- Bertrand Russell (1872 – 1970)

A learned blockhead is a greater blockhead than an ignorant one.

- Benjamin Franklin (1706 – 1790)

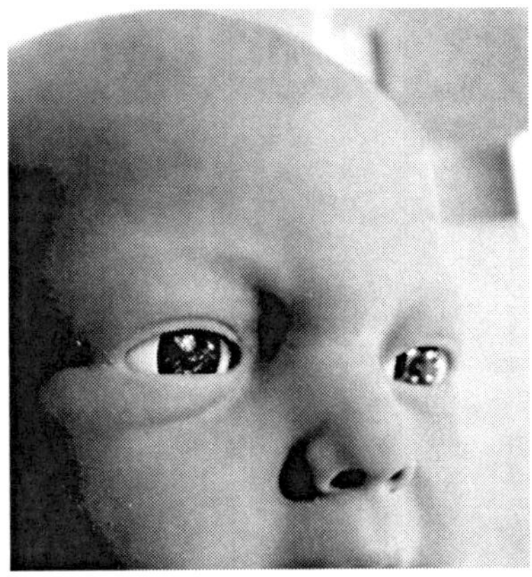

The schools ain't what they used to be and never was.

- Will Rogers (1879 – 1935)

I have never let my schooling interfere with my education.

- Mark Twain (1835 – 1910)

Lyndon B. Johnson

You ain't learning nothing when you're talking.

- LYNDON B. JOHNSON (1908 – 1973)

Wit is educated insolence.

- ARISTOTLE (384 – 322 BC)

My education was dismal. I went to a series of schools for mentally disturbed teachers.

- WOODY ALLEN (1935 –)

"Whom are you?" said he, for he had been to night school.

- GEORGE ADE (1866 – 1944)

I don't give a damn for a man that can spell a word only one way.

- Mark Twain (1835 – 1910)

Fig. 18.

Transferring gases.

Education is what you must acquire without any interference from your schooling.

- Mark Twain (1835 – 1910)

His lack of education is more than compensated for by his keenly developed moral bankruptcy.

- Woody Allen (1935 –)

When you educate a man you educate an individual; when you educate a woman you educate a whole family.

- ROBERT M. MACIVER (1882 – 1970)

A child only educated at school is an uneducated one.

- GEORGE BERNARD SHAW (1856 – 1950)

Education is the ability to listen to almost anything without losing your temper or your self-confidence.

- ROBERT FROST (1878 – 1963)

Those who educate children well are more to be honored than they who produce them; for these only gave them life, those the art of living well.

- Aristotle (384 – 322 BC)

Wonder is what the philosopher endures most; for there is no other beginning of philosophy than this.

- Plato (428 – 348 BC)

In large states, public education will always be mediocre, for the same reason that in large kitchens the cooking is bad.

- Friedrich Wilhelm Nietzche (1844 – 1900)

Those teachers and schools that truly succeed are those which inspire their students to move beyond the expectation of conventional wisdom.

- James D. Watson (1928 –) (co-discovered DNA)

Learning is not child's play; we cannot learn without pain.

- Aristotle (384 – 322 BC)

Old men are always advising young men to save money. That is bad advise. Don't save every nickel. Invest in yourself. I never saved a dollar until I was forty years old.

- Henry Ford (1863 – 1947)

You may have noticed the less I know about a subject the more confidence I have, and the more light I throw on it.

- Mark Twain (1835 – 1910)

As long as one keeps searching, the answers come.

- Joan Baez (1941 –)

He who can, does. He who cannot, teaches.

- George Bernard Shaw (1856 – 1950)

Chapter 7

Sports

Golf is the most fun you can have without taking your clothes off.

- Chi Chi Rodriguez (1935 –)

The more I practice, the luckier I get.

- Jerry Barber (1916 – 1994)

I never pray to God to make a putt. I pray to God to help me react good if I miss a putt.

- Chi Chi Rodriguez (1935 –)

Golf and sex are about the only things you can enjoy without being good at it.

- JIMMY DEMARET (1910 – 1983)

Ninety percent of the putts that fall short don't go in.

- YOGI BERRA (1925 –)

He who has the fastest golf cart never has a bad lie.

- MICKEY MANTLE (1931 – 1995)

When you win, nothing hurts.

- JOE NAMATH (1943 –)

There are two sorts of losers – the good losers, and the ones who can't act.

- LAURENCE J. PETERS (1919 – 1988)

I hate all sports as rabidly as a person who likes sports hates common sense.

- H. L. MENCKEN (1880 – 1956)

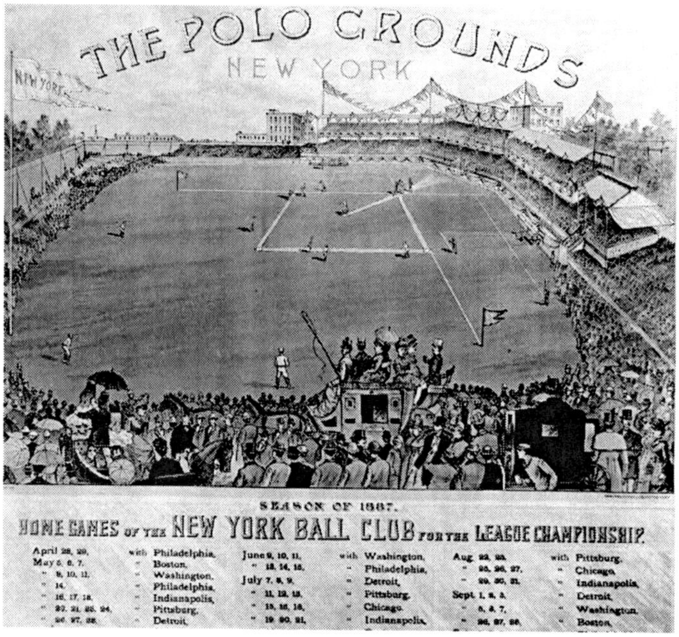

Baseball is ninety percent mental.
The other half is physical.

- YOGI BERRA (1925 –)

When I was a kid, I wanted to play base ball and join the circus. With the Yankees, I've been able to do both.

- GRAIG NETTLES (1944 –)

I'm not disloyal. I'm the most loyal player money can buy.

- DON SUTTON (1945 –)

I knew I was in trouble when they started clocking my fast ball with a sundial.

- Joe Magrane (1964 –)

It ain't bragging if you can do it.

- Dizzy Dean (1910 – 1974)

Going to bed with a woman never hurt a ball player. It's staying up all night looking for them that does you in.

- Casey Stengel (1890 – 1975)

Boxing is sort of like jazz. The better it is, the less amount of people can appreciate it.

- George Foreman (1949 –)

My toughest fight was with my first wife.

- Muhammad Ali (1942 –)

I know a lot of people think I'm dumb. Well, at least I aint' no educated fool.

- Leon Spinks (1953 –)

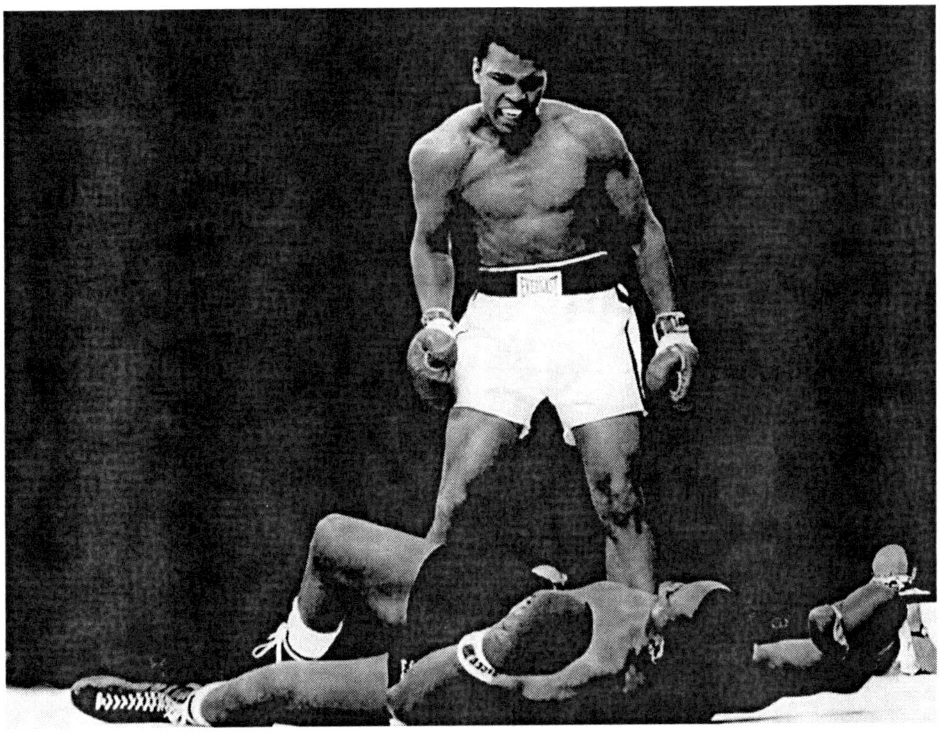

I'm so fast I could hit you before God gets the news.

- Muhammad Ali (1942 –)

Sometimes Howard [Cosell] makes me wish I was a dog and he was a fireplug.

- Muhammad Ali (1942 –)

Hurting people is my business.

- Sugar Ray Robinson (1921 – 1989)

I went to a fight the other night and a hockey game broke out.

- RODNEY DANGERFIELD (1921 – 2004)

The fans love the fighting. The players don't mind. The coaches like the fights. What's the big deal?

- DON CHERRY (1934 –)

He who lives by the cheap shot dies by the cross-check.

- STAN FISCHLER (1932 –)

We get nose jobs all the time in the NHL, and we don't even have to go to the hospital.

- Brad Park (1948 –)

I skate to where the punk is going to be, not where it has been.

- Wayne Gretzky (1961 –)

The trouble with officials is they just don't care who wins.

- Tommy Canterbury (?)

The fascination of shooting as a sport depends almost wholly on whether you are at the right or wrong end of the gun.

- P.G. Wodehouse (1881 – 1975)

To brag little – to show well – to crow gently, if in luck – to pay up, to own up, and to shut up, if beaten are the virtues of a sporting man.

- Oliver Wendell Holmes (1809 – 1894)

When man wants to murder a tiger, he calls it sport; when a tiger wants to murder him, he calls it ferocity.

- George Bernard Shaw (1856 – 1950)

There is no use in your walking five miles to fish when you can depend on being just as unsuccessful near home.

- Mark Twain (1835 – 1910)

The race is not always to the swift nor the battle to the strong, but that's the way to bet.

- DAMON RUNYON (1884 – 1946)

Horse sense is a good judgment which keeps horses from betting on people.

- W. C. FIELDS (1880 – 1946)

Wherever I go people are waving at me. Maybe if I do a good job, they'll use all their fingers.

- FRANK KING (1883 – 1969)

When you are not practicing, remember someone is practicing, and when you meet him, he will win.

- ED MACAULEY (1928 –)

LITH. BY A. HOEN & CO. BALTIMORE, MD.

PUBLISHED BY F. KLEMM, No. 254 N. CENTRAL AVE., BALTIMORE.

Chapter 8

Drink

Drink is your enemy – love your enemies.

- W. C. Fields (1880 – 1946)

One more drink and I'd be under the host.

- Dorothy Parker (1893 – 1967)

Any one who hates dogs and loves whiskey can't be all bad.

- W. C. Fields (1880 – 1946)

Candy is dandy but liquor is quicker.

- OGDEN NASH (1902 – 1971)

Drink, pretty creature, drink.

- WILLIAM WORDSWORTH (1770 – 1850)

I'm not so think as you drunk I am.

- SIR JOHN SQUIRE (1884 – 1958)

An alcoholic is someone you don't like who drinks as much as you do.

- Dylan Thomas (1914 – 1953)

Hangover: The wrath of grapes.

- Dorothy Parker (1893 – 1967)

A woman drove me to drink, and I never even had the courtesy to thank her.

- W. C. Fields (1880 – 1946)

Water, taken in moderation, cannot hurt anybody.

- MARK TWAIN (1835 – 1910)

The best audience is intelligent, well educated, and a little drunk.

- ALBEN W. BARKLEY (1877 – 1956)

I drink to make other people more interesting.

- GEORGE JEAN NATHAN (1882 – 1958)

I have taken more out of alcohol than alcohol has taken out of me.

- WINSTON CHURCHILL (1874 – 1965)

Winston Churchill

Champagne: In victory you deserve it; in defeat you need it.

- NAPOLEON BONAPARTE (1769 – 1821)

This wine is forty years old. It certainly doesn't show its age.

- CICERO (106 – 43 BC)

He that drinks fast, pays slow.

- BENJAMIN FRANKLIN (1706 – 1790)

I saw a notice which said "Drink Canada Dry" and I've just started.

- BRENDEN BEHAN (1923 – 1964)

A man must believe in something. I believe I'll have another drink!

- W. C. FIELDS (1880 – 1946)

Abstainer: A weak person who yields to the temptation of denying himself a pleasure.

- Ambrose Bierce (1842 – 1914)

I have to think hard to name an interesting man who does not drink.

- Richard Burton (1925 – 1984)

If you drink, don't drive. Don't even putt.

- Dean Martin (1917 – 1995)

Now don't say you can't swear off drinking, it's easy. I've done it a thousand times.

- W. C. Fields (1880 – 1946)

The secret of drunkenness is that it insulates us in thought, whilst it unites us in feeling.

- Ralph Waldo Emerson (1803 – 1882)

I don't drink water; it rusts pipes.

- W. C. Fields (1880 – 1946)

The Germans are exceedingly fond of Rhine wines. One tells them from the vinegar by the label.

- Mark Twain (1835 – 1910)

I've made a rule never to drink by daylight and never to refuse a drink after dark.

- H. L. Menchen (1880 – 1956)

I like liquor – its taste and effects – and that is just the reason why I never drink it.

- Thomas "Stonewall" Jackson (1824 – 1863)

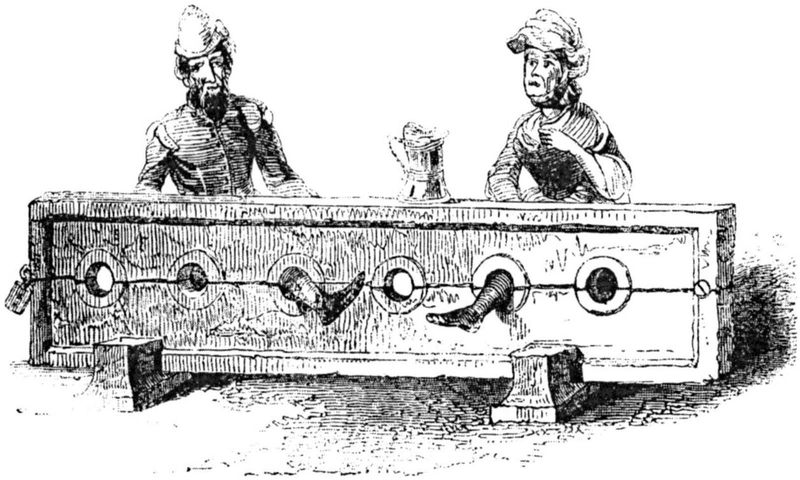

Beer is proof that God loves us and wants us to be happy.

- BENJAMIN FRANKLIN (1706 – 1790)

Drink! For you know not whence you come nor why. Drink! For you know not why you go, nor where.

- OMAR KHAYYAM (1048 – 1131)

Sometimes too much to drink is barely enough.

- MARK TWAIN (1835 – 1910)

Always do sober what you said you'd do drunk. That will teach you to keep your mouth shut.

- ERNEST HEMINGWAY (1899 – 1961)

Alcohol is the anesthesia by which we endure the operation of life.

- GEORGE BERNARD SHAW (1856 – 1950)

He who has not been at a tavern knows not what a paradise is.

- HENRY WADSWORTH LONGFELLOW (1807 – 1882)

I'm only a beer teetotaler, not a champagne teetotaler. I don't like beer.

- George Bernard Shaw (1856 – 1950)

One of the disadvantages of wine is that it makes a man mistake words for thoughts.

- Samual Johnson (1709 – 1784)

I never said all Democrats are saloonkeepers; what I said was all saloonkeepers are Democrats.

- Horace Greeley (1811 – 1872)

Prohibition officers raiding the Lunch Room of 822 Pa. Ave Wash. D.C. 23792 4/25/23.

CHAPTER 9

Sex

My brain is my second favorite organ.

- WOODY ALLEN (1935 –)

I can remember when the air was clean and sex was dirty.

- GEORGE BURNS (1896 – 1996)

Sex alleviates tension, love causes it.

- WOODY ALLEN (1935 –)

If it is worth doing, it is worth doing slowly ... very slowly.

- GYPSY ROSE LEE (1911/1914 – 1970)

Sex is good, but not as good as fresh sweet corn.

- GARRISON KEILLOR (1942 –)

You cannot separate young limbs and lechery.

- WILLIAM SHAKESPEARE (1564 – 1616)

Of all the sexual aberrations, the most peculiar is chastity.

- Rémy De Gourmont (1858 – 1915)

If men could get pregnant, abortion would be a sacrament.

- Florynce "Flo" Kennedy (1916 – 2000)

It is one of the superstitions of the human mind to have imagined that virginity could be a virtue.

- Voltaire (1694 – 1778)

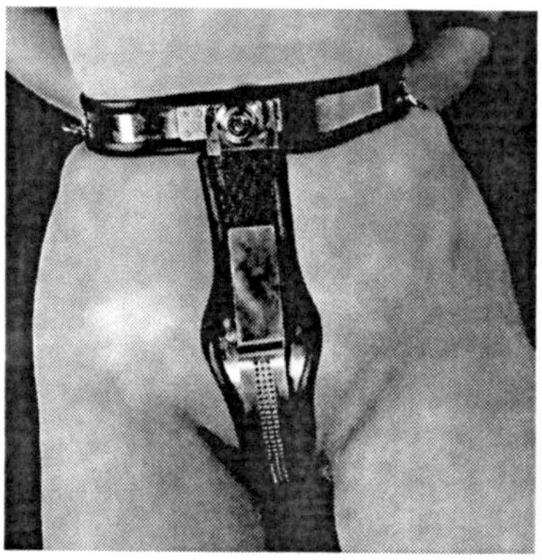

Dear Lord: Give me chastity and self restraint, but not yet.

- SAINT AUGUSTINE (354 – 430)

You gotta learn that if you don't get it by midnight, chances are you ain't gonna get it; and if you do, it ain't worth it.

- CASEY STENGEL (1891 – 1975)

Why should we take advise on sex from the pope? If he knows anything about it, he shouldn't.

- GEORGE BERNARD SHAW (1856 – 1950)

She may be good for nothing, but she's not bad for nothing.

- Mae West (1893 – 1987)

The big difference between sex for money and sex for free is that sex for money usually costs less.

- Brendan Behan (1923 – 1964)

Whoever called it necking was a poor judge of anatomy.

- Groucho Marx (1890 – 1977)

Woody Allen

Bisexuality immediately doubles your chances for a date on Saturday night.

- WOODY ALLEN (1935 –)

If only it was as easy to banish hunger by rubbing the belly as it is to masturbate.

- DIOGENES "THE CYNIC" (412 – 323 BC)

Masturbation! The amazing availability of it.

- JAMES JOYCE (1882 – 1941)

The good thing about masturbation is that you don't have to dress up for it.

- Truman Capote (1924 – 1984)

Hey! Don't knock masturbation. It's sex with someone I love.

- Woody Allen (1935 –)

Celibacy is not hereditary.

- Oscar Wilde (1854 – 1900)

What do I know about sex?
I'm a married man.

- TOM CLANCY (1947 –)

Familiarity breeds contempt – and children.

- MARK TWAIN (1835 – 1910)

If I'm not in bed by eleven at night,
I go home.

HENNY YOUNGMAN (1906 – 1998)

Sex: The thing that takes up the least amount of time and causes the most amount of trouble.

- John Barrymore (1882 – 1942)

The pleasure is momentary, the position ridiculous, and the expense damnable.

- Lord Chesterfield (1694 – 1773)

Power is the ultimate aphrodisiac.

- Henry Kissinger (1923 –)

Is it not strange that desire should so many years outlive performance?

- WILLIAM SHAKESPEARE (1564 – 1616)

There are girls who manage to sell themselves, whom no one would take as a gift.

- NICOLAS CHAMFONT (1741 – 1794)

Remember if you smoke after sex, you're doing it too fast.

- WOODY ALLEN (1935 –)

Lust wants what it can't have.

Publilius Syrus (85 – 43 BC)

Immorality: the morality of those who are having a better time.

- H. L. Mencken (1880 – 1956)

Sex without love is an empty experience, but, as empty experiences go, it's one of the best.

- Woody Allen (1935 –)

Tell him I've been too fucking busy – or vice versa.

- Dorothy Parker (1893 – 1967)

To err is human – but it feels divine.

- Mae West (1893 – 1987)

My Dad told me "Anything worth having is worth waiting for." I waited until I was fifteen.

- Zsa Zsa Gabor (1917 –)

When choosing between two evils, I always like to take the one I've never tried before.

- Mae West (1893 – 1987)

The last time I was in a woman, I was visiting the Statue of Liberty.

- Woody Allen (1935 –)

Mae West

Dancing: A perpendicular expression of a horizontal desire.

- George Bernard Shaw (1856 – 1950)

A terrible thing happened to me last night – Nothing.

- Phyllis Diller (1917 –)

Wishing
You
Love

Chapter 10

Love

Kind words can be short and easy to speak, but their echoes are truly endless.

- Mother Teresa (1910 – 1997)

The gods never let us love and be wise at the same time.

- Publilius Syrus (85 – 43 BC)

A woman has got to love a bad man once or twice in her life to be thankful for a good one.

- Marjorie Kinnan Rawlings (1896 – 1953)

We cannot really love anybody with whom we never laugh.

- AGNES REPPLIER (1855 – 1950)

Love is the triumph of imagination over intelligence.

- H. L. MENCKEN (1880 – 1956)

One is very crazy when in love.

- SIGMUND FREUD (1856 – 1939)

Love is a serious mental disease.

- PLATO (428 – 348 BC)

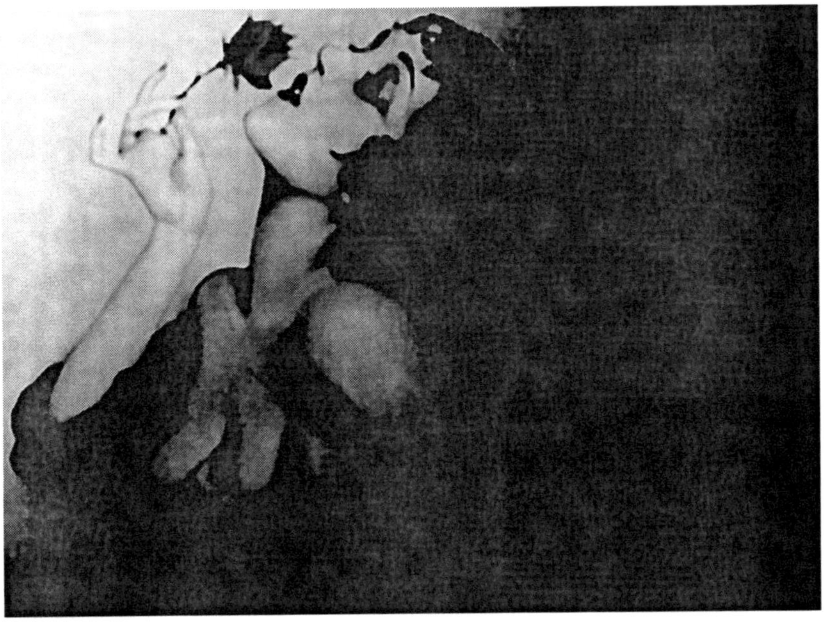

Great loves too must be endured.

- Coco Chanel (1883 – 1971)

Oh, what lies there are in kisses!

- Heinrich Heine (1797 – 1856)

Love is the state in which man sees things most decidedly as they are not.

- Friedrich Wilhelm Nietzsche (1844 – 1900)

Love takes up where knowledge leaves off.

- Thomas Aquinas (1225 – 1274)

Love: A temporary insanity curable by marriage.

- Ambrose Bierce (1842 – 1914)

Love is a fire. But whether it is going to warm your heart or burn down your house, you can never tell.

- Joan Crawford (1905 – 1977)

If two people love each other, there can be no happy end to it.

- Ernest Hemingway (1899 – 1961)

A fellow who sets out on love's road with an empty purse is taking on greater labors than Hercules.

- Titus Maccias Plautus (255 – 184 BC)

Love is the crocodile on the river of desire.

- Bhartrihari (6th or 7th Century)

First love is only a little foolishness and a lot of curiosity.

- George Bernard Shaw (1856 – 1950)

I don't think anyone knows I love the girl; I haven't done anything really silly yet.

- TITUS MACCIUS PLAUTUS (255 – 184 BC)

When two people love each other, they don't look at each other, they look in the same direction.

- GINGER ROGERS (1911 – 1995)

What a woman says to a panting lover should be written on the wind and running water.

- CATULLUS (84 – 54 BC)

Love is the irresistible desire to be irresistibly desired.

- Robert Frost (1878 – 1963)

When we want to read of the deeds that are done for love whither do we turn? To the murder column.

- George Bernard Shaw (1856 – 1950)

A woman loves you or she hates you; there's no other choice.

- Publilius Syrus (85 – 43 BC)

Never go to bed mad. Stay up and fight.

- Phyllis Diller (1917 –)

Love is the delightful interval between meeting a beautiful girl and discovering that she looks like a haddock.

- JOHN BARRYMORE (1882 – 1942)

There is always something ridiculous about the passions of people whom one has ceased to love.

- OSCAR WILDE (1854 – 1900)

Love is the answer, but while you are waiting for the answer, sex raises some pretty good questions.

- WOODY ALLEN (1935 –)

The average man is more interested in a woman who is interested in him than he is in a woman with beautiful legs.

- Marlene Dietrich (1901 – 1992)

In love, beauty counts for more than good advice.

- Publilius Syrus (85 – 43 BC)

Look for a sweet person. Forget rich.

- Estee Lauder (1908 – 2004)

Love is the greatest refreshment in life.

- PABLO PICASSO (1881 – 1973)

No one is able to flee from death or love.

- PUBLILIIUS SYRUS (85 – 43 BC)

Love is a game that two can play and both win.

- EVA GABOR (1919 – 1995)

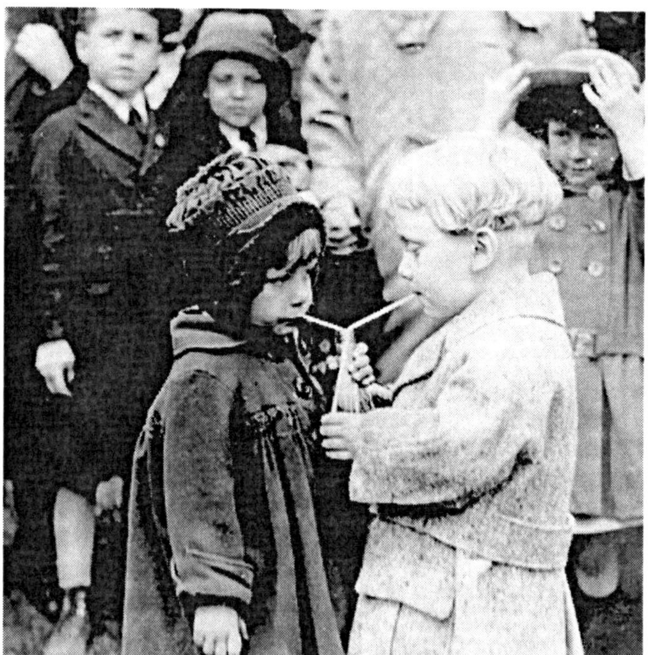

Christianity has done love a great service by making it a sin.

- ANATOLE FRANCE (1844 – 1924)

Men always want to be a woman's first love – woman like to be a man's last romance.

- OSCAR WILDE (1854 – 1950)

Women give men the very gold of their lives. But they invariably want it back in small change.

- OSCAR WILDE (1854 – 1950)

Never forget that the most powerful force on earth is love.

- NELSON ROCKEFELLER (1908 – 1979)

Ἔλα καί δός μου μιά φορά
'ακόμα τά φιλιά σου
Ἔλα νά βρῶ παρηγοριά
μέσα στήν αγκαλιά σου.

Chapter 11

Marriage

The husband who wants a happy marriage should learn to keep his mouth shut and his check book open.

- Groucho Marx (1890 – 1977)

Husbands are like fires. They go out if unattended.

- Zsa Zsa Gabor (1917 –)

Husbands never become good; they merely become proficient.

- H. L. Mencken (1880 – 1956)

My wife was too beautiful for words but not for arguments.

- John Barrymore (1882 – 1942)

Woman begins by resisting a man's advances and ends by blocking his retreat.

- Oscar Wilde (1854 – 1900)

Marriage is really tough because you have to deal with feelings and lawyers.

- Richard Pryor (1940 – 2005)

THE PLEASURES OF THE COUNTRY.
SWEET HOME.

'Home Sweet Home' must surely have been written by a bachelor.

- Samuel Butler (1835 – 1902)

By all means, marry. If you get a good wife, you'll become happy; if you get a bad wife, you'll become a philosopher.

- Socrates (470 – 399 BC)

Bachelors should be heavily taxed. It is not fair that some men should be happier than others.

- Oscar Wilde (1854 – 1900)

A woman usually respects her father, but her view of her husband is mingled with contempt, for she is, of course, privy to the transparent devices by which she snared him.

- H. L. MENCKEN (1880 – 1956)

H. L. Mencken

A dowry is a wonderful source of money, only if it comes without the wife.

- PLAUTUS (255 – 184 BC)

American women expect to find in their husbands a perfection that English women only hope to find in their butlers.

- W. SOMERSET MAUGHAM (1874 – 1965)

I wonder if the screwing I'm getting is worth the screwing I'm getting.

- Lana Turner (1921 – 1995)

Marriage is a great institution but I'm not ready for an institution yet.

- Mae West (1893 – 1987)

Whenever you want to marry someone, go have lunch with his ex-wife.

- Shelley Winters (1920 – 2006)

I have learned that only two things are necessary to keep one's wife happy. First, let her think she's having her way, and second, let her have it.

- LYNDON B. JOHNSON (1908 – 1973)

Marriage is so popular because it combines the maximum of temptation with the maximum of opportunity.

- GEORGE BERNARD SHAW (1856 – 1950)

The trouble with some women is that they get all excited about nothing – and then marry him.

- CHER (1946 –)

Hollywood brides keep the bouquets and throw away the grooms.

- GROUCHO MARX (1890 – 1977)

2891—(b) After Marriage.

Bigamy is having one wife too many. Monogamy is the same.

- OSCAR WILDE (1854 – 1900)

We sleep in separate rooms, we have dinner apart, we take separate vacations – we're doing everything we can to keep our marriage together.

- RODNEY DANGERFIELD (1921 – 2004)

I wasn't always rich. There was a time I didn't know where my next husband was coming from.

- MAE WEST (1893 – 1987)

Paying alimony is like feeding hay to a dead horse.

- GROUCH MARX (1890 – 1977)

You never realize how short a month is until you pay alimony.

- JOHN BARRYMORE (1882 – 1942)

It's a funny thing that when a man hasn't anything on earth to worry about, he goes off and gets married.

- Robert Frost (1878 – 1963)

Brides aren't happy – they are just triumphant.

- John Barrymore (1882 – 1942))

A man's friends like him but leave him as he is – his wife loves him and is always trying to turn him into somebody else.

- G. K. Chesterton (1874 – 1936)

Marriage makes an end of many short follies – being one long stupidity.

- Friedrich Wilhelm Nietzsche (1844 – 1900)

Marriage: A friendship recognized by the police.

- Robert Louis Stevenson (1850 – 1894)

ABRAHAM LINCOLN.

Marriage is neither heaven nor hell, it is simply purgatory.

- Abraham Lincoln (1809 – 1865)

Of all men, Adam was the happiest; he had no mother-in-law.

- Mark Twain (1835 – 1910)

Marriage is the only adventure open to the cowardly.

- Voltaire (1694 – 1778)

Politics doesn't make strange bedfellows – marriage does.

- Groucho Marx (1890 – 1977)

Rich Widows: The only secondhand goods that sell at first-class prices.

- BENJAMIN FRANKLIN (1706 – 1790)

Conscience is a mother-in-law whose visit never ends.

- H. L. MENCHEN (1880 – 1956)

You don't know anything about a woman until you meet her in court.

- NORMAN MAILER (1923 – 2007)

CHAPTER 12

Women

When a woman speaks sweetly, she's plotting mischief.

- FLORUS (C. AD 74)

Women's styles may change but their designs remain the same.

- OSCAR WILDE (1854 – 1900)

On one issue, at least, men and women agree: They both distrust women.

- H. L. MENCKEN (1880 – 1956)

Of all the wild beasts of land or sea, the wildest is women.

- MENANDER (342 – 291 BC)

Let thy maid servant be faithful, strong and homely.

- BENJAMIN FRANKLIN (1706 – 1790)

The way to fight a woman is with your hat. Grab it and run.

- JOHN BARRYMORE (1882 – 1942)

A woman is always buying something.

- Ovid (43 BC – AD 18)

Woman is surely the daughter of delay.

- Titus Maccius Plautus (255 – 184 BC)

When women kiss, it always reminds one of prize fighters shaking hands.

- H. L. Mencken (1880 – 1956)

As Miss America, my goal is to bring peace to the entire world and then to get my own apartment.

- JAY LENO (1950 –)

Better that a girl has beauty than brains, because boys see better than they think.

- JOSH BILLINGS (1818 – 1885)

I don't know anything better than a woman, if you want to spend money where it'll show.

- FRANK MCKINNEY "KIN" HUBBARD (1868 – 1930)

Women would be more charming if one could fall into her arms without falling into her hands.

- Ambrose Bierce (1842 – 1914)

A woman talks to one man, looks at a second, and thinks of a third.

- Bhartrihari (6th or 7th century)

Women are like elephants to me, I like to look at 'em but I wouldn't want to own one.

- W. L. Fields (1880 – 1946)

I do not know if she was virtuous, but she was ugly, and with a woman, that is half the battle.

- HEINRICH HEINE (1797 – 1856)

Her face was her chaperone.

- RUPERT HUGHES (1872 – 1956)

No cavalry or infantry has the gall to maneuver as coolly as a woman can.

- PLAUTUS (255 – 184 BC)

Good girls go to heaven, bad girls go everywhere.

- HELEN GURLEY BROWN (1922 –)

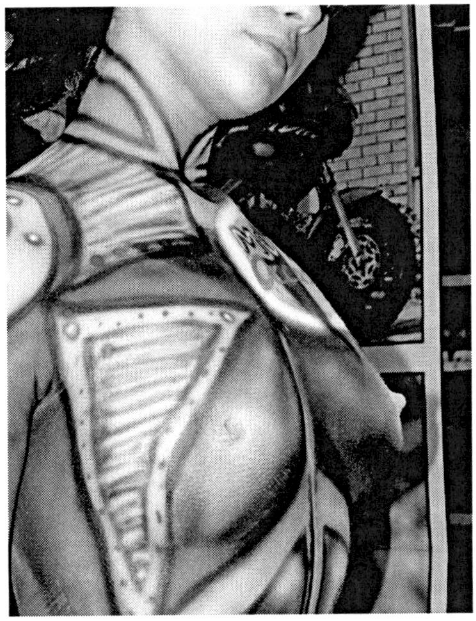

Who loves not women, wine, and song remains a fool his whole life long.

- MARTIN LUTHER (1483 – 1546)

In order to avoid being called a flirt, she always yielded easily.

- CHARLES MAURICE DE TALLYRAND (1754 – 1838)

She's the kind of girl who climbed the ladder of success wrong by wrong.

- MAE WEST (1892 – 1980)

She got her good looks from her father. He's a plastic surgeon.

- GROUCHO MARX (1890 – 1977)

That woman speaks eighteen languages and she can't say "no" in any of them.

- DOROTHY PARKER (1893 – 1967)

Gentlemen prefer blondes, but take what they can get.

- Don Herold (1889 – 1966)

There is a lot to say in her favor, but the other is more interesting.

- Mark Twain (1835 – 1910)

Women should be observed and not heard.

- Groucho Marx (1890 – 1977)

I'd rather have two girls at 21 each than one girl at 42.

- W. C. FIELDS (1880 – 1946)

Anyone who says he can see through women is missing a lot.

- GROUCHO MARX (1890 – 1977)

It's well to be off with the old woman before you're on with the new.

- GEORGE BERNARD SHAW (1856 – 1950)

Women are made to be loved, not understood.

- Oscar Wilde (1854 – 1900)

Brains are an asset, if you hide them.

- Mae West (1892 – 1980)

If women didn't exist, all the money in the world would have no meaning.

- Aristotle Onassis (1906 – 1975)

She's afraid that if she leaves, she'll become the life of the party.

- Groucho Marx (1890 – 1977)

If all these sweet young things were laid end to end, I wouldn't be the slightest bit surprised.

- Dorothy Parker (1893 – 1967)

She was what we used to call a suicide blonde – dyed by her own hand.

- Saul Bellow (1915 – 2005)

CHAPTER 13

Man

He is man, the most terrible of the beasts.

- G. K. CHESTERTON (1874 – 1936)

Man is a two-legged animal without feathers.

- PLATO (428 – 347 BC)

I believe the best definition of man is the ungrateful biped.

- FYODOR DOSTOYEVSKY (1821 – 1881)

It is even harder for the average ape to believe that he has descended from man.

- H. L. MENCKEN (1880 – 1956)

What an ugly beast is the ape, and how like us.

- CICERO (106 – 43 BC)

We need not worry so much about what man descends from – it's what he descends to that shames the human race.

- MARK TWAIN (1835 – 1910)

Who so would be a man must be a nonconformist.

- RALPH WALDO EMERSON (1803 – 1882)

Man: A reasoning rather than a reasonable animal.

- ALEXANDER HAMILTON (1755 – 1805)

The civilized world represents the victory of persuasion over force.

- PLATO (428 – 348 BC)

Man is the only animal that blushes. Or needs to.

- MARK TWAIN (1835 – 1910)

What men call good fellowship is commonly but the virtue of pigs in a litter which lie close together to keep each other warm.

- HENRY DAVID THOREAU (1817 – 1862)

Good breeding consists of concealing how much we think of ourselves and how little we think of the other person.

- MARK TWAIN (1835 – 1910)

Don't overestimate the decency of the human race.

- H. L. Mencken (1880 – 1956)

All that I care to know is that a man is a human being – that is enough for me; he can't be any worse.

- Mark Twain (1835 – 1910)

I love mankind; it's people I can't stand.

- Charles Schulz "Peanuts" (1922 – 2000)

Histories are more full of examples of the fidelity of dogs than of people.

- Alexander Pope (1688 – 1744)

If you pick up a starving dog and make him prosperous, he will not bite you; that is the principal difference between a dog and a man.

- Mark Twain (1835 – 1910)

It is easier to denature plutonium than to denature the evil spirit of man.

- Albert Einstein (1879 – 1955)

Man: The glory, jest and riddle of the world.

- Alexander Pope (1688 – 1744)

You can't say civilization don't advance ... in every war they kill you a new way.

- Will Rogers (1879 – 1935)

Men are moved by only two things; fear and self-interest.

- Napoleon Bonaparte (1769 – 1821)

Napoleon in Egypt

Civilization is a limitless multiplication of unnecessary necessities.

- MARK TWAIN (1835 – 1910)

Men have become the tools of their tools.

- HENRY DAVID THOREAU (1817 – 1862)

Things are in the saddle, and ride mankind.

- RALPH WALDO EMERSON (1803 – 1882)

Those who hate vice, hate mankind.

- Pliny the Younger (62 – 113)

The earth has a skin, and that skin has diseases; one of its diseases is called man.

- Friedrich Wilhelm Nietzsche (1844 – 1900)

The most costly of all follies is to believe passionately in the palpably not true. It is the chief occupation of mankind.

- H. L. Mencken (1880 – 1956)

History teaches us that men and nations behave wisely once they have exhausted all other alternatives.

- ABBA EBAN (1915 – 2002)

This world is a comedy for those who think and tragedy for those who feel.

- HORACE WALPOLE (1717 – 1797)

Perhaps I know best why it is man alone who laughs: He alone suffers so deeply that he had to invent laughter.

- FRIEDRICH WILLHELM NIETZSCHE (1844 – 1900)

Adam was only human. He did not want the apple for the apple's sake; he wanted it only because it was forbidden.

- Mark Twain (1835 – 1910)

I sometimes think that God, in creating man, somewhat overestimated his ability.

- Oscar Wilde (1854 – 1900)

If mankind had created man, he would be ashamed of his performance.

- Mark Twain (1835 – 1910)

Maybe the world is another planet's hell.

- ALDOUS HUXLEY (1894 – 1963)

We are here and it is now. Further than that, all human knowledge is moonshine.

- H. L. MENCKEN (1880 – 1956)

He is a self made man and worships his creator.

- JOHN BRIGHT (1811 – 1889)

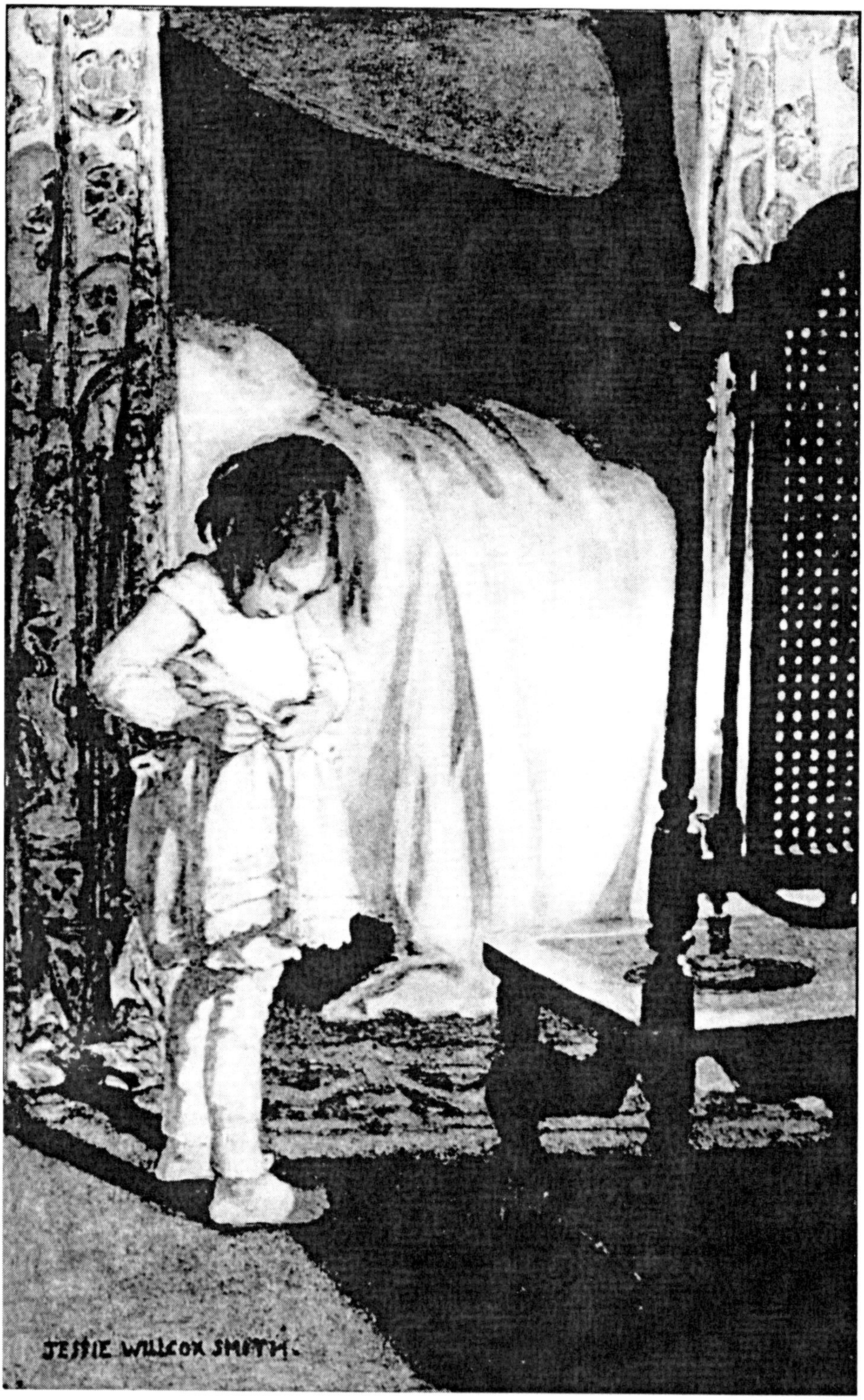
JESSIE WILLCOX SMITH.

Chapter 14

Children

A boy is, of all wild beasts, the most difficult to manage.

- Plato (428 – 348 BC)

A child is a curly, dimpled lunatic.

- Ralph Waldo Emerson (1803 – 1882)

Children today are tyrants. They contradict their parents, gobble their food and tyrannize their teachers.

- Socrates (470 – 399 BC)

Insanity is hereditary;
you can get it from your children.

- SAM LEVENSON (1911 – 1980)

Insomnia: A contagious disease transmitted from babies to parents.

- IMMANUEL KANT (1724 – 1804)

Parents of young children should realize that few people, and maybe no one, will find their children as enchanting as they do.

- BARBARA WALTERS (1929 –)

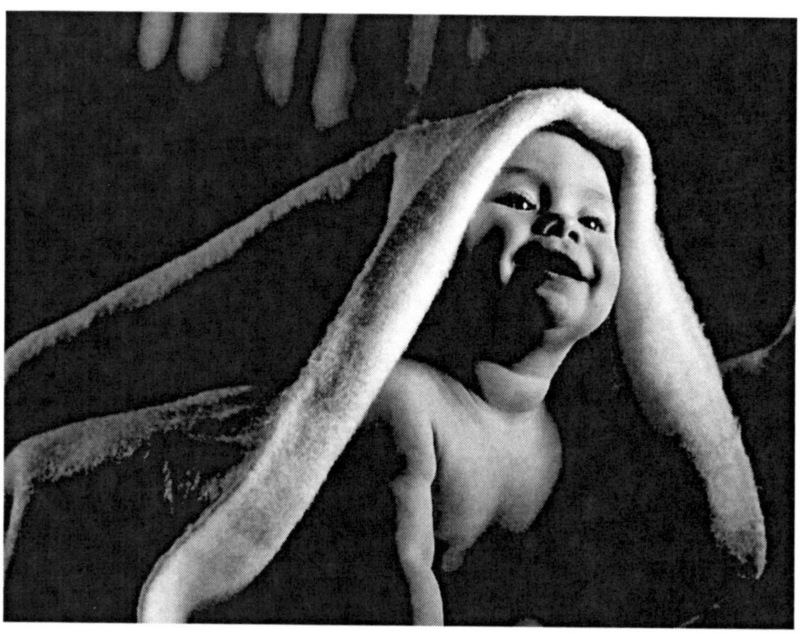

My mother had a great deal of trouble with me, but I think she enjoyed it.

- Mark Twain (1835 – 1910)

Children are given us to discourage our better emotions.

- H. H. Munro "Saki" (1870 – 1916)

Never have children, only grandchildren.

- Gore Vidal (1925 –)

All God's children are not beautiful. Most of God's children are, in fact, barely presentable.

- FRAN LEBOWITZ (1950 –)

We've been trying to have a kid. Well, she was trying, I just laid there.

- BOB SAGET (1956 –)

Having children is like having a bowling alley installed in your brain.

- MARTIN MULL (1943 –)

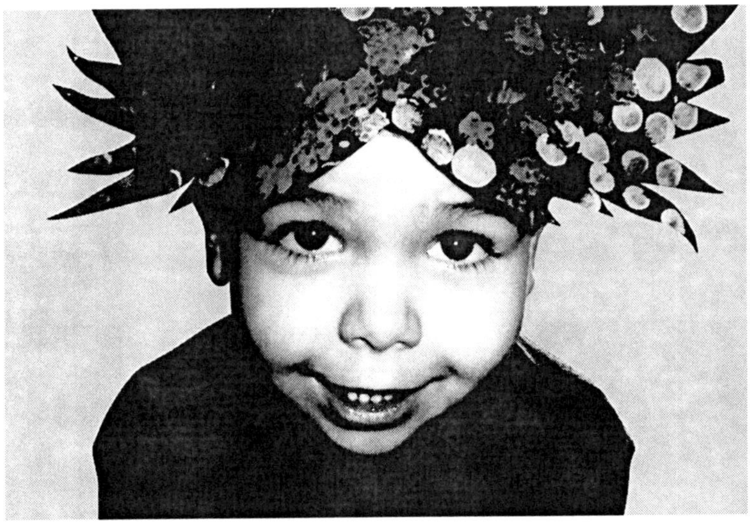

The thing that impresses me about America is the way parents obey their children.

- Duke of Windsor (1894 – 1972)

When I was a boy fourteen, my father was so ignorant I could hardly stand to have the old man around. But when I got to be 21, I was astonished at how much he had learned in seven years.

- Mark Twain (1835 – 1910)

Anyone who hates children and dogs can't be all bad.

- W. C. Fields (1880 – 1946)

Children make the most desirable opponents in Scrabble as they are both easy to beat and fun to cheat.

- FRAN LEBOWITZ (1950 –)

A baby is an inestimable blessing and a bother.

- MARK TWAIN (1835 – 1916)

A happy childhood is poor preparation for human contact.

- COLETTE (1873 – 1954)

No matter how old a mother is, she watches her middle-aged children for signs of improvement.

- Florida Scott-Maxwell (1883 – 1967)

The best way to keep children at home is to make the atmosphere pleasant – and let the air out of the tires.

- Dorothy Parker (1893 – 1967)

Of children as of procreation - the pleasure momentary, the posture ridiculous, the expense damnable.

- Evelyn Waugh (1903 – 1966)

Children are never too tender to be whipped. Like tough beef steaks, the more you beat them the more tender they become.

- EDGAR ALLAN POE (1809 – 1849)

I'm for bringing back the birch, but only for consenting adults.

- GORE VIDAL (1925 –)

Little boys should be obscene and not heard.

- OSCAR WILDE (1854 – 1900)

It is no wonder that people are so horrible when they start life as children.

- Kingsley Amis (1922 – 1995)

When I was kidnapped, my parents snapped into action. They rented out my room.

- Woody Allen (1935 –)

My eleven year old daughter mopes around the house all day, waiting for her breasts to grow.

- Bill Cosby (1937 –)

Never lend your car to anyone to whom you have given birth.

- ERMA BOMBECK (1927 – 1996)

My parents put a live teddy bear in my crib.

- WOODY ALLEN (1935 –)

My children didn't have my advantages; I was born into abject poverty.

- KIRK DOUGLAS (1916 –)

Providence protects children and idiots. I know because I have tested it.

- Mark Twain (1835 – 1910)

The first half of our life is ruined by our parents and the second half by our children.

- Clarence Darrow (1857 – 1938)

Like its politicians and its wars, society has the teenagers it deserves.

- J. B. Priestley (1894 – 1984)

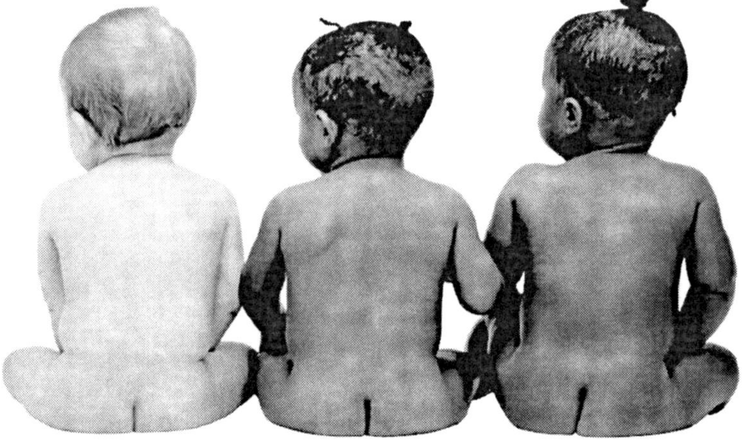

Sometimes, when I look at my children, I say to myself "Lillian, you should have stayed a virgin."

- LILLIAN CARTER (1898 – 1983)
(MOTHER OF PRESIDENT JIMMY CARTER)

There are three terrible ages of childhood – 1 to 10, 10 to 20, 20 to 30.

- CLEVELAND AMORY (1917 – 1998)

I could now afford all the things I never had as a kid, if I didn't have kids.

- ROBERT ORBEN (1927 –)

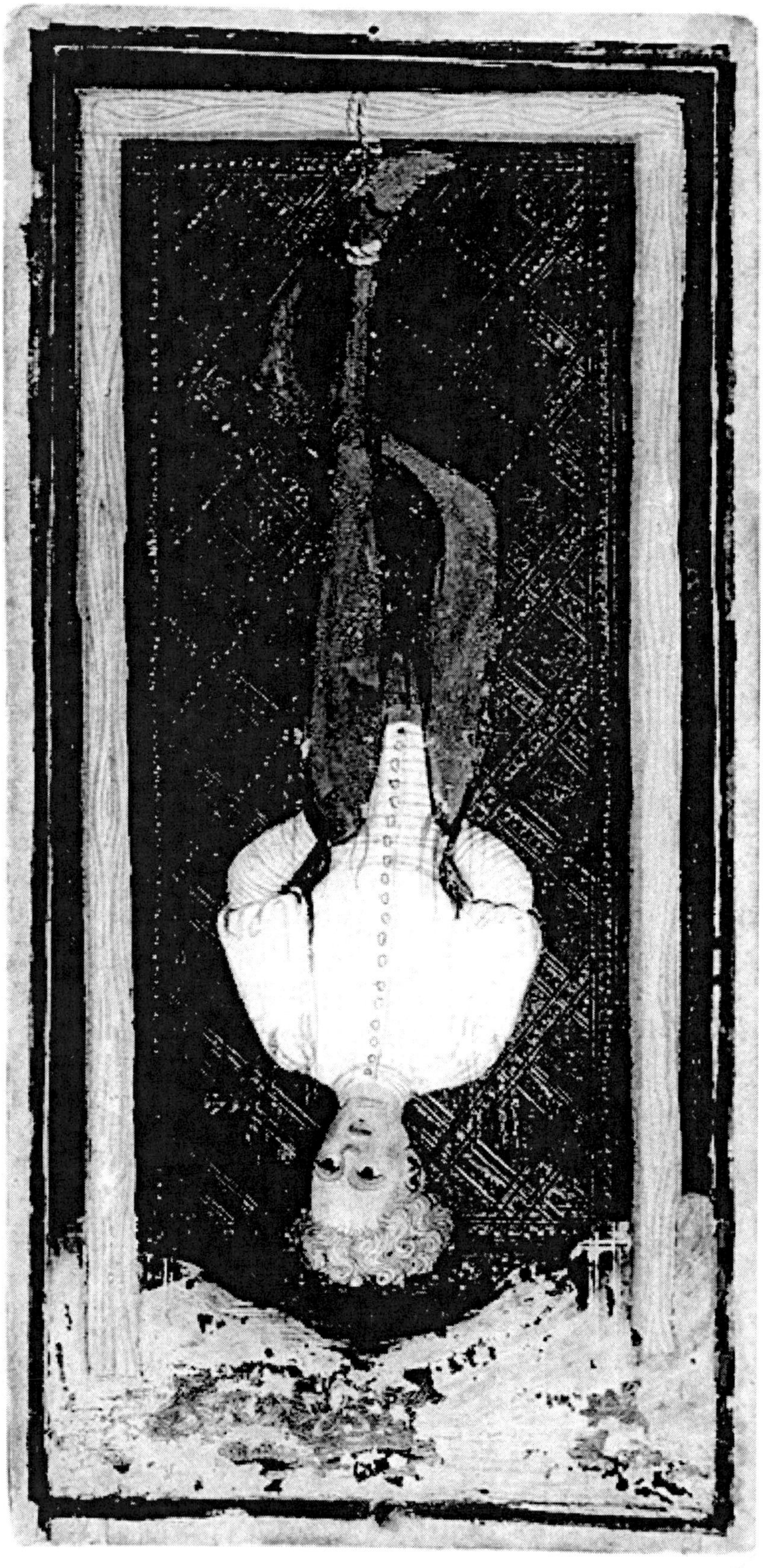

Chapter 15

Human Nature

A man who is not a fool can rid himself of every folly but vanity.

- Jean-Jacques Rousseau (1712 – 1778)

Most people would succeed in small things if they were not troubled by great ambitions.

- Henry Wadsworth Longfellow (1807 – 1882)

No luck is so good that you can't find some complaint.

- Publilius Syrus (85 – 43 BC)

Everyone thinks of changing the world but no one thinks of changing himself.

- Leo Tolstoy (1828 – 1910)

There are few who would not rather be hated than laughed at.

- Sydney Smith (1877 – 1935)

Nearly all men can stand adversity, but if you want to test a man's character, give him power.

- Abraham Lincoln (1809 – 1865)

We don't know what we want, but we are ready to bite somebody to get it.

- Will Rogers (1879 – 1935)

Will Rogers

It is a sin to believe evil of others, but it is seldom a mistake.

- H. L. Mencken (1880 – 1956)

Every generation laughs at the old fashions but religiously follows the now.

- Henry David Thoreau (1817 – 1862)

Benjamin Franklin

He that falls in love with himself will have no rivals.

- BENJAMIN FRANKLIN (1706 – 1790)

In every work of genius we recognize our rejected thoughts.

- RALPH WALDO EMERSON (1803 – 1882)

The things that are hardest to bear are sweetest to remember.

- SENECA (54 BC – 39 AD)

What hurt him most was his outrageous opinion of his own worth.

- CORENLIUS NEPOS (100 – 25 BC)

The trouble with most of us is that we would rather be ruined by praise than saved by criticism.

- NORMAN VINCENT PEALE (1898 – 1993)

Few things are harder to put up with than a good example.

- MARK TWAIN (1835 – 1910)

Shallow men believe in luck.

- GEORGE BERNARD SHAW (1856 – 1950)

A good man is always a beginner.

- MARTIAL (40 – 104)

Shallowness is natural; conceit comes with education.

- CICERO (106 – 43 BC)

It is easier to forgive an enemy than to forgive a friend.

- William Blake (1757 – 1827)

Glory is fleeting, but obscurity is forever.

- Napoleon Bonaparte (1769 – 1821)

Nobody ever forgets where he buried a hatchet.

- Frank McKinney "Kin" Hubbard (1868 – 1930)

What a pleasant stain comes from an enemy's blood.

- PUBLILIUS SYRUS (85 – 43 BC)

The hatred of relatives is the most violent.

- TACITUS (55 – 113)

I hold it better for the ruler to be feared than to be loved.

- NICCOLÒ MACHIAVELLI (1469 – 1527)

Few men have virtue to withstand the highest bidder.

- GEORGE WASHINGTON (1732 – 1799)

Most fools think they are only ignorant.

- BENJAMIN FRANKLIN (1706 – 1790)

Before a man speaks, it is always safe to assume that he is a fool. After he speaks, it is seldom necessary to assume it.

- H. L. MENCKEN (1880 – 1956)

Better a witty fool than a foolish wit.

- SHAKESPEARE (1564 – 1616)

What really flatters a man is that you think him worth flattering.

- GEORGE BERNARD SHAW (1856 – 1900)

Self-respect: the secure feeling that no one as yet is suspicious.

- H. L. MENCKEN (1880 – 1956)

Bore: A person who talks when you wish him to listen.

- Ambrose Bierce (1842 – 1914)

Bores bore each other too, but it never seems to teach them anything.

- Don Marquis (1878 – 1937)

We often forgive those who bore us, but we cannot forgive those whom we bore.

- Francois de la Rochefoucauld (1613 – 1680)

Gentlemen, you have just been listening to that Chinese sage, On Too Long.

- WILL ROGERS (1879 – 1935)

Bore: One who has the power of speech but not the capacity for conversation.

- BENJAMIN DISRAELI (1804 – 1881)

The nice thing about being a celebrity is that when you bore people, they think it's their fault.

- HENRY KISSINGER (1923 –)

Tears for someone else's trouble dry quickly.

- Cicero (106 – 43 BC)

Men easily believe what they want to.

- Caesar (100 – 44 BC)

A man's worst difficulties begin when he is able to do as he likes.

- Thomas H. Huxley (1825 – 1895)

ADAM AND EVE IN THE GARDEN OF EDEN.

Chapter 16

Truth & Lies

There are only two ways of telling the complete truth – anonymously and posthumously.

- Thomas Sowell (1930 –)

Boys, I may not know much but I know chicken shit from chicken salad.

- Lyndon B. Johnson (1908 – 1973)

The fellow that agrees with everything you say is either a fool or he is getting ready to skin you.

- Frank McKinney "Kin" Hubbard (1868 – 1930)

The liar's punishment is not in the least that he is not believed but that he cannot believe anyone else.

- GEORGE BERNARD SHAW (1856 – 1950)

Bill Clinton

No man has a good enough memory to make a successful liar.

- ABRAHAM LINCOLN (1809 – 1865)

No one lies so boldly as the man who is indignant.

- FRIEDRICH WILHELM NIETZSCHE (1844 – 1900)

Get your facts first and then you can distort them as much as you please.

- Mark Twain (1835 – 1910)

When liars speak the truth, they are not believed.

- Aristotle (384 – 322 BC)

Honesty is a good thing, but it is not profitable to its possessor unless it is kept under control.

- Don Marquis (1878 – 1937)

If I were two-faced, would I be wearing this one?

- ABRAHAM LINCOLN (1809 – 1865)

Truth is beautiful – without doubt; but so are lies.

- RALPH WALDO EMERSON (1803 – 1882)

The pure and simple truth is rarely pure and never simple.

- OSCAR WILDE (1854 – 1900)

Actions lie louder than words.

- CAROLYN WELLS (1862 – 1942)

Honesty is the best image.

- TOM WILSON "ZIGGY" (1931 –)

We ought never to do wrong when people are looking.

- MARK TWAIN (1835 – 1910)

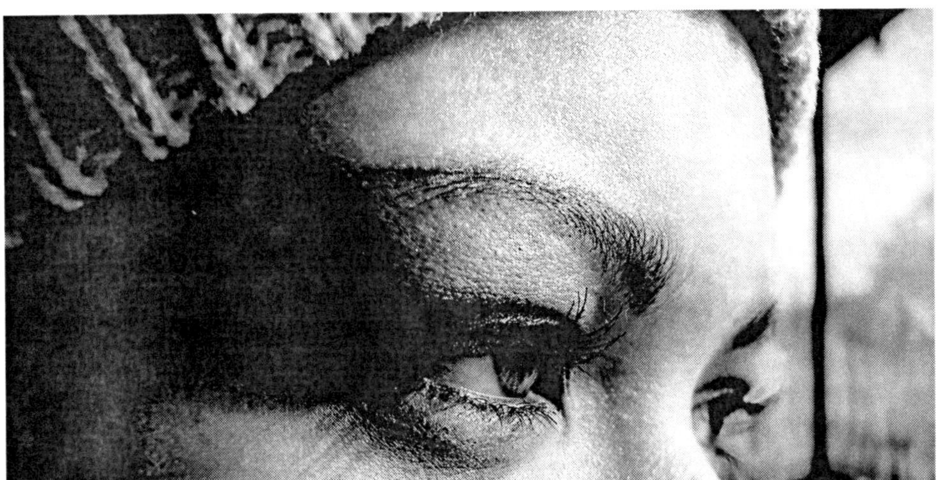

Confession may be good for my soul but it's bad for my reputation.

- Mark Twain (1835 – 1910)

A little inaccuracy sometimes saves tons of explanations.

- H. H. Munro "Saki" (1870 – 1916)

Though I am not naturally honest, I am so sometimes by chance.

- Shakespeare (1564 – 1616)

It is hard to believe a man is telling the truth when you know that you would lie if you were in his place.

- H. L. Mencken (1880 – 1956)

The Right Honorable Gentleman is indebted to his memory for his jests and his imagination for his facts.

- Richard Brinsley Sheridan (1751 – 1816)

A lie can run around the world six times while the truth is still trying to put on its pants.

- Mark Twain (1835 – 1910)

I never did give anybody hell. I just told the truth and they thought it was hell.

- HARRY S. TRUMAN (1884 – 1972)

As scarce as the truth is, the supply has always been in excess of the demand.

- JOSH BILLING (1818 – 1885)

Ye shall know the truth and the truth shall make you mad.

- ALDOUS HUXLEY (1894 – 1963)

Whatever deceives seems to produce a magical enchantment.

- Plato (428 – 348 BC)

The great masses of the people ... will more easily fall victims to a great lie than to a small one.

- Adolf Hitler (1889 – 1945)

Carlyle said "A lie cannot live"; it shows he did not know how to tell them.

- Mark Twain (1835 – 1910)

Joseph Stalin

The best way to keep one's word is not to give it.

- NAPOLEON BONAPARTE (1769 – 1821)

Gaiety is the outstanding feature of the Soviet Union.

- JOSEPH STALIN (1878 – 1953)

Convictions are more dangerous foes of truth than lies.

- FRIEDRICH WILHELM NIETZSCHE (1844 – 1900)

When you read a biography, remember that the truth is never fit for publication.

- George Bernard Shaw (1856 – 1950)

Winston Churchill

Men occasionally stumble over the truth, but most of them pick themselves up and hurry off as if nothing had happened.

- Winston Churchill (1874 – 1965)

It is unfortunate, considering that enthusiasm moves the world, that so few enthusiasts can be trusted to speak the truth.

- Arthur Balfour (1848 – 1930)

The best mind-altering drug is truth.

- Lily Tomlin (1939 –)

The least initial deviation from the truth is multiplied later a thousand fold.

- ARISTOTLE (384 – 322 BC)

Most writers regard the truth as their most valuable possession, and therefore are most economical in its use.

- MARK TWAIN (1835 – 1910)

The difference between truth and fiction is that fiction has to make sense.

- MARK TWAIN (1835 – 1910)

A thing is not necessarily true because badly uttered, nor false because spoken magnificently.

- SAINT AUGUSTINE (354 – 430)

DEMOCRATIC
MERRY-GO-ROUND
HEARST
BRYAN

CHAPTER 17

Politicians

A politician is an animal who can sit on a fence and keep both ears to the ground.

- H. L. MENCKEN (1880 – 1956)

A politician is a person with whose politics you don't agree; if you agree with him, he is a statesman.

- DAVID LLOYD GEORGE (1863 – 1945)

Politicians are interested in people. Not that this is always a virtue. Fleas are interested in dogs.

- P. J. O'ROURKE (1947 –)

Ninety percent of politicians give the other ten percent a bad name.

- HENRY KISSINGER (1923 –)

Nine politicians out of ten are knaves who maintain themselves by preying on the idiotic vanities and pathetic hopes of half-wits.

- H. L. MENCKEN (1880 – 1956)

Politicians are the same all over: They promise to build a bridge even when there is no river.

- NIKITA KHRUSCHEV (1894 – 1971)

Those who are too smart to engage in politics are punished by being governed by those who are dumber.

- Plato (428 – 348 BC)

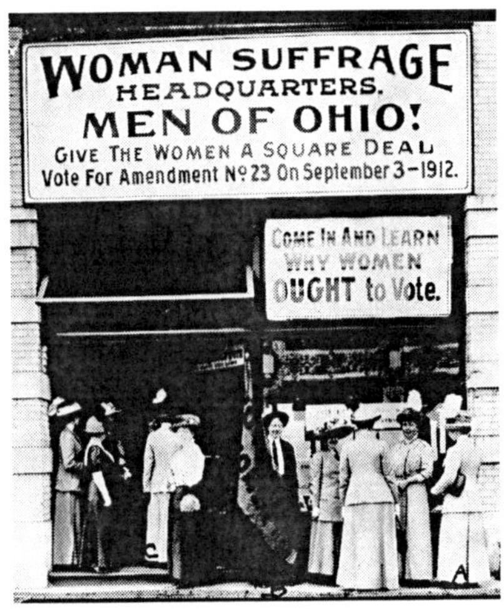

He knows nothing and he thinks he knows everything. That points clearly to a political career.

- George Bernard Shaw (1856 – 1950)

If a politician found he had cannibals among his constituents, he would promise them missionaries for dinner.

- H. L. Mencken (1880 – 1956)

You can fool too many of the people too much of the time.

- JAMES THURBER (1894 – 1961)

With Congress, every time they make a joke, it's a law, and every time they make a law, it's a joke.

- WILL ROGERS (1879 – 1935)

The function of socialism is to raise suffering to a higher level.

- NORMAN MAILER (1923 - 2007)

If presidents don't do it to their wives, they do it to the country.

- MEL BROOKS (1926 -)

In order to become the master, the politician poses as the servant.

- CHARLES DE GAULLE (1890 – 1970)

The secret of the demagogue is to make himself as stupid as his audience so that they believe they are as clever as he.

- KARL KRAUS (1874 – 1936)

Your public servants serve you right.

- ADLAI STEVENSON (1900 – 1965)

Now and then an innocent man is sent to the legislature.

- FRANK MCKINNEY "KIN" HUBBARD (1868 – 1930)

There is no act of treachery or meanness of which a political party is not capable; for in politics there is no honor.

- BENJAMIN DISRAELI (1804 – 1881)

Mothers all want their sons to grow up to be president but they don't want them to become politicians in the process.

- JOHN F. KENNEDY (1917 – 1963)

During an election campaign, the air is full of speeches and vice versa.

- Henry Adams (1838 – 1918)

In America you can go on the air and kid the politicians, and the politicians can go on the air and kid the people.

- Groucho Marx (1890 – 1977)

Nothing is so admirable in politics as a short memory.

- John Kenneth Galbraith (1908 – 2006)

Since a politician never believes what he says, he is surprised when others believe him.

- CHARLES DE GAULLE (1890 – 1970)

Politics is far more complicated than physics.

- ALBERT EINSTEIN (1879 – 1955)

Oh, that lovely title, Ex-president.

- DWIGHT D. EISENHOWER (1890 – 1969)

Communism, like any other revealed religion, is largely made up of prophecies.

- H. L. MENCKEN (1880 – 1956)

I would not like to be a political leader in Russia. They never know when they're being taped.

- RICHARD NIXON (1913 – 1994)

Richard Nixon

In politics, an absurdity is not a handicap.

- NAPOLEON BONAPARTE (1769 – 1821)

The first mistake in public business is going into it.

- BENJAMIN FRANKLIN (1706 – 1790)

FARMER GARFIELD
Cutting a Swath to the White House.

I got fed up with all the sex and sleaze and backhanders of rock'n'roll, so I went into politics.

- TONY BLAIR (1953 –)

The more you observe politics, the more you've got to admit that each party is worse than the other.

- WILL ROGERS (1879 – 1935)

Their insatiable lust for power is only equaled by their incurable impotence in exercising it.

- WINSTON CHURCHILL (1874 – 1965)

Vilify! Vilify! Some of it will always stick.

- PIERRE AUGUSTIN BEAUMAZCHAIS (1732 – 1799)

The popularity of a bad man is as treacherous as he is himself.

- Pliny the Younger (62 –113)

The best political community is formed by citizens of the middle class and those states are likely to be well administered in which the middle class is large and larger if possible than both the other classes … or at any rate than either singly.

- Aristotle (384 – 322 BC)

Men hesitate less to injure a man who makes himself loved than to injure one who makes himself feared.

- Niccolo Machiavelli (1469 – 1527)

GRAND, NATIONAL UNION BANNER FOR 1864.

LIBERTY, UNION AND VICTORY.

Chapter 18

Democracy

Democracy is the theory that the common people know what they want, and deserve to get it good and hard.

- H. L. Menchen (1880 – 1956)

Democracy substitutes election by the incompetent many for appointment by the corrupt few.

- George Bernard Shaw (1856 – 1950)

Under democracy, one party always devotes its chief energies to trying to prove that the other party is unfit to rule – and both commonly succeed, and are right.

- H. L. Mencken (1880 – 1956)

Democracy gives every man the right to be his own oppressor.

- JAMES RUSSELL LOWELL (1819 – 1891)

Democracy is a process by which the people are free to choose the men who will get the blame.

- LAURENCE J. PETER (1821 – 1880)

The whole dream of democracy is to raise the proletarian to the level of stupidity attained by the bourgeois.

- GUSTAVE FLAUBERT (1821 – 1880)

Man's capacity for justice makes democracy possible, but man's inclination to injustice makes democracy necessary.

- Reinhold Niebuhr (1892 – 1971)

Giving every man a vote has no more made men wise and free than Christianity has made them good.

- H. L. Mencken (1880 – 1956)

In general, the art of government consist in taking as much money as possible from one class of citizens to give to the other.

- Voltaire (1694 – 1778)

It is dangerous to be right when the government is wrong.

- VOLTAIRE (1694 – 1778)

The urge to save humanity is almost always a false front for the urge to rule.

- H. L. MENCKEN (1880 – 1956)

What luck for rulers that men do not think.

- ADOLF HITLER (1889 – 1945)

The pleasure of governing must certainly be exquisite if we may judge from the vast numbers who are eager to be concerned with it.

- VOLTAIRE (1694 – 1778)

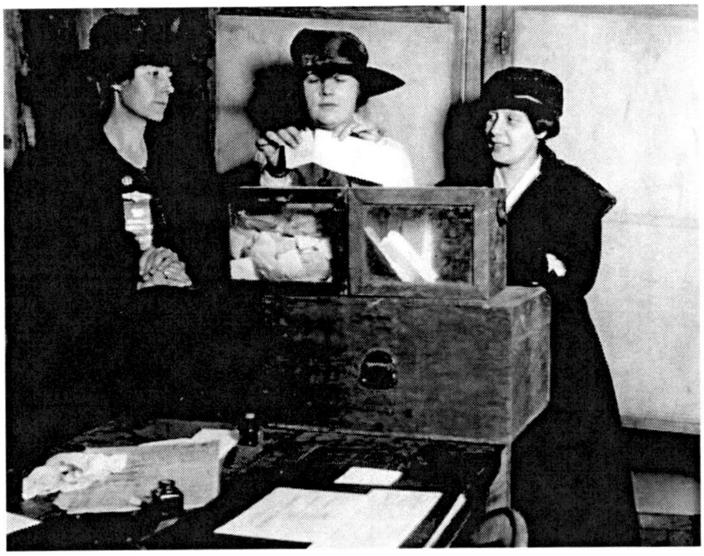

The trouble with free elections is you never know who is going to win.

- LEONID BREZHNEV (1906 – 1982)

I don't make jokes. I just watch the government and report the facts.

- WILL ROGERS (1879 – 1935)

When there is no middle class, and the poor greatly exceed in number, troubles arise and the state soon comes to an end.

- ARISTOTLE (384 – 322 BC)

THE WAY TO GROW POOR. ✦ THE WAY TO GROW RICH.

Republics end through luxury, monarchy through poverty.

- Montesquieu (1689 – 1755)

That government is best which governs least.

- Henry David Thoreau (1817 – 1862)

Government has no other end but the preservation of property.

- John Locke (1632 – 1704)

I disapprove of what you say, but I will defend to the death your right to say it.

- Voltaire (1694 – 1778)

I know of no example in time or place of a society that has been marked by a large measure of political freedom, and that has not also used something comparable to a free market.

- Milton Friedman (1912 – 2006)

Those who expect to reap the blessings of freedom must, like men, undergo the fatigue of supporting it.

- Thomas Paine (1737 – 1809)

People demand freedom of speech as a compensation for the freedom of thought which they seldom use.

- Soren Aabye Kierkegaard (1813 – 1855)

It is amazing how wise statesmen can be when it is ten years too late.

- DAVID LLOYD GEORGE (1863 – 1945)

Sincere diplomacy is no more possible than dry water.

- JOSEPH STALIN (1878 – 1953)

The more law, the less justice.

- CICERO (106 – 43 BC)

When you say that you agree to a thing in principle you mean that you have not the slightest intention of carrying it out.

- OTTO VON BISMARCK (1815 – 1898)

The law is reason free from passion.

- Aristotle (384 – 322 BC)

If you like laws and sausages, you should never watch either one being made.

- Otto Von Bismarck (1815 – 1898)

The government solution to a problem is usually as bad as the problem.

- Milton Friedman (1912 – 2006)

In rivers and bad governments, the lightest things swim at the top.

- Benjamin Franklin (1706 – 1790)

"MONKEY SHINES."

A government is the only known vessel that leaks from the top.

- James Reston (1909 – 1995)

I'd rather entrust the government of the United States to the first four hundred people listed in the Boston telephone directory than to the faculty of Harvard University.

- William F. Buckley, Jr. (1925 – 2008)

Fleas can be taught nearly everything a congressman can.

- Mark Twain (1835 – 1910)

The difference between bad speech and bad deeds is opportunity.

- Marcus Fabius Quintilianus (35 – 100)

Creative semantics is the key to contemporary government; it consists of talking in strange tongues lest the public learn the inevitable inconveniently early.

- George Will (1941 –)

Chapter 19

Religion

A casual stroll through the lunatic asylum shows that faith does not prove anything.

- Friedrich Wilhelm Nietzsche (1844 – 1900)

Faith must trample under foot all reason, sense and understanding.

- Bertrand Russell (1872 – 1970)

The way to see by faith is to shut the eye of reason.

- Benjamin Franklin (1706 – 1790)

**Everyone prefers belief
to the exercise of judgment.**

- SENECA (54 BC – 39 AD)

**Religion is a conceited effort to deny
the most obvious realities.**

- H. L. MENCKEN (1880 – 1956)

A cult is a religion with no political power.

- TOM WOLFE (1931 –)

If God did not exist it would have been necessary to invent Him.

- Voltaire (1694 – 1778)

The impotence of God is infinite.

- Anatole France (1844 – 1924)

Man rarely (if ever) manages to dream up a god superior to themselves. Most gods have the manners of a spoiled child.

- Robert A. Heinlein (1907 – 1988)

A Sunday School is a prison in which children do penance for the evil conscience of their parents.

- H. L. MENCKEN (1880 – 1956)

There is something feeble and a little contemptible about a man who cannot face the perils of life without the help of comfortable myths.

- BERTRAND RUSSELL (1872 – 1970)

When a man is freed of religion, he has a better chance to live a normal and wholesome life.

- SIGMUND FREUD (1856 – 1939)

The worshiper is the father of the Gods.

- H. L. Mencken (1880 – 1956)

Which is it, is man one of God's blunders or is God one of man's?

- Friedrich Wilhelm Nietzsche (1844 – 1900)

It takes a long while for a naturally trustful person to reconcile himself to the idea that after all God will not help him.

- H. L. Mencken (1880 –1956)

God, that dumping ground of our dreams.

- Jean Rostand (1868 – 1918)

The average man does not know what to do with his life, yet wants another one which will last forever.

- Anatole France (1844 – 1924)

Say what you will about the Ten Commandments, you must always come back to the pleasant fact that there are only ten of them.

- H. L. Mencken (1880 – 1956)

Men enriched by your sweat and misery, made you superstitious not that you might fear God, but that you might fear them.

- Voltaire (1694 – 1778)

Religion is excellent stuff for keeping common people quiet.

- Napoleon Bonaparte (1769 – 1821)

Science has done more for the development of Western civilization in one hundred years than Christianity did in eighteen hundred years.

- John Burroughs (1837 – 1921)

Christianity must be divine, since it has lasted 1,700 years, despite the fact that it is so full of villainy and nonsense.

- VOLTAIRE (1694 – 1778)

There is not enough religion in the world to destroy the world's religions.

- FRIEDRICH WILHELM NIETZSCHE (1844 – 1900)

Unless you hate your father and mother and wife and brothers and sisters and yes, even you own life, you can't be my disciple.

- JESUS CHRIST (0? – 32?) LUKE 14:26

So far as I can remember, there is not one word in the Gospels in praise of intelligence.

- Bertrand Russell (1872 – 1970)

The inspiration of the Bible depends on the ignorance of the gentlemen who read it.

- Robert G. Ingersoll (1833 – 1899)

It ain't those parts of the Bible that I can't understand that bother me, it's the parts that I do understand.

- Mark Twain (1835 – 1910)

We have just enough religion to make us hate, but not enough to make us love one another.

- JONATHAN SWIFT (1667 – 1745)

Puritanism: The haunting fear that someone, somewhere, may be happy.

- H. L. MENCKEN (1880 – 1956)

The Catholic faith is confession on Saturday. Absolution on Sunday. At it again on Monday.

- H. G. WELLS (1866 – 1946)

God is always on the side of the big battalions.

- Voltaire (1694 – 1778)

Christian theology is not only opposed to the scientific spirit; it is opposed to every other form of rational thinking.

- H. L. Mencken (1880 – 1956)

The age of ignorance commenced with the Christian system.

- Thomas Paine (1723 – 1809)

The first clergyman was the first rascal who met the first fool.

- VOLTAIRE (1694 – 1778)

Next to a circus, there ain't nothing that packs up and tears out of town any quicker than the Christmas spirit.

- FRANK MCKINNEY "KIN" HUBBARD (1868 – 1930)

When I hear a man preach, I like to see him act as if he were fighting bees.

- ABRAHAM LINCOLN (1809 – 1865)

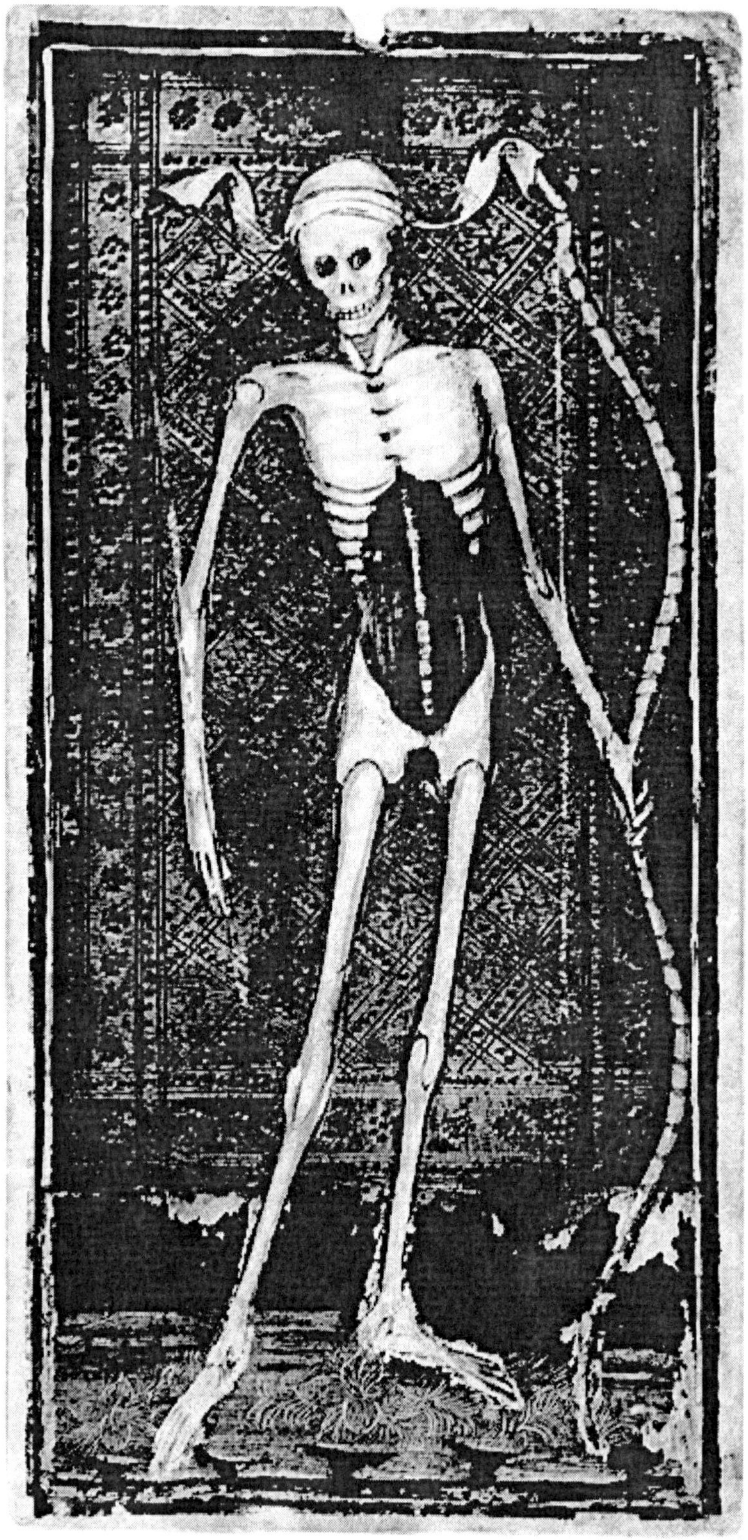

Chapter 20

Death

Don't go to sleep, so many people die there.

- Mark Twain (1835 – 1910)

If this is dying, then I don't think much of it.

- Lytton Strachey (1880 – 1932)

I don't want to achieve immortality through my work. I want to achieve it through not dying.

- Woody Allen (1935 –)

The reports of my death are greatly exaggerated.

- MARK TWAIN (1835 – 1910)

They say such nice things about people at their funerals that it makes me sad to realize that I'm going to miss mine by just a few days.

- GARRISON KEILLOR (1942 –)

A cynic is a man who when he smells flowers looks around for a coffin.

- H. L. MENCKEN (1880 – 1956)

I know a man who gave up smoking, drinking, sex, and rich food. He was healthy right up to the time he killed himself.

- Johnny Carson (1925 – 2005)

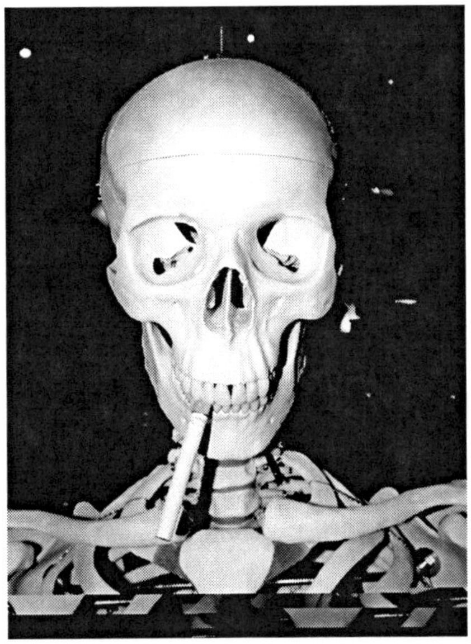

I have a fine heart … it will last me as long as I live.

- W. C. Fields (1880 – 1946)

I take my only exercise acting as pallbearer at the funerals of my friends who exercise regularly.

- Mark Twain (1835 – 1910)

It's not that I'm afraid to die. I just don't want to be there when it happens.

- Woody Allen (1935 –)

I refused to attend his funeral. But, I wrote a nice letter explaining that I approved of it.

- Mark Twain (1835 – 1910)

If Roosevelt were alive today, he'd turn over in his grave.

- Samuel Goldwyn (1882 – 1974)

You need religion if you are terrified of death.

- Gore Vidal (1925 –)

I don't believe in an after life, although I am bringing a change of underwear.

- Woody Allen (1935 –)

I am ready to meet my Maker. Whether my Maker is ready to meet me is another matter.

- Winston S. Churchill (1874 – 1965) On his 75th Birthday

Don't let it end like this. Tell them I said something.

- PANCHO VILLA (1878 – 1923)
LAST WORDS

Let us endeavor so to live that when we come to die even the undertaker will be sorry.

- MARK TWAIN (1835 – 1910)

There is nothing more exhilarating than to be shot at without results.

- WINSTON CHURCHILL (1874 – 1965)

When you have to kill a man, it costs nothing to be polite.

- Winston Churchill (1874 – 1965)

One murder makes a villain; millions, a hero.

- Napoleon Bonaparte (1769 – 1821)

A single death is a tragedy. A million deaths is a statistic.

- Joseph Stalin (1879 – 1953)

If fame is to come only after death, I am in no hurry for it.

- MARTIAL (86 – 103)

Murderer: One presumed to be innocent until declared insane.

- OSCAR WILDE (1854 – 1900)

The only completely consistent people are the dead.

- ALDOUS HUXLEY (1894 – 1963)

No matter how much a woman loved a man, it would still give her a glow to see him commit suicide for her.

- H. L. Mencken (1880 – 1956)

Suicide is belated acquiescence in the opinion of one's wife's relatives.

- H. L. Mencken (1880 – 1956)

The thought of suicide is a great consolation: with the help of it, one has got through many a bad night.

- Friedrich Wilhelm Nietzsche (1844 – 1900)

The disciples of a martyr suffer much more than the martyr.

- FRIEDRICH WILHELM NIETZSCHE (1844 – 1900)

A thing is not necessarily true because a man dies for it.

- OSCAR WILDE (1854 – 1900)

Martyrdom covers a multitude of sin.

- MARK TWAIN (1835 – 1910)

Epitaphs: An inscription which hopes that virtues acquired by death will have a retroactive effect.

- AMBROSE BIERCE (1842 – 1914)

If you take epitaphs seriously, we ought to bury the living and resurrect the dead.

- Mark Twain (1835 – 1910)

ACTUAL EPITAPHS:

Excuse my dust.

- Dorothy Parker (1893 – 1957)

The rarest quality in an epitaph is truth.

- Henry David Thoreau (1817 – 1862)

Pardon me for not getting up.

- Ernest Hemingway (1899 – 1961)

On the whole, I'd rather be in Philadelphia.

- W. C. Fields (1880 – 1946)

I'm involved in a plot.

- Alfred Hitchcock (1899 – 1980)

Chapter 21

Youth & Aging

Youth is a wonderful thing. What a crime to waste it on children.

- George Bernard Shaw (1856 – 1950)

In America, the young are always to give to those who are older than themselves the full benefit of their inexperience.

- Oscar Wilde (1854 – 1900)

Blessed are the young, for they shall inherit the National debt.

- Herbert Hoover (1874 – 1964)

There is no sadder sight than a young pessimist, except an old optimist.

- MARK TWAIN (1835 – 1910)

W. Somerset Maugham

I suppose it's difficult for the young to realize that one may be old without being a fool.

- W. SOMERSET MAUGHAM (1874 – 1965)

The young always have the same problem – how to rebel and conform at the same time. They have now resolved this by defying their parents and copying one another.

- QUENTIN CRISP (1908 – 1999)

Men are like wine, some turn to vinegar, the best improve with age.

- Pope John XXIII (1881 – 1963)

At age fifty, every man has the face he deserves.

- George Orwell (1903 – 1950)

No wise man ever wished to be younger.

- Jonathan Swift (1667 – 1745)

We do not count a man's years until he has nothing else to count.

- RALPH WALDO EMERSON
(1803 – 1882)

... of age, that age appears to be best in four things – old wood best to burn, old wine to drink, old friends to trust, and old authors to read.

- FRANCIS BACON (1561 – 1626)

It is unbecoming for young men to utter maxims.

- ARISTOTLE (384 – 322 BC)

A man is as old as the woman he feels.

- Groucho Marx (1890 – 1977)

I am not young enough to know everything.

- Oscar Wilde (1854 – 1900)

I'm pushing sixty.
That is enough exercise for me.

- Mark Twain (1835 – 1900)

Young men want to be faithful and are not; old men want to be faithless and cannot.

- OSCAR WILDE (1854 – 1900)

After fifty, a man begins to deteriorate, but in the forties, he is at the maximum of his villainy.

- H. L. MENCKEN (1880 – 1956)

If I'd known I was gonna live this long, I'd have taken better care of myself.

- EUBIE BLAKE (1887 – 1983)

As long as a woman can look ten years younger than her own daughter, she is perfectly satisfied.

- Oscar Wilde (1854 – 1900)

Man weeps to think that he will die so soon; women that she was born so long ago.

- H. L. Mencken (1880 – 1956)

Time and tide wait for no man, but time always stands still for a woman of thirty.

- Robert Frost (1878 – 1963)

The secret of staying young is to live honestly, eat slowly, and lie about your age.

- LUCILLE BALL (1911 – 1989)

When people tell you how young you look, they are also telling you how old you are.

- CARY GRANT (1904 – 1986)

After age seventy, it's patch, patch, patch.

- JIMMY STEWART (1908 – 1997)

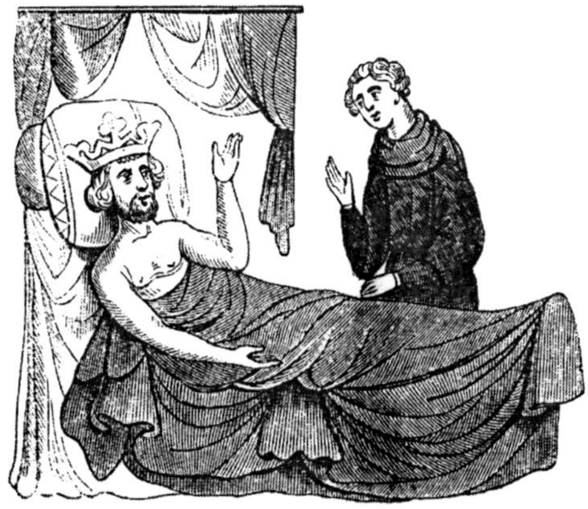

From birth to age 18, a girl needs good parents. From 18 to 35, she needs good looks. From 35 to 55, she needs a good personality. From 55 on, she needs good cash.

- SOPHIE TUCKER (1884 – 1996)

The old believe everything, the middle-aged suspect everything, the young know everything.

- OSCAR WILDE (1894 – 1900)

No one is so old as not to think he can live one more year.

CICERO (106 – 43 BC)

When a woman gets too old to be attractive to man, she turns to God.

- HONORÈ DE BALZAC (1799 – 1850)

Youth had been a habit of hers for so long that she could not part with it.

- RUDYARD KIPLING (1865 – 1936)

It is after you have lost your teeth that you can afford to buy steaks.

PIERRE AUGUSTE RENOIR (1841 – 1919)

Wrinkles should merely indicate where smiles have been.

- Mark Twain (1835 – 1910)

Old age is like a plane flying through a storm. Once you are aboard, there is nothing you can do.

- Golda Mier (1898 – 1978)

To get back my youth, I would do anything in the world, except take exercise, get up early or be respectable.

- Oscar Wilde (1854 – 1900)

One should never trust a woman who tells one her real age. A woman who would tell one that would tell one anything.

- OSCAR WILDE (1854 – 1900)

Retirement at sixty five is ridiculous. When I was sixty five, I still had pimples.

- GEORGE BURNS (1896 – 1996)

You know you're getting old when the candles cost more than the cake.

- BOB HOPE (1903 – 2003)

Chapter 22

Life & Happiness

The art of living is more like wrestling than dancing.

- Marcus Aurelius (121 – 180)

Life does not cease to be funny when people die any more than it ceases to be serious when people laugh.

- George Bernard Shaw (1856 – 1950)

Life is an effort that deserves a better cause.

- Karl Kraus (1874 – 1936)

Life itself is the proper binge.

- JULIA CHILD (1912 – 2004)

**If I had to live my life again,
I'd make the same mistakes, only sooner.**

- TALLULAH BANKHEAD (1903 – 1968)

There are two tragedies in life. One is not to get your heart's desire. The other is to get it.

- GEORGE BERNARD SHAW (1856 – 1950)

Life can only be understood backward, but it must be lived forward.

- Soren Kierkegaard (1813 – 1855)

Life is a constant oscillation between the sharp horns of a dilemma.

- H. L. Mencken (1880 – 1956)

The good life is one inspired by love and guided by knowledge.

- Bertrand Russell (1872 – 1970)

There is no cure for birth and death, save to enjoy the interval.

- George Santayana (1863 – 1952)

We must laugh at man to avoid crying for him.

- Napoleon Bonaparte (1769 – 1821)

To be stupid, selfish and have good health are three requirements for happiness.

- Gustave Flaubert (1821 – 1880)

The unexamined life is not worth living.

- Socrates (470 – 399 BC)

The longer I live, the more beautiful life becomes.

- Frank Lloyd Wright (1867 – 1959)

Life would be infinitely happier if we could only be born at the age of eighty and gradually approach eighteen.

- Mark Twain (1835 – 1910)

Mistakes are part of the dues one pays for a full life.

- SOPHIA LOREN (1934 –)

We are always getting ready to live, but never living.

- RALPH WALDO EMERSON (1803 – 1882)

The basic fact about human existence is not that it is a tragedy, but it is a bore.

- H. L. MENCKEN (1880 – 1910)

Start everyday with a smile – and get it over with.

- W. C. Fields (1880 – 1946)

Always do right. That will gratify some of the people and astonish the rest.

- Mark Twain (1835 – 1910)

Life is much too important a thing to talk seriously about it.

- Oscar Wilde (1854 – 1900)

It is not reason which is the guide to life, but custom.

- DAVID HUME (1711 – 1776)

Men can only be happy when they do not assume that the object of life is happiness.

- GEORGE ORWELL (1903 – 1950)

Happiness is not something you experience, it's something you remember.

- OSCAR LEVANT (1906 – 1972)

**It is neither wealth nor splendor,
but tranquility and occupation
which give happiness.**

- Thomas Jefferson (1743 – 1826)

**The greater part of our happiness
or misery depends on our dispositions
and not on our circumstances.**

- Martha Washington (1731 – 1802)

**If only we'd stop trying to be happy,
we could have a pretty good time.**

- Edith Wharton (1862 – 1937)

The secret of being miserable is to have the leisure to bother about whether you are happy or not.

- GEORGE BERNARD SHAW (1856 – 1950)

Happy is he who causes scandal.

- SALVADOR DALI (1904 – 1989)

Amusement is the happiness of those who cannot think.

- ALEXANDER POPE (1688 – 1744)

Grief can take care of itself; but to get the full value of a joy, you must have somebody to divide it with.

- Mark Twain (1835 – 1910)

Birds sing after a storm; why shouldn't people feel as free to delight in whatever remains to them?

- Rose Kennedy (1890 – 1995)

Youth is a blunder, manhood a struggle, old age a regret.

- Benjamin Disraeli (1804 – 1881)

The trouble with life is that there are so many beautiful women and so little time.

- JOHN BARRYMORE (1882 – 1942)

Life being what it is, one dreams of revenge.

- PAUL GAUGUIN (1848 – 1903)

Life is a dead end street.

- H. L. MENCKEN (1880 – 1956)

APPENDIX

Biographies

The purpose of these biographies is to give a quick background on the people who are quoted. Most of the names are familiar. Dozens of scholarly volumes have been written about many of these public figures. These biographies in no way do justice to their lives, careers or contributions to mankind. As a quick, fun reference, I hope it is useful.

All biographies come from Wikipedia, the free encyclopedia, unless otherwise referenced.

Adams, Henry Brooks

Henry Brooks Adams (February 16, 1838 – March 27, 1918) was an American novelist, journalist, historian and academic. He is best-known for his autobiographical book, *The Education of Henry Adams*. He was a member of the Adams political family.

Ade, George

George Ade (February 9, 1866 – May 16, 1944) was an American writer, newspaper columnist, and playwright.

Ade was born in Kentland, Indiana. In 1890 Ade joined the *Chicago Morning News*, which later became the *Chicago Record*. He wrote the column, *Stories of the Streets and of the Town*. In the column, George Ade illustrated Chicago-life. It featured characters like Artie, an office boy; Doc Horne, a gentlemanly liar; and Pink Marsh, a black shoeshine boy. Ade's well-know "fables in slang" also made their first appearance in this popular column.

Adenauer, Konrad

Konrad Hermann Josef Adenauer (January 5, 1876 – April 19, 1967) was a German statesman. Although his political career spanned 60 years, beginning as early as 1906, he is most noted for his role as the first Chancellor of West Germany from 1949 – 1963 and chairman of the Christian Democratic Union from 1950 to 1966. He was the oldest chancellor ever to serve Germany, leaving at the age of 87.

Ali, Muhammad

Muhammad Ali (born **Cassius Marcellus Clay Jr.** on January 17, 1942) Is a retired American boxer and former three-time World Heavyweight Champion and winner of an Olympic Light-heavyweight gold medal. In 1999, Ali was crowned "Sportsman of the Century" by *Sports Illustrated* and the BBC.

Allen, Fred

Fred Allen (born **John Florence Sullivan** on May 31, 1894 in Cambridge, Massachusetts, died March 17, 1956 in New York City) was an American comedian whose absurdist, pointed radio show (1934 – 1949) made him on of the most popular and forward-looking humorists in the so-called classic era of American radio.

His best-remembered gag may be his long-running mock feud with friend and fellow comedian Jack Benny. Allen has been considered one of the more accomplished, daring and relevant humorists of his time. A master ad libber, he constantly battled censorship and developed routines the style and substance of which influenced future comic talents, notably Stan Freberg. Perhaps more than any of his generation, Fred Allen wielded influence that outlived both his contemporaries and the medium that made him famous.

Allen, Woody

Woody Allen (born **Allen Stewart Königsberg** on December 1, 1935) Is a three-time Academy Award-winning American film director, writer, actor, jazz musician, comedian and playwright. His large body of work and cerebral film style, mixing satire, wit and humor, have made him one of the most respected and prolific filmmakers in the modern era. Allen writes and directs his movies and has also acted in the majority of them. For inspiration, Allen draws heavily on literature, sexuality, philosophy, psychology, Judaism, European cinema and New York City, where he was born and has lived his entire life.

Amis, Kingsley

Sir Kingsley William Amis, CBE (April 16, 1922 – October 22, 1995) was an English novelist, poet, critic, and teacher. He wrote more than twenty novels, three collections of poetry, short stories, radio and television scripts, and books of social and literary criticism. He fathered English novelist Martin Amis.

Amory, Cleveland

Cleveland Amory (September 2, 1917 – October 14, 1998) was an American author who devoted his life to promoting animal rights. He was perhaps best known for his books about his cat named *Polar Bear*, whom he saved from the New York Streets on Christmas Eve, 1978.

Aquinas, Thomas

Thomas Aquinas, O.P. (also **Saint Thomas Aquinas**, **Thomas of Aquin**, or **Aquino**; c. 1225 – 7 March 1274) was an Italian Catholic priest in the Dominican Order, a philosopher and theologian In the scholastic tradition, known as **Doctor Angelicus**, **Doctor Universalis** and **Doctor Communis.** He was the foremost classical proponent of natural theology, and the father of the Thomistic school of philosophy and theology.

Aristotle

(Greek: 'Ἀριστοτέλης Aristotélēs) (384 BC – 322 BC) was a Greek philosopher, a student of Plato and teacher of Alexander the Great. He wrote on many different subjects, including physics, metaphysics, poetry, theater, music, logic, rhetoric, politics, Government, ethics, biology and zoology. Aristotle (together with Socrates and Plato) is one of the most important philosophers in Western thought. He was one of the first to systematize philosophy and science. His thinking on physics and science had a profound impact on medieval thought, which lasted until the Renaissance, and the accuracy of some of his biological observations was only confirmed in the last century. His logical works contain the earliest formal study of logic that we have and was not superseded until the late nineteenth century. In the Middle Ages, Aristotelian metaphysics had a profound influence on philosophical and theological thinking in the Islamic and Jewish traditions, and on Christian thought, where its legacy is still felt in Christian theology, for example in Orthodox theology, and especially within the Catholic tradition shaped by scholasticism. All aspects of Aristotle's philosophy continue to be the object of active academic study today

Augustine of Hippo

Aurelius Augustinus, Augustine of Hippo, or **Saint Augustine** (November 13, 354 – August 28, 430) was a philosopher and theologian, and was bishop of the North African city of Hippo Regius for the last third of his life. Augustine is one of the most important figures in the development of Western Christianity, and is considered to be one of the church fathers. He framed the concepts of original sin and just war.

Aurelius, Marcus

Marcus Aurelius Antoninus Augustus (Rome, April 26, 121 – Vindobona or Sirmium, March 17, 180) was Roman Emperor from 161 to his death in 180. He was the last of the "Five Good Emperors", and is also considered one of the most important stoic philosophers.

His tenure was marked by wars in Asia against a revitalized Parthian Empire, and with Germanic tribes along the *Limes Germanicus* into Gaul and across the Danube. A revolt in the East, led by Avidius Cassius, failed.

Marcus Aurelius' work *Meditations*, written on campaign between 170 – 180, is still revered as a literary monument to a government of service and duty and has been praised for its "exquisite accent and its infinite tenderness.

Bacall, Lauren

Betty Jane Perske (born September 16, 1924), better known as **Lauren Bacall**, is a Golden Globe – and Tony Award–winning, as well as Academy Award–nominated, American film and stage actress and model. Known for her husky voice and sultry looks, she became a famous icon in the 1940s and has kept on acting to this day.

She is perhaps best known for being a film noir leading lady in films such as *The Big Sleep* (1946) and *Dark Passage* (1947), as well as a comedienne, as seen in 1953's *How to Marry a Millionaire*. Bacall also enjoyed success starring in the Broadway musicals *Applause* in 1970 and Woman of the Year in 1981.

Bacon, Francis

Francis Bacon, 1st Viscount St Alban (22 January 1561 – 9 April 1626) was an English philosopher, statesman, and essayist. He is also known as a proponent of the scientific revolution. Indeed, according to John Aubrey, his dedication may have brought him into a rare historical group of scientists who were killed by their own experiments.

His works established and popularized an inductive methodology for scientific inquiry, often called the *Baconian method* or simply, the scientific method. In the context of his time such methods were connected with the occult trends of hermeticism and alchemy. Nevertheless, his demand for a planned procedure of investigating all things natural marked a new turn in the rhetorical and theoretical framework for science, much of which still informs conceptions of proper methodology today.

Baez, Joan

Joan Chandos Baez (born January 9, 1941) is an American folk singer and songwriter known for her highly individual vocal style. She is a soprano with a three-octave vocal range and a distinctively rapid vibrato. Many of her songs are topical and deal with social issues.

She is best known for her hits "There But For Fortune", Diamonds & Rust" and "The Night They Drove Old Dixie Down", and to a lesser extent, "We Shall Overcome", "Love Is Just A Four-Letter

Word", "Farewell Angelina", "Sweet Sir Galahad", and "Joe Hill" (songs she performed at the 1969 Woodstock festival).

Balfour, Arthur

Arthur James Balfour, 1st Earl of Balfour, KG, OM, PC (25 July 1848 – 19 March 1930) was a British Conservative politician and statesman, and the Prime Minister from 1902 to 1905, a time when his party and government became divided over the issue of tariff reform. Later, as Foreign Secretary, he authored the Balfour Declaration of 1917, which supported the establishment of a Jewish homeland in Palestine.

Ball, Lucille

Lucille Désirée Ball (August 6, 1911 – April 26, 1989) was an Iconic American, comedienne, actress, glamour girl and star of the landmark sitcoms *I Love Lucy*, *The Lucy Show*, and *Here's Lucy*. Lucille Ball is one of the American's favorite stars and had one of Hollywood's longest careers. She was a major movie star from the 1930's to the 1970s, and appeared on television for more than 30 years. She won 13 Emmy Awards (more than any other person ever), and dozens of Golden Globes and Lifetime Achievement Awards. She was also nominated dozens of other times for Emmys and Golden Globes.

Balzac, Honoré de

Honoré de Balzac (May 20, 1799 – August 18, 1850) was a nineteenth-century French novelist and playwright. His *magnum Opus* was a sequence of almost 100 novels and plays collectively entitled *La Comédie humaine*, which presents a panorama of French life in the years after the fall of Napoléon Bonaparte in 1815.

Due to his keen observation of detail and unfiltered representation of society, Balzac is regarded as one of the founders of realism in European literature. He is renowned for his multi-faceted characters; even his lesser characters are complex, morally ambiguous and fully human.

Bankhead, Tullulah

Tallulah Brockman Bankhead (January 31, 1902 – December 12, 1968) was an American actress, talk-show host and *bonne vivante*.

Bankhead was born in Huntsville, Alabama. She has been described as "an extremely homely child", overweight and with a deep, husky voice resulting from chronic bronchitis.

Bankhead came from a powerful Democratic political family in the South in general and Alabama in particular. Her father was the Speaker of the United States House of Representatives from 1936 – 1940. She was the niece of Senator John H. Bankhead II, and granddaughter of Senator John H. Bankhead. Bankhead herself was a Democrat, albeit one of a more liberal stripe than the rest of her family.

Her family sent her to various schools in an attempt to keep her out of trouble. At 15, Bankhead won a movie-magazine beauty contest and convinced her family to let her move to New York. She quickly won bit parts, first appearing in a non-speaking role in *The Squab Farm*. During these early New York years, she became a peripheral member of the Algonquin Round Table and known as a hard-partying girl-about-town.

In 1923, she made her debut on the London stage. She returned to the US in 1931 to be Paramount Pictures' "next Marlene Dietrich", but Hollywood success eluded her in her first four films of the 30s. Critics agree that her acting was flat, that she was unable to dominate the camera, and that she was generally outclassed by Dietrich, Carole Lombard, and others. She rented a home at 1712 Stanley Street, in Hollywood, and began hosting parties that were said to "have no boundaries". On September 9, 1932, she was featured on the cover of *Film Weekly*.

Bankhead's first film was Tarnished Lady (1931), directed by George Cukor, and Cukor and Bankhead became fast friends. Bankhead behaved herself on the set and filming went smoothly, but she found filmmaking to be very boring and didn't have the patience for it. She didn't like Hollywood either. When she met producer Irving Thalberg, she asked him, "How do you get laid in this dreadful place?"

Barber, Jerry

Carl Jerome "Jerry" Barber (April 25, 1916 – September 23, 1994) Was a professional golfer on the PGA Tour.

He was born in Jacksonville, Illinois. Among his seven tour victories, Barber won the 1961 PGA Championship at Olympia Fields Country Club (a location not far from where Barber grew up) on the strength of one of the most astonishing displays of clutch putting in major championship history. Trailing Don January by four shots with three holes to play in the final round, Barber made a 20-foot birdie putt at the 16th hole, a 40-foot par-saving putt at 17, and a 60-foot birdie putt at 18 to tie January and force a playoff, which Barber won the next day by one stroke. Barber played on two Ryder Cup teams, 1955 and 1961, and also was team captain in 1961.

Barkley, Alben W.

Alben William Barkley (November 24, 1877 – April 30, 1956) was a Democratic member of the U.S. House of Representatives and the United States Senate from Paducah, Kentucky, and the thirty-fifth Vice President of the United States.

Barnum, P. T.

Phineas Taylor Barnum (July 5, 1810 – April 7, 1891) was an American showman who is best remembered for his entertaining hoaxes and for founding the circus that eventually became the Ringling Bros. And Barnum & Bailey Circus. Barnum never flinched from his stated goal "to put money in his own coffers". He was a businessman above all else, his profession was pure entertainment, and he was perhaps the first "show business" millionaire. He never said "There's a sucker born every minute" as is famously ascribed, but his rebuttal to his critics was often "I am a showman by profession…and all the gilding shall make nothing else of me." Although famous for his brazen self-promotion and blatant puffery, he understood his times and profited from them brilliantly.

Barry, Dave

David Barry, Jr. (born July 3, 1947) is a best selling American Author and Pulitzer Prize-winning humorist who wrote a nationally Syndicated column for the Miami Herald from 1983 to 2005.

Barrymore, John

John Sidney Blyth Barrymore (February 15, 1882 in Philadelphia, Pennsylvania – May 29, 1942 in Los Angeles, California), was an American actor.

He gained fame as a stage actor, lauded for his portrayals of Hamlet and Richard III, and is frequently called the greatest actor of his generation. He was the brother of Lionel Barrymore and Ethel Barrymore, and the grandfather of Drew Barrymore.

Beaumarchais, Pierre

Pierrce-Augustin Caron de Beaumarchais (January 24, 1732 – May 17 – 18, 1799) was a watch-maker, inventor, musician, politician, invalid, fugitive, spy, publisher, arms-dealer, and revolutionary (both French and American). He was best known, however, for his theatrical works, especially the three Figaro plays.

Behan, Brendan

Brendan Francis Behan (Irish: *Breandán Ó Beaucháin*) (February 9, 1923 – March 20, 1964) was an Irish poet, short story writer, novelist and playwright who wrote in both Irish and English. He was also a committed Irish Republican and an erstwhile member of the Irish Republican Army.

Behan was one of the most successful Irish dramatists of the 20th century.

Bellow, Saul

Saul Bellow, born Solomon Bellows (Lachine, Quebec, Canada, June 10, 1915 – April 5, 2005 in Brookline, Massachusetts), was an acclaimed Canadian-born American writer. He won the Nobel Prize in Literature in 1976 and the National Medal of Arts in 1988.

Bellow is best known for writing novels that investigate isolation, spiritual dissociation, and the possibilities of human awakening. Bellow drew inspiration from Chicago, his hometown, and he set much of his fiction there. His works exhibit a mix of high and low culture, and his fictional characters are also a potent mix of intellectual dreamers and street-smart confidence men. While on a Guggenheim fellowship in Paris, he wrote his best-known novel, *The Adventures of Augie March* (1953).

Bentham, Jeremy

Jeremy Bentham (26 February 1748 – 6 June 1832) was an English jurist, philosopher, and legal and social reformer. He was a political radical and a leading theorist in Anglo-American philosophy of law. He is best known for his advocacy of utilitarianism and his opposition to the concept of natural rights with oft quoted statements to the effect that such rights were nonsense. He influenced the development of welfarism.

Berenson, Bernard

Bernard Berenson (born June 26, 1865 Butrimonys (now Vilna), Lithuania – October 6, 1959 Florence, Italy) was an American art historian specializing in the Renaissance. He was a major figure in establishing the market for paintings by the "Old Masters".

Berra, Yogi

Lawrence Peter "Yogi" Berra (born May 12, 1925 in St. Louis, Missouri) is a former Major League Baseball player and manager. He played almost his entire career for the New York Yankees and was elected to the baseball Hall of Fame in 1972. He was one of only four players to be named the Most Valuable Player of the American League three times, and one of only six managers to lead both American and National League teams to the World Series.

Berra, who quit school in the eighth grade, has a tendency toward malapropism and fracturing the English language in highly provocative, interesting ways. Simultaneously denying and confirming his reputation, Berra once stated, "I never said half the things I really said." *(See Yogiisms.)*

Bhartrhari

Bhartrhari is the name of a 6th or 7th century Sanskrit grammarian, and of a Sanskrit poet of roughly the same period. It is not known whether the two are identical.

Bierce, Ambrose

Ambrose Gwinett Bierce (June 24, 1842 – 1914(?)) was An American editorialist, journalist, short-story writer and satirist, today best known for his *Devil's Dictionary*.

Bierce's lucid, unsentimental style has kept him popular when many of his contemporaries have been consigned to oblivion. His dark, sardonic views and vehemence as a critic earned him the nickname, "**Bitter Bierce**". Such was his reputation that it was said his judgment on any piece of prose or poetry could make or break a writer's career. Among the younger writers whom he encouraged were the poet George Sterling and the fiction writer W. C. Morrow.

Billings, Josh

Josh Billings was the pen name of humorist born **Henry Wheeler Shaw** (20 April 1818 – 14 October 1885). He was perhaps the second most famous humor writer and lecturer in the United States in the second half of the 19th century after Mark Twain, although his reputation has not fared so well with later generations.

Bismarck, Otto von

Otto Eduard Leopold von Bismarck, 1st Graf von Bismarck-Schönhausen, 1st Herzog von Lauenburg. **1st Fürst von Bismarck** (born April 1, 1815 in Schönhausen, today Saxony-Anhalt; died July 30, 1898 in Friedrichsruh near Hamburg), was a Prussian and German statesman of the 19th century. As Minister-President of Prussia from 1862 – 90, he engineered the unification of Germany. From 1867 on, he was Chancellor of the North German Confederation. When the second German Empire was declared in 1871, he served as its first Chancellor, gaining the nickname "*Iron Chancellor*".

Bismarck held conservative monarchical views in the tradition of Clemens von Metternich, the Austrian statesman who devised the diplomatic arrangements which governed Europe after the Napoleonic Wars – arrangements which Bismarck upset. Bismarck's primary objectives were to ensure the supremacy of the Prussian state within Central Europe, and of the aristocracy within the state itself. His most significant achievement was the creation of the modern German state, with Prussia at its core, through a series of wars and political maneuvering in the 1860s. The final act, the Franco-Prussian War of 1870 – 71, saw Prussia break France's power on the European continent.

Blair, Tony

Anthony Charles Lynton Blair (born 6 May 1953) is a British politician who served as Prime Minister of the United Kingdom from 2 May 1997 to 27 June 2007. Leader of the Labour Party from 1994 to 2007 and Member of Parliament for Sedgefield from 1983 to 2008. On the day he stood down as Prime Minister, he was appointed official Envoy of the Quartet on the Middle East on behalf of the United Nations, the European Union, the United States and Russia, and stepped down as an MP.

Blake, Eubie

James Hubert Blake (February 7, 1887 – February 12, 1983) was a composer, lyricist, and pianist of ragtime, jazz, and popular music. With long time collaborator Noble Sissle, Blake wrote the Broadway musical *Shuffle Along* in 1921; this was one of the first Broadway musical ever to be written and directed by African Americans. Blake's compositions included such hits as, "Bandana Days", "Charleston Rag", ":Love Will Find A Way", "Memories of You", and "I'm Just Wild About Harry". The musical *Eubie!,* which featured the collective works of Blake opened on Broadway in 1978.

Blake, William

William Blake (November 28, 1757 – August 12, 1827) was an English poet, painter, and printmaker. Largely unrecognized during his lifetime, Blake's work is today considered seminal and significant in the history of both poetry and the visual arts. He was voted 38th in a poll of the 100 Greatest Britons organized by the BBC in 2002.

Blount, Jr., Roy

Roy Alton Blount, Jr. (born October 4, 1941, in Indianapolis, Indiana) is an American writer. Best known as a humorist, Blount is also a reporter, actor, and musician with the Rock Bottom Remainders, a rock band composed entirely of writers. Blount graduated from Decatur High School in Decatur, Georgia, where he was editor of the school newspaper, *The Scribbler*, and Vanderbilt University. Recently he guided American television audiences down the Mississippi River, narrating the documentary *The Main Stream* for PBS. As of 2007 he is featured regularly as a panelist on the NPR news/comedy quiz show, *Wait Wait... Don't Tell Me.* On the show, Blount is known for outrageous dead-pan comments which frequently reduce the panel to tears of laughter, such as his discussion of "E.J. Junior Senior Junior High School".

Bonaparte, Napoleon

Napoleon I (born **Napoleone di Buonaparte**, later **Napoléon Bonaparte**) (15 August 1769 – 5 May 1821) was a French military and political leader who had significant impact on modern European history. He was a general during the French Revolution, the ruler of France as First Consul (*Premier Consul*) of the French Republic, Emperor of the French (*Empereur des Français*), King of Italy, Mediator of the Swiss Confederation and Protector of the Confederation of the Rhine.

Bombeck, Erma

Erma Louise Bombeck (February 21, 1927 – April 22, 1996), born **Erma Fiste**, was an American humorist who achieved great popularity for a newspaper column that depicted suburban home life in the second half of the 20th century.

Born in Dayton, Ohio, Bombeck graduated from the University of Dayton in 1949 with a degree in English. She started her career in 1949 as a reporter for the Dayton Journal Herald, but after marrying school administrator Bill Bombeck, a college friend, she left the job and raised three children.

As the children grew she started writing *At Wit's End*, telling self-deprecating tales about the life of a housewife. It debuted in the *Kettering-Oakwood Times* in 1964. She was paid $3 per column.

Growing popularity led *At Wit's End* to be nationally syndicated in 1965, and eventually it ran three times a week in more than 700 newspapers. The column was collected in many best-selling books, and her fame was such that a television sitcom was based on her. The series, *Maggie*, ran for eight shows in 1982 before being cancelled.

Boorstin, Daniel J.

Daniel Joseph Boorstin (October 1, 1914 – February 28, 2004) was a prolific American historian, professor, attorney, and writer. He served as the U.S. Librarian of Congress from 1975 until 1987.

Brando, Marlon

Marlon Brando, Jr. (April 3, 1924 – July 1, 2004) was an Academy Award-winning American actor whose body of work spanned over half a century. He is widely regarded as one of the most influential actors of all time. Brando is best known for his roles in *A Streetcar Named Desire* and *On the Waterfront*, both directed by Elia Kazan in the early 1950s, as well as his Academy-Award winning performance as Vito Corleone in *The Godfather* and as Colonel Walter E. Kurtz in *Apocalypse Now*, the latter two directed by Francis Ford Coppola in the 1970;s. Brando also garnered worldwide attention by playing Jor-El in *Superman: The Movie* (1978), directed by Richard Donner.

Brezhnev, Leonid

Leonid Ilyich Brezhnev (December 19, 1906 – November 10, 1982) was General Secretary of the Communist Party of the Soviet Union (and thus political leader of the USSR) from 1964 to 1982, serving in that position longer than anyone other than Joseph Stalin. He was twice Chairman of the Presidium of the Supreme Soviet (head of state), from 1960 to 1964 and from 1977 to 1982.

Bright, John

John Bright (November 16, 1811 – March 27, 1889), Quaker, was a British Radical and Liberal statesman, associated with Richard Cobden in the formation of the Anti-Corn Law League. He was one of the greatest orators of his generation, and a strong critic of British foreign policy.

Brooks, Mel

Mel Brooks (born June 28, 1926) is a multi-award winning American director, writer, comedian, actor and producer best known as a creator of broad film farces and comedy parodies. Brooks is a member of the short list of entertainers with the distinction of having won an Emmy, a Grammy, an Oscar and a Tony award.

Brown, Helen Gurley

Helen Gurley Brown (b. February 18, 1922 in Green Forest, Arkansas), is an author, publisher, and businesswoman. She was editor-in-chief of *Cosmopolitan* magazine for 32 years.

In 1962, at the age of 40, Brown authored the best selling book *Sex and the Single Girl*. In 1965 she became editor-in-chief of *Cosmopolitan* and reversed the fortunes of the failing magazine. During the decade of the 1950s she was an outspoken advocate of women's sexual freedom and sought to provide them with role-models and a guide in her magazine. Brown claimed that women could have it all, "love, sex, and money". Due to her advocacy, the liberated single woman was often referred to generically as the "Cosmo Girl". Her work played a part in what is often called the sexual revolution.

Buckley, Jr., William F.

William Frank "Bill" Buckley, Jr. (born November 24, 1925 February 27 2008) was an American author and conservative commentator. He founded the political magazine *National Review* in 1955, hosted the television show *Firing Line* from 1966 until 1999, and was a nationally syndicated newspaper columnist. His writing style was famed for its eloquence, wit, and use of uncommon words. Over the course of his career, Buckley's views have changed on some issues, such as drug legalization, which he now favors. In his December 1, 2007 column, Buckley claimed to favor banning tobacco.

Buckley was the author of a series of novels featuring the character of CIA agent Blackford Oakes, along with dozens of other books on writing, speaking, history, politics, and sailing. Buckey refers to himself "on and off" as either libertarian or conservative. He was based in New York City and Stamford, Connecticut. Buckley often signed his name as "**WFB**".

Burns, George

George Burns (born Nathan Birnbaum January 20, 1896 – March 9, 1006) was an Academy Award-winning Jewish-American comedian and actor.

His career spanned vaudeville, film, radio, and television, with and without his equally legendary wife, Gracie Allen. His arched eyebrow and cigar smoke punctuation became familiar trademarks for over three quarters of a century. Enjoying a remarkable career resurrection that began at age 79, and ended shortly before his death at age 100, George Burns was as well known in the last two decades of his life as at any other time during his career.

Burroughs, John

John Burroughs (April 3, 1837 – March 29, 1921) was an American naturalist and essayist important in the evolution of the U.S. conservation movement. According to biographers at the American Memory project at the Library of Congress, John Burroughs was the most important practitioner after Thoreau of that especially American literary genre, the nature essay. By the turn of the century he had become a virtual cultural institution in his own right: the Grand Old Man of Nature at a time when the American romance with the idea of nature, and the American conservation movement, had come fully into their own.

His extraordinary popularity and popular visibility were sustained by a prolific stream of essay collections, beginning with *Wake-Robin* in 1871.

Burton, Richard

Richard Burton, CBE (November 10, 1925 – August 5, 1984) was a Welsh actor. He was at one time the highest-paid actor in Hollywood. Known for his distinctive voice, he was nominated seven times for Academy Awards for acting, but never won.

Butler, Samuel (novelist)

Samuel Butler (December 4, 1835 – June 18, 1902) was a British writer strongly influenced by his New Zealand experiences. He is best known for his utopian satire *Erewhon* and his posthumous novel *The Way of All Flesh*.

Caesar, Julius

Gaius Julius Caesar (July 13, 100 BC – March 15, 44 BC) was a Roman military and political leader and one of the most influential men in world history. He played a critical role in the transformation of the Roman Republic into the Roman Empire.

A politician of the *populares* tradition, he formed an unofficial triumvirate with Marcus Licinius Crassus and Gnaeus Pompeius Magnus which dominated Roman politics for several years, opposed in the Roman Senate by *optimates* like Marcus Porcius Cato and Marcus Calpurnius Bibulus. His conquest of Gaul extended the Roman world all the way to the Atlantic Ocean, and he also conducted the first Roman invasion of Britain in 55 BC; the collapse of the triumvirate, however, led to a stand-off with Pompey and the Senate. Leading his legions across the Rubicon, Caesar began a civil war in 49 BC from which he became the undisputed master of the Roman world.

After assuming control of government, he began extensive reforms of Roman society and government. He was proclaimed dictator for life (*dictator perpetuus*), and heavily centralized the bureaucracy of the Republic. However, a group of senators, led by Cesar's former friend Marcus Junius Brutus, assassinated the dictator on the Ides of March (March 15) in 44 BC, hoping to restore the normal running of the Republic. However, the result was another Roman civil war, which ultimately led to the establishment of a permanent autocracy by Caesar's adopted heir, Gaius Octavianus. In 42 BC, two years after his assassination, the Senate officially sanctified Caesar as one of the Roman deities.

Camden, William

William Camden (2 May 1551 – 9 November 1623) was an English antiquarian and historian. He wrote the first topographical survey of the island of Great Britain and the first detailed historical account of the reign of Elizabeth I of England.

Canterburry, Tommy

Tommy Canterburry No biography.

Cantor, Eddie

Eddie Cantor (January 31, 1892 – October 10, 1964) was an American comedian, singer, actor, songwriter. Known to Broadway, radio and early television audiences as **Banjo Eyes**, this "Apostle of Pep" was regarded almost as a family member by millions because his top-rated radio shows revealed intimate stories and amusing antics about his wife Ida and five children.

Capp, Al

Al Capp (Septembver 28, 1909 – November 5, 1979) was an American cartoonist best known for the satiric comic strip, *Li'l Abner*. He also wrote the comic strips *Abbie and Slats* and *Long Sam*. He won the 1947 National Cartoonist Society Reuben Award for the comic strip *Li'l Abner*, and their 1979 Elzie Segar Award posthumously.

Capote, Truman

Truman Capote (30 September 1924 – 25 August 1984) was an American writer whose stories, novels, plays and non-fiction are recognized literary classics, including the novella *Breakfast at Tiffany's* (1958) and *In Cold Blood* (1965), which he labeled a "non-fiction novel." At least 20 films and TV dramas have been produced from Capote novels, stories and screenplays.

Carlyle, Thomas

Thomas Carlyle (December 4, 1795 – February 5, 1881) was a Scottish essayist, and historian, whose work was hugely influential during the Victorian era. Coming from a strict Calvinist family, Carlyle was expected by his parents to become a preacher. However, while at the University of Edinburgh, he lost his Christian faith; nevertheless, Calvinist values remained with him throughout his life. This combination of a religious temperament with loss of faith in traditional Christianity made Carlyle's work appealing to many Victorians who were grappling with scientific and political changes that threatened the traditional social order.

Carson, Johnny

John William "Johnny" Carson (October 23, 1925 – January 23, 2005) was an American television host best known for his iconic status as host of *The Tonight Show Starring Johnny Carson* for thirty years.

Carter, Lillian Gordy

Bessie Lillian Gordy Carter (August 15, 1898 – October 30, 1983) was the mother of former president of the United States, Jimmy Carter. She is also known for contribution to nursing in her home state of Georgia and as a Peace Corps volunteer in India as well as writing two books during the Carter presidency.

Catullus

Gaius Valerius Catullus (ca. 84 – 54 BC) was a Roman poet of the 1st century BC. His work remains widely studied, and continues to influence poetry and other art. Fresco from Herculaneum, presumably showing a love couple.

Chamfort, Nicolas

Nicolas Chamfort (April 6, 1741, Clermont-Ferrand, Auvergne France – April 13, 1794, Paris) was a French writer, best known for his witty epigrams and aphorisms.

Chanel, Coco

Gabrielle Bonheur "Coco" Chanel (August 19, 1883 – January 10, 1971) was a pioneering French fashion designer whose modernist philosophy, menswear-inspired fashions, and pursuit of expensive simplicity made her arguably the most important figure in the history of 20th-centruy fashion. Her influence on haute couture was such that she was the only person in the field to be named on TIME Magazine's 100 most influential people of the 20th century.

Chekhov, Anton

Anton Pavlovich Chekhov was a Russian short story writer and playwright. He was born in Taganrog, southern Russia, on 29 January 1860, and died of tuberculosis at the health spa of Badenweiler, Germany, on 15 July 1904. His playwriting career produced four classics, while his best short stories are held in high esteem by writers and critics. Chekhov practiced as a doctor throughout most of his literary career: "Medicine is my lawful wife," he once said, "and literature is my mistress".

Chekhov renounced the theatre after the disastrous reception of *The Seagull* in 1896; but the play was revived to acclaim by Constantin Stanislavski's Moscow Art Theatre, which subsequently also produced *Uncle Vanya* and premiered Chekhov's last two plays, *Three Sisters* and *The Cherry Orchard.* These four works present a special challenge to the acting ensemble as well as to audiences, because in place of conventional action Chekhov offers a "theatre of mood" and a "submerged life in the text". Not everyone appreciated that challenge: Leo Tolstoy reportedly told Chekhov, "You know, I cannot abide Shakespeare, but your plays are even worse".

Cher

Cher (born **Cherilyn Sarkisian LaPierre** on May 20, 1946) is an American singer, actress, songwriter, author and entertainer. Among her many accomplishments in music, television and film, she has won an Academy Award, a Grammy Award, an Emmy Award, a Cannes Film Award, three Golden Globe Awards, and Billboard Music Awards, among others.

Cher first rose to prominence in 1965 as one half of the pop/rock duo Sonny & Cher. She also established herself as a solo recording artist, releasing 25 albums, numerous compilations and tallying 34 *Billboard* Top 40 entries over her career, both solo and with Sonny. They include eighteen Top 10 singles and five number one singles (four solo). Cher has had 16 top ten hits in the UK between 1965 and 2003, four of which reached number one (two solo, one with Sonny, one as part of a charity single).

She became a television star in the 1970s and a film actress in the 1980s. In 1987, she won the Academy Award for Best Actress for her role in the romantic comedy *Moonstruck*.

In a career surpassing 40 years, Cher has been described as an enduring pop icon and one of the most popular female artists in music history. Since her debut in 1964, Cher has sold over 100 million records worldwide and an estimated 70 million solo singles, becoming one of the biggest-selling artists of all time.

Cherry, Don (ice hockey)

Donald Stewart "Grapes" Cherry, (born February 5, 1934 in Kingston, Ontario, Canada) is a hockey commentator for CBS Television. Cherry co-hosts the "Coach's Corner" intermission segment (with Ron MacLean) on the long running Canadian sports program *Hockey Night in Canada*. He is known for his outspoken manner, flamboyant dress, and staunch patriotism.

Besides playing and coaching hockey, he is also well-known as an author, syndicated radio commentator for The Fan Radio Network, creator of the *Rock'em Sock'em Hockey* video series, and celebrity endorser. Many consider him to be a Canadian cultural icon.

Chesterfield, Earl of

Earls of Chesterfield, in the County of Derby, was a title in the Peerage of England. It was created in 1616 for **Philip Stanhope**. He had already been created **Baron Stanhope**, of Shelford in the County of Nottingham, in 1616, also in the Peerage of England. Stanhope's youngest son the Hon. Alexander Stanhope was the father of James Stanhope, 1st Earl Stanhope while his half-brother Sir John Stanhope of Elvaston was the great-grandfather of

William Stanhope, 1st Earl of Harrington.

Lord Chesterfield's great-great-grandson, the fourth Earl, was a politician and man of letters and notably served as Lord Lieutenant of Ireland and as Secretary of State for the Northern Department.

Chesterton, G. K.

Gilbert Keith Chesterton (May 29, 1874 – June 14, 1936) was an influential English writer of the early 20th century. His prolific and diverse output included journalism, philosophy, poetry, biography, Christian apologetics, fantasy, and detective fiction.

Chesterton has been called the "prince of paradox". He wrote in an off-hand, whimsical prose studded with startling formulations. For example: "Thieves respect property. They merely wish the property to become their property that they may more perfectly respect it." He is one of the few Christian thinkers who are equally admired and quoted by both liberal and conservative Christians, and indeed by many non-Christians. Chesterton's own theological and political views were far too nuanced to fit comfortably under the "liberal" or "conservative" banner. And in his own words he cast aspersions on the labels saying, "The whole modern world had divided itself into Conservatives and Progressives. The business of Progressives is to go on making mistakes. The business of the Conservatives is to prevent the mistakes from being corrected." He is not to be confused with his cousin A. K. Chesterton, whose political views were very different.

Child, Julia

Julia Child (August 15, 1912 – August 13, 2004) was a famous American cook, author, and television personality who introduced French cuisine and cooking techniques to the American mainstream through her many cookbooks and television programs. Her most famous works are the 1961 cookbook *Mastering the Art of French Cooking* and showcasing her sui generis television persona, the series *The French Chef*, which premiered in 1963.

Churchill, Winston

Sir Winston Leonard Spencer-Churchill, KG, OM, CH, TD, FRS, PC (Can) (30 November 1874 – 24 January 1965) was a British politician who served as Prime Minister of the United Kingdom from 1940 to 1945 and again from 1951 to 1955. A noted statesman, orator and strategist, Churchill was also an officer in the British Army. A prolific author, he won the Nobel Prize in Literature in 1953 for his historical writings.

During his army career Churchill saw combat with the Malakand Field Force on the Northwest Frontier, at the Battle of Omdurman in the Sudan and during the Second Boer War in South Africa. During this period he also gained fame, and not a small amount of notoriety, as a correspondent. At the forefront of the political scene for almost sixty years, Churchill held numerous political and cabinet positions. Before the First World War, he served as President of the Board of Trade and Home Secretary during the Liberal governments. In the First World War Churchill served in numerous positions, as First Lord of the Admiralty, Minister of Munitions, Secretary of State for War and Secretary of State for Air. He also served in the British Army on the Western Front and commanded the British Army on the Western Front and commanded the 6th Battalion of the Royal Scots Fusiliers. During the interwar years, he served as Chancellor of the Exchequer.

After the outbreak of the Second World War, Churchill was appointed First Lord of the Admiralty. Following the resignation of Neville Chamberlain on 10 May 1940, he became Prime Minister of the United Kingdom and led Britain to victory against the Axis powers. His speeches were a great inspiration to the embattled Allied forces. After losing the 1945 election, Churchill became the leader of the opposition. In 1951, Churchill again became Prime Minister before finally retiring in 1955. Upon his death, he was granted the honour, by Queen Elizabeth II of the United Kingdom, of a state funeral which saw one of the largest assemblies of statesmen in the world.

Ciardi, John

John Anthony Ciardi (June 24, 1916 – March 30, 1986) was an American poet, translator, and etymologist.

John Ciardi was primarily a poet, but he also translated Dante's *Divine Comedy*, wrote several volumes of children's poetry, pursued etymology, contributed to the *Saturday Review* as a columnist and long-time poetry editor, and directed the Bread Loaf Writers' Conference in Vermont . In 1959, Ciardi published a book on how to read, write, and teach poetry, *How Does a Poem Mean?,* which has proven to be among the most-used books of its kind. At the peak of his popularity in the early 1960s, Ciardi also had a network television program on CBS, *Accent*. For the last decade of his life, he reported on word histories on National Public Radio's *Morning Edition*, as an outgrowth of his series of books of etymologies, *A Browser's Dictionary* (1980), *A Second Browser's Dictionary* (1983) and *Good Words to You* (posthumously published in 1987). Among 20th–century American men of letters he maintained a notably high profile and level of popularity with the general public, as well as a reputation for considerable craftsmanship in his output.

Cicero

Marcus Tullius Cicero (Classical Latin pronounced [' kikero:]), January 3, 106 BC – December 7, 43 BC) was a Roman statesman, lawyer, political theorist, and philosopher. Cicero is widely considered one of Rome's greatest orators and prose stylists.

Cicero is generally seen as one of the most versatile minds of Roman culture and his writing the paragon of Classical Latin. He introduced the Romans to the chief schools of Greek philosophy and created a Latin philosophical vocabulary. An impressive orator and successful lawyer, Cicero likely thought his political career his most important achievement.

Clancy, Tom

Thomas Leo Clancy Jr. (born April 12, 1947), better known as Tom Clancy, is a US author of best selling political thrillers, best known for his technically detailed espionage and military science storylines set during and in the aftermath of the Cold War. His name is also a brand for similar books written by ghost writers and a series of non-fiction books on military subjects and merged biographies of key leaders. He is also part-owner of the Baltimore

Orioles, a Major League Baseball team. He officially is the Orioles' Vice Chairman of Community Projects and Public Affairs.

Colette

Colette was the pen name of the French novelist **Sidonie-Gabrielle Colette** (January 28, 1873 – August 3, 1954). She is best known, at least in the English-speaking world, for her novel Gigi, which provided the plot for a Lerner & Loewe musical firm and stage musical.

Confucius

Confucious (pinyin: Kǒng Fūzǐ; Wade-Giles: K'ung-fu-tzu), lit. "*Master Kung,*" 551 BCE – 479 BCE) was a Chinese thinker and social philosopher, whose teachings and philosophy have deeply influenced Chinese, Korean, Japanese, and Vietnamese thought and life.

His philosophy emphasized personal and governmental morality, correctness of social relationships, justice and sincerity. These values gained prominence in China over other doctrines, such as Legalism or Taoism during the Han Dynasty. Confucius' thoughts have been developed into a system of philosophy known as *Confucianism*. It was introduced to Europe by the Jesuit Matteo Ricci, who was the first to Latinise the name as "Confucius".

His teachings may be found in the *Analects of Confucius*, a collection of "brief aphoristic fragments", which was compiled many years after his death. Modern historians do not believe that any specific documents can be said to have been written by Confucius, but for nearly 2,000 years he was thought to be the editor or author of all the Five Classics such as the *Classic of Rites* (editor), and the *Spring and Autumn Annals* (author).

Cosby, Bill

William Henry "Bill" Cosby, Jr., Ed.D. (born July 12, 1937) is an American comedian, actor, television producer, activist, and luminary. A veteran stand-up performer, he got his start at various clubs,then landed a vangurd role in the 1960's action show *I Spy*. He later starred in his own series, *The Bill Cosby Show*, in the late 1960's. He was one of the major characters on the children's television show for its first two seasons, and created the humourous educational cartoon series *Fat Albert and the Cosby Kids*, about a group of young friends growing up in the city. Cosby also acted in numerous films, although none has received the acclaim of his television work. During the 1980s, Cosby produced and starred in what is considered one of the decade's defining sitcoms, *The Cosby Show*, which aired from 1984 to 1992. The sitcom featured an upper-middle class African-American family without resorting to the kinds of stereotypes previously seen among African-Americans in prime-time television. While some argued that *The Cosby Show* ignored the issues of racial inequity still prevalent in society, many agreed that it showcased positive role models.

Coward, Noel

Sir Noel Peirce Coward (16 December 1899 – 26 March 1973) was an Academy Award winning English actor, playwright, and composer of popular music.

A student at the Italia Conti Academy stage school, Coward's first professional engagement was on 27 January 1911, in the children's play *The Goldfish*. After this appearance, he was sought after for children's roles by other professional theatres. He was cast as the Lost Boy Slightly in the 1913 production of *Peter Pan*.

Crawford, Joan

Joan Crawford (born **Lucille Fay LeSueur**; (March 23, 1905 – May 10, 1977) was an Academy Award-winning American actress. The American Film Institute named Crawford among the Greatest Female Stars of All Time, ranking her at number 10.

Crisp, Quentin

Quentin Crisp (December 25, 1908 – November 21, 1999) born **Denis Charles Pratt**, was an English writer, artist's model, actor and raconteur known for his memorable and insightful witticisms. He became a gay icon in the 1970s after publication of his memoir, *The Naked Civil Servant*, brought to the attention of the general public his defiant exhibitionism and longstanding refusal to conceal his homosexuality.

Dalí, Salvador

Salvador Domingo Felipe Jacinto Dalí Domènech, 1st Marquis **of Púbol** (May 11, 1904 – January 23, 1989) was a Spanish surrealist painter born in Figueres, Catalonia, Spain.

Dalí was a skilled draftsman, best known for the striking and bizarre images in his surrealist work. His painterly skills are often attributed to the influence of Renaissance masters. His best know work, *The Persistence of Memory*, was completed in 1931.

Dangerfield, Rodney

Rodney Dangerfield (November 22, 1921 – October 5, 2004) born **Jacob Cohen**, was an American comedian and actor, best known for the catchphrase "*I don't get no respect*" and his monologues on that theme.

Darrow, Clarence

Clarence Seward Darrow (April 18, 1857 Kinsman Township, Trumbull County, Ohio – March 13, 1938 Chicago) was an American lawyer and leading member of the American Civil Liberties Union, best known for defending teenage thrill killers Leopold and Loeb in their trial for murdering 14-year-old Bobby Franks (1924) and defending John T. Scopes in the so-called "Monkey" Trial (1925), in which he opposed the statesman William Jennings Bryan. He remains notable for his wit, compassion, and agnosticism that marked him as one of the most famous American lawyers and civil libertarians.

De Gaulle, Charles

Charles André Joseph Marie de Gaulle (November 22, 1890 – November 9, 1970) was a French general and statesman who led the Free French Forces during World War II and later founded the French Fifth Republic and served as its first President. In France, he is commonly referred to as *Général de Gaulle* or simply *Le Général*.

De Kooning, Willem

Willem de Kooning (April 24, 1904 – March 19, 1997) was an abstract expressionist painter, born in Rotterdam, the Netherlands.

In the post World War II era, De Kooning painted in the style that is referred to as Abstract expressionism, Action painting, and the New York School. Other painters in this category include Jackson Pollock, Franz Kline, Arshile Gorky, Mark Rothko, Hans Hofmann, Robert Motherwell, Philip Guston and Clyfford Still among others.

Dean, Dizzy

Jerome Hanna "Dizzy" Dean (January 16, 1910 – July 17, 1974) was an American pitcher in Major League Baseball, elected to the Baseball Hall of Fame. He was born in Lucas, Arkansas, and was a life-long resident of Bond, Mississippi. He was a pitcher for the St. Louis Cardinals (1930-1937), the Chicago Cubs (1938 – 1941), and briefly for the St. Louis Browns (1947).

Demaret, Jimmy

James Newton Demaret (May 24, 1910 – December 28, 1983) Was an American professional golfer. He won 31 PGA Tour events in a long career between 1935 and 1957 and was the first three-time winner of the Masters.

Demaret was elected to the World Golf Hall of Fame in 1983. In 2000, he was ranked as the 20th greatest golfer of all time by *Golf Digest* magazine.

Dewar, Tommy

Sir Thomas Robert Dewar (1864 – 1930) was a Scottish whisky distiller who, along with his brother John Dewar, built their family label, Dewar's, into an international success. They blended their whisky to make it more appealing to the international palate and Sir Thomas demonstrated particular skills in marketing, traveling the world to find new markets and promote his product, exploiting romantic images of Scotland and tartan in his advertising.

Tommy Dewar, as stated above, was an enthusiastic and gifted thinker and salesman. The founder of the "Dewarism" philosophy, he attempted to show that the way to success in life is not through an arduous or painstaking work agenda; success can be attained without compromising joy in life. This idea being the core of the philosophy, Tommy wrote smaller statements or observations that he accumulated throughout his life.

Dietrich, Marlene

Marlene Dietrich (December 27, 1901 – May 6, 1992) was a German-born American actress, singer and entertainer. She is regarded as being the first German actress to become successful in Hollywood.

Throughout her long career, starting as a cabaret singer, chorus girl and film actress in 1920s Berlin, Hollywood movie star in the 1930s, World War II frontline entertainer during the 1940s, and finally as an international stage show performer from the 1950s to the 1970s, Dietrich constantly re-invented herself and eventually became one of the entertainment icons of the 20th century. The American Film Institute ranked Dietrich No. 9 amongst the Greatest Female Stars of All Time.

Diller, Phyllis

Phyllis Diller (1917 –), a Golden Globe—nominated American comedienne, is considered one of the pioneers of female stand-up comedy. She created a stage character persona that was a wild-haired, eccentrically dressed housewife who made jokes about a fictional husband named "Fang" while smoking from a long cigarette holder. Another distinct characteristic is her cackling laugh, one of the best recognized noises in comedy. Diller is given credit for opening the locked doors for the stand-up comedy field to women such as Rita Rudner, Totie Fields, Joan Rivers, Lily Tomlin, Sandra Bernhard, Joy Behar, Rosie O'Donnell and Roseanne Barr.

Diogenes of Sinope

Diogenes "the Cynic", Greek philosopher, was born in Sinope (modern day Sinop, Turkey) about 412 BC (according to other sources 404 BC), and died in 323 BC, at Corinth. Details of his life come in the form of anecdotes (*chreia*), especially from Diogenes Laërtius, in his book *Lives and Opinions of Eminent Philosophers*.

Diogenes of Sinope is said to have been a disciple of Antisthenes, who (according to Plato's *Phaedo*) was present at the death of Socrates. Diogenes, a beggar who made his home in the streets of Athens, made a virtue of extreme poverty. He taught contempt for human achievements; his was a relentless campaign to debunk social values and institutions.

Dirksen, Everett

Everett McKinley Dirksen (January 4, 1896 – September 7, 1969) was a Republican U.S. Congressman and Senator from Illinois. As Republican Senate leader he played a highly visible and key role in the politics of the 1960s, including helping to write and pass the Civil Rights Act of 1964. He later offered his support for the Open Housing Act of 1968, another landmark piece of Civil Rights legislation. He was one of the Senate's strongest supporters of the Vietnam War. He was a member of the Pi Kappa Alpha Fraternity.

Disraeli, Benjamin

Benjamin Disraeli, 1st Earl of Beaconsfield, KG, PC, FRS (born **Benjamin D'Israeli**; 21 December 1804 – 19 April 1881) was a British Conservative statesman and literary figure. He served in government for three decades, twice as Prime Minister – the first and thus far only person of Jewish parentage to do so (although Disraeli was baptized in the Anglican Church at 13). Disraeli's most lasting achievement was the creation of the modern Conservative Party after the Corn Laws schism of 1846.

Dostoevsky, Fyodor

Fyodor Mikhailovich Dostoevsky (November 11, 1821 – February 9, 1881) was a Russian novelist and writer of fiction whose works, including *Crime and Punishment* and *The Brothers Karamazov*, have had a profound and lasting effect on intellectual thought and world literature.

Douglas, Kirk

Kirk Douglas (born **Issur Danielovitch** on December 9, 1916) is an iconic American actor and film producer known for his cleft chin, his gravelly voice and his recurring roles as the kinds of characters Douglas himself once described as "sons of bitches". He is also father to Hollywood actor and producer Michael Douglas. He came in at #17 on AFI's list of the greatest male American screen legends of all time and is one of the two living actors (men) on the list (Sidney Poitier being the other).

Dunne, Finley Peter

Finley Peter Dunne (July 10, 1867 – April 24, 1936) was a Chicago-based U. S. author, writer and humorist. He wrote *Mr. Dooley in Peace and War* in 1898. "Mr. Dooley" became one of the first nationally syndicated newspaper features. Set in a South Side Chicago Irish pub, Mr. Dooley, the owner and bartender, would expound upon political and social issues of the day, using the thick verbiage and accent of an Irish immigrant. Dunne's sly humor and political acumen won the support of President Theodore Roosevelt, a frequent target of Mr. Dooley's barbs.

Eban, Abba

Abba Eban (born **Aubrey Solomon Meir** on 2 February 1915, died 17 November 2002) was an Israeli diplomat and politician.

Edison, Thomas

Thomas Alva Edison (February 11, 1847 –October 18, 1931) was an American inventor of Dutch origin and businessman who developed many devices that greatly influenced life around the world, including the phonograph and a long lasting light bulb. Dubbed "The Wizard of Menlo Park" by a newspaper reporter, he was one of the first inventors to apply the principles of mass production to the process of invention, and therefore is often credited with the creation of the first industrial research laboratory. Edison is considered one of the most prolific inventors in history, holding 1,093 U.S./ patents in his name, as well as many patents in the United Kingdom, France and Germany.

Einstein, Albert

Albert Einstein (March 14, 1879 – April 18, 1955) was a German-born theoretical physicist. He is best known for his theory of relativity and specifically mass-energy equivalence, $E = mc^2$. Einstein received the 1921 Nobel Prize in Physics "for his services to Theoretical Physics, and especially for his discovery of the law of the photoelectric effect".

Einstein's many contributions to physics include his special theory of relativity, which reconciled mechanics with electromagnetism, and his general theory of relativity, which extended the principle of relativity to non-uniform motion, creating a new theory of gravitation. His other contributions include relativistic cosmology, capillary action, critical opalescence, classical problems of statistical mechanics and their application to quantum theory, an explanation of the Brownian movement of molecules, atomic transition probabilities, the quantum theory of a monatomic gas, thermal properties of light with low radiation density (which laid the foundation for the photon theory), a theory of radiation including stimulated emission, the conception of a unified field theory, and the geometrization of physics.

Works by Albert Einstein include more than fifty scientific papers and also non-scientific books. In 1999 Einstein was named *Time* magazine's "Person of the Century", and a poll of prominent physicists named him the greatest physicist of all time. In popular culture the name "Einstein" has become synonymous with genius.

Eisenhower, Dwight D.

Dwight David Eisenhower, born **David Dwight Eisenhower** (October 14, 1890 – March 28, 1959), nicknamed "**Ike**", was a five-star General in the United States Army and U.S. politician, who served as the 34th President of the United States (1953 – 1961). During the Second World War, he served as Supreme Commander of the Allied forces in Europe, with responsibility for planning and supervising the successful invasion of France and Germany in 1944-45. In 1951, he became the first supreme commander of NATO.

Eisenhower was elected the 34th President as a Republican, serving for two terms. As President, he oversaw the cease-fire of the Korean War, kept up the pressure on the Soviet Union during the Cold War, made nuclear weapons a higher defense priority, launched the Space Race, enlarged the Social Security program, and began the Interstate Highway System.

Eliot, T.S.

Thomas Stearns Eliot, OM (September 26, 1888 – January 4, 1965), was a poet, dramatist and literary critic. He received the Nobel Prize in Literature in 1948. He wrote the poems *The Love* Song of J. Alfred Prufrock, The Waste Land, The Hollow Men, *Ash Wednesday*, and *Four Quartets*; the plays *Murder in the Cathedral* and *The Cocktail Party*; and the essay *Tradition and the Individual Talent*. Eliot was born an American, moved to the United Kingdom in 1914 (at the age of 25), and became a British subject in 1927 at the age of 39.

Emerson, Ralph Waldo

Ralph Waldo Emerson (May 25, 1803 – April 27, 1882) was an American essayist, poet, and leader of the Transcendentalist movement in the early 19th century.

Emerson gradually moved away from the religious and social beliefs of his contemporaries, formulating and expressing the philosophy of Transcendentalism in his 1836 essay, *Nature*. As a result of this ground breaking work he gave a speech entitled *The American Scholar* in 1837, which is considered to be America's "Intellectual Declaration of Independence". He once said "Make the most of yourself, for that is all there is of you."

Considered one of the great orators of the time, Emerson's enthusiasm and respect for his audience enraptured crowds. His support for abolitionism late in life created controversy, and he was subject to abuse from crowds while speaking on the topic. When asked to sum up his work, he said his central doctrine was "the infinitude of the private man".

Fields, W. C.

W. C. Fields (January 29, 1880 – December 25, 1946) was an American juggler, comedian, and actor. Fields created one of the great American comic personas of the first half of the 20th century – a misanthrope who teetered on the edge of buffoonery but never quite fell in, an egotist blind to his own failings, a charming drunk; and a man who hated children, dogs and women, unless they were the wrong sort of women.

This characterization that he portrayed in films and radio was so strong that it generally identified with Fields himself. It was maintained by the then-typical movie-studio publicity departments at Field's studios (Paramount and Universal) and further established by Robert Lewis Taylor's 1949 biography *W. C. Fields, His Follies and Fortunes*. Beginning in 1973, with the publication of Fields's letters, photos, and personal notes in grandson Ronald Fields's book *W. C. Fields by Himself*, it has been shown that Fields was married (and subsequently estranged from his wife), he financially supported their son, and he loved his grandchildren.

Fischler, Stan

Stan Fischler (born March 31, 1932 Brooklyn, New York) is a controversial hockey and New York City Subway historian, broadcaster, author and professor.

For his hockey knowledge, Fischler is known as "The Hockey Maven" in both local and national circles. Fischler is an analyst for the New Jersey Devils and New York Islanders on FSN New York and the New York Rangers on MSG. He also provides general hockey analysis on MSG and writes columns for the network's website. A consummate entertainer, Fischler is known by some to play to the cameras and has become embroiled in more than a few controversies due to a seeming desire to take contrary positions for publicity.

In addition to broadcasting, Fischler has authored or co-authored more than 90 books on hockey or the NYC subway system, frequently co-writing with his wife Shirley. His books include: The Hockey Encyclopedia", "Everybody's Hockey Book", "Hockey

Chronicle", "The New NHL Encyclopedia, and most recently "MetroIce: A Century of Hockey in Greater New York", focusing on the Rangers, Islanders and Devils franchises. His most famous subway book is *Uptown, Downtown.*

On September 18, 2007 Fischler was announced one of the four recipients of the 2007 Lester Patrick Trophy.

Flaubert, Gustave

Gustave Flaubert (December 12, 1821 – May 8, 1880) was a French writer who is counted among the greatest Western novelists. He is known especially for his first published novel, *Madame Bovary* (1857), and for his scrupulous devotion to his art and style, best exemplified by his endless search for "*le mot juste*" ("the precise word").

Florus

Florus, Roman historian, lived in the time of Trajan and Hadrian. He compiled, chiefly from Livy, a brief sketch of the history of Rome from the foundation of the city to the closing of the temple of Janus by Augustus (25 BC). The work, which is called *Epitome de T. Livio Bellorum onmium annorum DCC Libri duo*, is written in a bombastic and rhetorical style – a panegyric of the greatness of Rome, the life of which is divided into the periods of infancy, youth and manhood. It is often wrong in geographical and chronological details. In spite of its faults, however, the book was much used in the Middle Ages and survived as a textbook into the nineteenth century.

Flynn, Errol

Errol Leslie Thomson Flynn (June 20, 1909 – October 14, 1959) was an Australian film actor, most famous for his romantic swashbuckler roles in Hollywood films and his flamboyant lifestyle.

Flynn became an overnight sensation with his first starring role in *Captain Blood* (1935). He became typecast as a swashbuckler and made a host of such films, including *The Adventures of Robin Hood* (1938), *The Dawn Patrol* (1938) with his close friend David

Niven, *Dodge City* (1939), *The Sea Hawk* (1940), and *Adventures of Don Juan* (1948).

Flynn played opposite Olivia de Havilland in eight films, including *Captain Blood, The Charge of the Light Brigade* (1936), *The Adventures of Robin Hood, Dodge City, Santa Fe Trail* (1940), and *They Died with their Boots On* (1941). Film historian Rudy Behlmer asserted that during the filming of Robin Hood, de Havilland and Flynn were romantically involved (see the Special Edition of Robin Hood on DVD, 2003), but de Havilland herself has disputed this. Their relationship was, she said in an interview for Turner Classic Movies, platonic, mostly because Flynn was already married to Lili Damita. *The Adventures of Robin Hood* was Flynn's first in Technicolor.

Forbes, Malcolm

Malcolm Stevenson Forbes (August 19, 1919 – February 24, 1990) was publisher of Forbes magazine, founded by his father B.C. Forbes and today run by his son Steve Forbes.

He was a graduate of the Lawrenceville School and Princeton University, where he donated the money for Forbes College, one of the six residential colleges at the University. He received an honorary degree from Miami University in Oxford, Ohio and was initiated as an honorary member of the Alpha Chapter of Phi Kappa Tau.

After dabbling in politics, including service in the New jersey Senate from 1951 to 1957 and candidacy for Governor of New Jersey, he committed to the magazine full time by 1957, three years after his father's death, and after the death of his brother Bruce Charles Forbes in 1964 acquired sole control of the company. The magazine grew steadily under his leadership, and he diversified into real estate sales and other ventures.

Ford, Henry

Henry Ford (July 30, 1863 – April 7, 1947) was the American founder of the Ford Motor Company and father of modern assembly lines used in mass production. His introduction of the Model T automobile revolutionized transportation and American industry. He was a prolific inventor and was awarded 161 U.S. patents. As owner of the Ford Company he became one of the richest and best-known people in the world. He is credited with "Fordism", that is, the mass production of large numbers of inexpensive automobiles using the assembly line, coupled with high wages for his workers. Ford had a global vision, with consumerism as the key to peace. Ford did not believe in accountants; he amassed one of the world's largest fortunes without ever having his company audited under his administration. Henry Ford's intense commitment to lowering costs resulted in many technical and business innovations, including a franchise system that put a dealership in every city in North America, and in major cities on six continents. Ford left most of his vast wealth to the Ford Foundation but arranged for his family to control the company permanently.

Foreman, George

George Edward Foreman (born January 10, 1949) is an American two-time World Heavyweight Boxing Champion. He is the oldest man ever to win the heavyweight title, and also has been named one of the 25 greatest fighters of all time by Ring magazine.

Nicknamed "Big George", he is now a successful businessman (well known for his Grill) and an ordained Christian minister who has his own church.

France, Anatole

Anatole France (16 April 1844 – 12 October 1924), born **François-Anatole Thibault**, was A French author. He was born in Paris, and died in Tours, Indre-et-Loire.

Anatole France became known after the publication of *The Crime of Sylvestre Bonnard* (1881). Its protagonist, skeptical old scholar Sylvester Boinnard, embodied France's own personality. The novel was praised for its elegant prose and won him a prize from the French Academy. In *La rotisserie de la Reine Pedauque* (1893) Anatole France ridiculed belief in the occult; and in *Les opinions de Jerome Coignard* (1893), France captured the atmosphere of the *fin de siècle.*

Franklin, Benjamin

Benjamin Franklin (January 17, 1706 – April 17, 1790) was one of the most important and influential Founding Fathers of the United States of America. A noted polymath, Franklin was a leading author and printer, satirist, political theorist, politician, scientist, inventor, civic activist, statesman and diplomat. As a scientist he was a major figure in the Enlightenment and the history of physics for his discoveries and theories regarding electricity. He invented the lighting rod, bifocals, the Franklin stove, a carriage odometer, and a musical instrument. He formed both the first public lending library and fire department in America.

He was an early proponent of colonial unity and as a political writer and activist he, more than anyone, invented the idea of an American nation and as a diplomat during the American Revolution, he secured the French alliance that helped to make Independence possible.

Freud, Sigmund

Sigmund Freud, born **Sigismund Schlomo Freud**)May 6, 1856 – September 23, 1939), was an Austrian neurologist and psychiatrist who founded the psychoanalytic school of psychology. Freud is best known for his theories of the unconscious mind and the defense mechanism of repression. He is also renowned for his redefinition of sexual desire as the primary motivational energy of human life which is directed toward a wide variety of objects; as well as his therapeutic techniques, including his theory of transference in the therapeutic relationship and the presumed value of dreams as sources of insight into unconscious desires.

Friedman, Milton

Milton Friedman (July 31, 1912 – November 16, 2006) was an American Nobel Laureate economist and public intellectual. An advocate of economic freedom, Friedman made major contributions to the fields of macroeconomics, microeconomics, economic history and statistics. In 1976, he was awarded the Nobel memorial Prize in Economic Sciences for his achievements in the fields of consumption analysis, monetary history and theory, and for his demonstration of the complexity of stabilization policy.

According to *The Economist*, Friedman "was the most influential economist of the second half of the 20th century...possibly of all of it." Alan Greenspan stated "There are very few people over the generations who have ideas that are sufficiently original to materially alter the direction of civilization. Milton is one of those very few people." In his 1962 book *Capitalism and Freedom*, Friedman advocated minimizing the role of government in a free market as a means of creating political and social freedom. In his 1980 television series *Free to Choose* Friedman explained how the free market works, emphasizing that he believed that it has been shown to solve social and political problems that other systems have failed to address adequately. His books and columns for *Newsweek* were widely read and even circulated underground behind the Iron Curtain.

Frost, Robert

Robert Lee Frost (March 26, 1874 – January 29, 1963) was an American poet. His work frequently used themes from rural life in New England, using the setting to examine complex social and philosophical themes. A popular and often-quoted poet, Frost was honored frequently during his lifetime, receiving four Pulitzer Prizes.

Although he is commonly associated with New England, Robert Frost was native of California, born in San Francisco, and lived there until he was 11 years old. His mother, Isabelle Moodie Frost, was of Scottish descent; his father, William Prescott Frost, Jr., was a descendant of colonist Nicholas Frost from Tiverton, Devon, England who had sailed to New Hampshire in 1634 on the *Wolfrana*.

Gabor, Eva

Eva Gabor (in Hungarian **Gábor Ěva**) (February 11, 1919 – July 4, 1995) was a Hungarian-born actress, best known as Lisa Douglas, the wife of Eddie Albert's character Oliver Wendell Douglas, on *Green Acres*. She was the sister of Zsa Zsa Gabor and the late Magda Gabor.

Gabor, Zsa Zsa

Zsa Zsa Gábor (born February 6, 1917) is a Hungarian-born American actress and socialite. Gabor won the Miss Hungary beauty contest in 1936, but was disqualified for being underage. On a trip to Vienna in the same year she was discovered by the famous tenor Richard Tauber and was invited to sing the soubrette role in his new operetta *Der singende Traum* (The Singing Dream") at the Theater an der Wien, her first stage appearance.

Gabor has been married nine times. She was divorced seven times, and one marriage was annulled. Her husbands, in chronological order are:

- Burhan Belge (1937 – 1941) (divorced)
- Conrad Hilton (April 10, 1942 – 1947) (divorced)
- George Sanders (April 2, 1949 – April 2, 1954) (divorced)
- Herbert Hutner (November 5, 1962 – March 3, 1966) (divorced)
- Joshua S. Cosden, Jr. (March 9, 1966 – October 18, 1967) divorced)
- Jack Ryan (January 21, 1975 – 1976) (divorced)
- Michael O'Hara (August 27, 1976 – 1982) (divorced)
- Felipe de Alba (April 13, 1983 – April 14, 1983) (annulled)
- Frédéric Prinz von Anhalt (August 14, 1986 to present)

Gabor is the only Gábor sister to bear a child. According to Gabor's book *One Lifetime Is Not Enough* her pregnancy resulted from her being raped by Conrad Hilton. Hilton and Gabor's only child, born after their divorce, is Francesca Hilton (Gabor) born March 10, 1947. In 2005, Zsa Zsa accused her daughter, Francesca, of larceny and fraud, and filed a lawsuit against her in a California court.

Galbraith, John Kenneth

John Kenneth Galbraith (October 15, 1908 – April 29, 2006) was an influential Canadian-American economist. He was a Keynesian and an institutionalist, a leading proponent of 20th-century American liberalism and progressivism. His books on economic topics were bestsellers in the 1950s and 1960s.

Galbraith was a prolific author who produced four dozen books and over a thousand articles on various subjects. Among his most famous works was a popular trilogy on economics, *American Capitalism* (1952), *The Affluent Society* (1958), and *The New Industrial State* (1967). He taught at Harvard University for many years. Galbraith was active in politics, serving in the administrations of Franklin D. Roosevelt, Harry S. Truman, John F. Kennedy and Lyndon B. Johnson; and among other roles served as United States Ambassador to India under Kennedy.

He was one of a few two-time recipients of the Presidential Medal of Freedom. He received one from President Truman in 1946 and another from President Bill Clinton in 2000. He was also awarded the Order of Canada in 1997 and, in 2001, the Padma Vibhushan, India's second highest civilian award, for his contributions to strengthening ties between India and the United States.

Galsworthy, John

John Galsworthy OM (14 August 1867 – 31 January 1933) was an English novelist and playwright. Notable works include *The Forsyte Saga* (1906 – 1921) and its sequels, *A Modern Comedy* and *End of the Chapter*. He won the Nobel Prize in Literature in 1932.

From the Four Winds was Galsworthy's first published work in 1897, a collection of short stories. These, and several subsequent works, were published under the pen name John Sinjohn and it would not be until *The Island Pharisees* (1904) that he would begin publishing under his own name, probably owing to the death of his father. His first play, *The Silver Box* (1906) became a success, and he followed it up with *The Man of Property* (1906), the first in the Forsyte trilogy. Although he continued writing both plays and novels it was as a playwright he was mainly appreciated at the time. Along with other writers of the time such as Shaw his plays addressed the class system and social issues, two of the best known being *Strife* (1909) and *The Skin Game* (1920).

He is now far better known for his novels and particularly *The Forsyte Saga*, the first of three trilogies of novels about the eponymous family and connected lives. These books, as with many of his other works, dealt with class, and in particular upper-middle class lives. Although sympathetic to his characters he highlights their insular, snobbish and acquisitive attitudes and their suffocating moral codes. He is viewed as one of the first writers of the Edwardian era; challenging in his works some of the ideals of society depicted in the proceeding literature of Victorian England. The depiction of a woman in an unhappy marriage furnishes another recurring theme in his work. The character of Irene in *The Forsyte Saga* is drawn from Ada Pearson even though her previous marriage was not as miserable as Irene's.

Gauguin, Paul

Eugène Henri Paul Gauguin (7 June 1848 – 8 May 1903) was a leading Post-Impressionist painter. His bold experimentation with coloring led directly to the Synthetist style of modern art while his expression of the inherent meaning of the subjects in his paintings, under the influence of the cloisonnist style, paved the way to Primitivism and the return to the pastoral. He was also an influential exponent of wood engraving and woodcuts as art forms.

George, David Lloyd

David Lloyd-George, 1st Earl Lloyd-George of Dwyfor OM, PC (17 January 1863 – 26 March 1945) was a British statesman who was the first, and only Welsh Prime Minister that Britain has had so far. He was Prime Minister throughout the later half of World War I and the first four years of the subsequent peace.

Gleason, Jackie

Herbert John "Jackie" Gleason (February 26, 1916 – June 24, 1987) was an iconic American comedian, actor, and musician.

One of the most popular stars of early television, Gleason was respected for both comedic and dramatic roles. However, his major legacy was his brash visual and verbal comedy styling, especially as delivered by the character Ralph Kramden on the pioneering sitcom *The Honeymooners*.

Goethe, Johann Wolfgang von

Johann Wolfgan von Goethe, (28 August 1749 – 22 March 1832) was a German writer. George Eliot called him "Germany's greatest man of letters... and the last true polymath to walk the earth." Goethe's works span the fields of poetry, drama, literature, theology, humanism, and science. Goethe's *magnum opus*, lauded as one of the peaks of world literature, is the two-part dramatic poem *Faust*. Goethe's other well-known literary works include his numerous poems, the Bildungsroman *Wilhelm Meister's Apprenticeship* and the epistolary novel *The Sorrows of Young Werther*.

Goethe was one of the key figures of German literature and the movement of Weimar Classiciam in the late 18th and early 19th centuries; this movement coincides with Enlightenment, Sentimentality ("*Empfindsamkeit*"), *Sturm und Drang*, and Romanticism. The author of the scientific text *Theroy of Colours*, he influenced Darwin with his focus on plant morphology.

Goldwyn, Samuel

Samuel Goldwyn (27 August 1882 – 31 January 1974) was an Academy Award and Golden Globe Award-winning producer, also a well-known Hollywood motion picture producer and founding contributor of several motion picture studios.

Gourmont, Remy de

Remy de Gourmont (April 4, 1858 – September 27, 1915) was a French Symbolist poet, novelist, and influential critic. He was widely read in his era, and an important influence on Blaise Cendrars.

Grant, Cary

Archibald Alex Leach (January 18, 1904 – November 29, 1986), better known by his stage name, **Cary Grant**, was an English-born film actor in American motion pictures. With his distinctive Mid-Atlantic accent, he was noted as perhaps the foremost exemplar of the debonair leading man, handsome, virile, charismatic and charming. He was named the second Greatest Male Star of All Time of American cinema, after Humphrey Bogart, by the American Film Institute. He was well known for starring in classic films such as *The Philadelphia Story*, *North By Northwest*, *Notorious*, *To Catch A Thief*, *Bringing Up Baby* and *The Bishop's Wife*.

Graves, Robert

Robert von Ranke Graves (24 July 1895 – 7 December 1985) was an English poet, scholar, and novelist. During his long life, he produced more than 140 works. He was the son of the Anglo-Irish writer Alfred Perceval Graves and Amalie von Ranke. The historian Leopold von Ranke was his mother's uncle. He was the brother of the author Charles Patrick Graves.

Graves considered himself a poet first and foremost. His poems, together with his innovative interpretation of the Greek Myths, his memoir of the First World War, *Good-bye to All That*, and his historical study of poetic inspiration, *The White Goddess*, have never been out of print. He earned his living from writing, particularly popular historical novels such as *I, Claudius*, *The Golden Fleece* and *Count Belisarius*. He was also a prominent translator of Classical Latin and Ancient Greek texts; his versions of *The Twelve Caesars* and *The Golden Ass* remain popular today for their clarity and entertaining style. Graves was awarded the 1934 James Tait Black Memorial Prize for both *I, Claudius* and *Claudius the God*.

Greeley, Horace

Horace Greeley (February 3, 1811 – November 29, 1872) was an American editor of a leading newspaper, a founder of the Republican party, reformer and politician. His *New York Tribune* was American's most influential newspaper from the 1840s to the 1870s and "established Greeley's reputation as the greatest editor of his day." Greeley used it to promote the Whig and Republican parties, as well as antislavery and a host of reforms. Crusading against the corruption of Ulysses S. Grant's Republican administration, he was the presidential candidate in 1872 of the new Liberal Republican Party. Despite having the additional support of the Democratic Party, he lost in a landslide.

Gretzky, Wayne

Wayne Douglas Gretzky, OC (born January 26, 1961 in Brantford, Ontario) is a retired Canadian-American professional ice hockey player who is currently part-owner and head coach of the Phoenix Coyotes.

Nicknamed "**The Great One**", Gretzky was called "the greatest player of all time" in *Total Hockey: The Official Encyclopedia of the NHL*. He is generally regarded as the best player in history and has been called "the greatest hockey player ever" by many sportswriters, players, and coaches. He set 40 regular season records, 15 playoff records, six All-Star records, won four Stanley Cups with the Edmonton Oilers, and won nine MVP awards and ten scoring titles. He is the only player ever to total over 200 points in a season (a feat that he accomplished four times in his career). In addition, he tallied over 100 points a season for 15 NHL seasons, 13 of them consecutively. He is the only player to have his number, 99, officially retired by the National Hockey League for *all teams* – no player in the NHL will ever again wear the number 99.

He retired from playing in 1999, becoming Executive Director for the Canadian national men's hockey team during the 2002 Winter Olympics. He also became part owner of the Phoenix Coyotes in 2000 and following the 2004-05 NHL lockout became their head coach.

Guinness, Alec

Sir Alec Guinness, CH, CBE (2 April 1914 – 5 August 2000) was an Academy Award and Tony Award-winning English actor. Guinness first worked writing copy for advertising before making his debut at the Albery Theatre in 1936 at the age of 22, playing the role of Osric in John Gielgud's wildly successful production of *Hamlet*.

Guinness continued playing Shakespearean roles throughout his career. In 1937 he played the role of Aumerle in *Richard II* and Lorenzo in *The Merchant of Venice* under the direction of John Gielgud. He starred in a 1938 production of *Hamlet* which won him acclaim on both sides of the Atlantic. He also appeared as Romeo in a production of *Romeo and Juliet* (1939), Andrew Aguecheck in *Twelfth Night* and as Exeter in *Henry V* in 1937, both opposite Laurence Olivier, and

Ferdinand in *The Tempest*, opposite Gielgud as Prospero.

In 1939, he adapted Charles Dickens' novel *Great Expectations* for the stage, playing the part of Herbert Pocket. The play was a success. One of its viewers was a young British film editor named David Lean, who had Guinness reprise his role in the former's 1946 film adaptation of the play.

Guinness served in the Royal Navy throughout World War II.

Guinness won particular acclaim for his work with director David Lean. After appearing in Lean's *Great Expectations* and *Oliver Twist*, he was given a starring role opposite William Holden in *Bridge on the River Kwai*. For his performance as Colonel Nicholson, the unyielding British POW leader, Guinness won an Academy Award for Best Actor.

Other famous roles of this time period included *The Swan* (1956) with Grace Kelly in her last film role, *The Horse's Mouth* (1958) in which Guinness played the part of drunken painter Gulley Jimson as well as contributing the screenplay, for which he was nominated for an Academy Award for Best Writing, Screenplay Based on Material from Another Medium, *Tunes of Glory* (1960), *Damn the Defiant!* (1962), *The Fall of the Roman Empire* (1964), *The Quiller Memorandum* (1966), *Scrooge* (1970), and the title role in *Hitler: The Last Ten Days* (1973) (which he considered his best film performance).

Guinness' role as Obi-Wan Kenobi in the original *Star Wars* trilogy, beginning in 1977, brought him worldwide recognition by a new generation. Guinness agreed to take the part on the condition that he would not have to do publicity to promote the film. He was also one of the few cast members who believed that the film would be a box office hit and negotiated a deal for two percent of the gross, which made him very wealthy in later life.

Hamilton, Alexander

Alexander Hamilton (January 11, 1755 – July 12, 1804) was an Army officer, lawyer, Founding Father, American politician, leading statesman, financier and political theorist. One of America's first constitutional lawyers, he was a leader in calling the Philadelphia Convention in 1787; he was one of the two chief authors of the anonymous *Federalist Papers*, the most cited contemporary interpretation of intent for the United States Constitution.

During the Revolutionary War, Hamilton served as an artillery captain, was an aide-de-camp to General George Washington, and led three battalions at the Battle of Yorktown. Under President Washington, Hamilton became the first Secretary of the Treasury. As Secretary of the Treasury and confidant of Washington, Hamilton had wide-reaching influence over the direction of policy during the formative years of the government. Hamilton believed in the importance of a strong central government, and convinced Congress to use an elastic interpretation of the Constitution to pass far-reaching laws. They included: the funding of the national debt; federal assumption of the state debts; creation of a national bank; and a system of taxes through a tariff on imports and a tax on whiskey that would help pay for it. He admired the success of the British system – particularly its strong financial and trade networks – and opposed what he saw as the excesses of the French Revolution.

Heine, Heinrich

Christian Johann Heinrich Heine (December 13, 1797 – February 17, 1856) was a journalist, essayist, and one of the most significant German romantic poets. He is remembered chiefly for selections of his lyric poetry, many of which were set to music in the form of *lieder* (art songs) by German composers.

Heinlein, Robert A.

Robert Anson Heinlein (July 7, 1907 – May 8, 1988) was one of the most popular, influential, and controversial authors of "hard science fiction". He set a high standard for science and engineering plausibility and helped to raise the genre's standards of literary quality. He was the first writer to break into mainstream, general magazines such as *The Saturday Evening Post*, in the late 1940s, with unvarnished science fiction. He was among the first authors of best selling, novel-length science fiction in the modern, mass-market era. For many years, Heinlein, Isaac Asimov, and Arthur C. Clarke were known as the "Big Three" of science fiction.

Hemingway, Ernest

Ernest Miller Hemingway (July 21, 1899 – July 2, 1961) was an American novelist, short story writer, and journalist . Nicknaming himself "*Papa*" while still in his 20s, he was part of the 1920s expatriate community in Paris known as "the Lost Generation", as described in his memoir *A Moveable Feast*. Hemingway received the Pulitzer Prize in 1953 for *The Old Man and the Sea*. He received the Nobel Prize in Literature in 1954. During his later life, Hemingway suffered from increasing physical and mental problems. In July 1961, after being released from a mental hospital where he's been treated for severe depression, he committed suicide at his home in Ketchum, Idaho with a shotgun.

Hepburn, Katharine

Katharine Houghton Hepburn (May 12, 1907 – June 29, 2003) was an iconic American actress of film, television and stage.

A screen legend, Hepburn holds the record for the most Best Actress Oscar wins with four, from twelve nominations (Meryl Streep currently holds the record for most overall acting nominations with fourteen). Hepburn won an Emmy Award in 1975 for her lead role in *Love Among the Ruins* opposite her friend Laurence Olivier, and was nominated for four other Emmys and two Tony Awards during the course of her more than 70-year acting career. In 1999, the American Film Institute ranked Hepburn as the top female star of all time.

Herford, Oliver

Oliver Herford (1863 – 1935) was a British born American writer, artist and illustrator who has been called "The American Oscar Wilde". As a frequent contributor to *The Mentor*, *Life*, and *Ladies' Home Journal*, he sometimes signed his artwork as "O'Herford". In 1906 he wrote and illustrated the *Little Book of Bores*". He also wrote short poems like "The Chimpanzee" and "The Hen", as well as writing and illustrating "The Rubaiyat of a Persian Kitten" (1904), "Cynic's Calendar" (1917) and "Excuse It Please" (1930). His sister Beatrice Herford was also a humorist.

Herold, Don

Don Herold (July 9, 1889 – June 1, 1966) was an American humorist, writer, illustrator, and cartoonist who wrote and illustrated many books and was a contributor to national magazines.

Hitchcock, Alfred

Sir Alfred Joseph Hitchcock, KBE (August 13, 1899 – April 29, 1980) was an iconic and highly influential English-born American film director and producer who pioneered many techniques in the suspense and thriller genres. He directed more than fifty feature films in a career spanning six decades, from the silent film era, through the invention of talkies, to the color era. Hitchcock was among the most consistently successful and publicly recognizable world directors during his lifetime, and remains one of the best known and most popular of all time.

Famous for his expert and largely unrivalled control of pace and suspense, Hitchcock's films draw heavily on both fear and fantasy, and are known for their droll humour and witticisms. They often portray innocent people caught up in circumstances beyond their control or understanding.

Hitler, Adolf

Adolf Hitler (April 20, 1889 – April 30, 1945) was a German politician, who became the Leader of the National Socialist German Workers Party and was appointed as the Chancellor of Germany in 1933. After the death of President Paul Von Hindenburg in 1934, Hitler declared himself Führer, combining the offices of President and Chancellor into one using the power vested in him by the Enabling Act, and remained in the position of Führer until his eventual suicide in 1945.

The Nazi Party gained power during Germany's period of crisis after World War I, exploiting effective propaganda and Hitler's charismatic oratory to gain popularity. The Party emphasized nationalism and anti-semitism as its primary political expressions, eventually resorting to murdering its opponents to ensure success.

After the restructuring of the state economy and the rearmament of the Wehrmacht, a dictatorship (commonly characterized as either totalitarian or fascist) was established by Hitler, who then pursued an aggressive foreign policy, with the goal of seizing *Lebensraum*. This resulted in the German Invasion of Poland in 1939, drawing the British and French Empires into World War II.

The Wehrmacht enjoyed great success in the early stages of the war, and the Axis Powers managed to occupy most of Mainland Europe and parts of Asia at the height of their power. Eventually however, the occupation was rolled back by the combined efforts of the Allies after a long struggle, and the Wehrmacht was ultimately defeated. By 1945, both Hitler's policy and the Nazi Party lay in ruins; his bid for territorial conquest and racial subjugation had caused the deaths of tens of millions of people, including the deliberate genocide of an estimated six million Jews in what is now known as the Holocaust.

During the final days of the war in 1945, as the German capital of Berlin was being invaded and destroyed by the Red Army of the Soviet Union, Hitler married Eva Braun and less than 24 hours later, the two committed suicide in the Führerbunker.

Holmes, Jr., Oliver Wendell

Oliver Wendell Holmes, Jr. (March 8, 1841 – March 6, 1935) was an American jurist who served on the Supreme Court of the United States from 1902 to 1932. Noted for his long service, his concise and pithy opinions, and his deference to the decisions of elected legislatures, he is one of the most widely cited United States Supreme Court justices in history, particularly for his "clear and present danger" majority opinion in the 1919 case of *Schenck v. United States*, as well as one of the most influential American common-law judges.

Hoover, Herbert

Herbert Clark Hoover (August 10, 1874 – October 20, 1964), the thirty-first President of the United States (1929 – 1933), was a mining engineer and humanitarian administrator. As the United States Secretary of Commerce in the 1920s under Presidents Warren Harding and Calvin Coolidge, he promoted economic modernization. In the presidential election of 1928 Hoover easily won the Republican nomination. The nation was prosperous and optimistic, leading to a landslide for Hoover over the Democrat Al Smith, a Catholic whose religion was distrusted by many. Hoover deeply believed in the Efficiency Movement (a major component of the Progressive Era), arguing that there were technical solutions to all social and economic problems. That position was challenged by the Great Depression, which began in 1929, the first year of his presidency. He tried to combat the Depression with volunteer efforts and government action, none of which produced economic recovery during his term. The consensus among historians is that Hoover's defeat in the 1932 election was caused primarily by failure to end the downward spiral into deep Depression, compounded by popular opposition to prohibition. Other electoral liabilities were Hoover's lack of charisma in relating to voters, and his poor skills in working with politicians.

Hope, Bob

Bob Hope KBE (May 29, 1903 – July 27, 2003) was an English-born entertainer who appeared in vaudeville, on Broadway, in radio, television, movies, and on numerous USO tours for U.S. military personnel.

Born Leslie Townes Hope in Eltham, London, England, Hope was the fifth of seven sons. His English father, William Henry Hope, was a stonemason from Weston-super-Mare and his Welsh mother, Avis Townes, was a light opera singer but later had to find work as a cleaning woman. The family lived in Weston-super-Mare, then Whitehall and St. George in Bristol, before moving to Cleveland, Ohio in 1908. The family traveled to the United States as passengers on board the SS Philadelphia. They were inspected at Ellis Island on 30 March 1908. Hope became a U.S. citizen in 1920 at the age of seventeen.

Hopper, Edward

Edward Hopper (July 12, 1882 – May 15, 1967) was an American painter and printmaker. While most popularly known for his oil paintings, he was equally proficient was a watercolorist and printmaker in etching.

Horne, Lena

Lena Mary Calhoun Horne (born June 30, 1917 in Bedford-Stuyvesant, Brooklyn, New York City, New York) is a popular singer of African-American descent. She has recorded and performed extensively with jazz musicians (notably Artie Shaw, Teddy Wilson), Billy Strayhorn, and Duke Ellington. She currently lives in New York City and no longer makes public appearances (JET, April 2007). She might be best-known for her version of the song "Stormy Weather", which was a hit in the 1940s.

Hubbard, Kin

Frank McKinney Hubbard (born 1 September 1868 in Bellefontaine, Ohio – died: 26 December 1930 in Indianapolis, Indiana) was an American cartoonist, humorist, and journalist better known by his pen name **"Kin" Hubbard**.

He was creator of the cartoon "Abe Martin of Brown County" which ran in U.S. newspapers from 1904 until his death in 1930, and was the originator of many political quips that remain in use. North American humorist Will Rogers declared Kin to be "America's greatest humorist".

Hughes, Rupert

Rupert Hughes (1872 – 1956) was a historian, novelist, film director, and composer based in Hollywood. Hughes was born in Lancaster, Missouri. His parents were Felix Turner Hughes and Jean Amelia Summerlin, who were married in 1865. His brother Howard R. Hughes, Sr., co-founded the Hughes Tool Company. He was the uncle of Howard Hughes. His three volume scholarly biography of George Washington broke new ground in demythologizing the general and was well received by historians.

Hughes, active in state politics, was one of the founders of the California State Guard in 1940.

Hugo, Victor

Victor-Marie Hugo (February 26, 1802 – May 22, 1885) was a French poet, playwright, novelist, essayist, visual artist, statesman, human rights campaigner, and perhaps the most influential exponent of the Romantic movement in France.

In France, Hugo's literary reputation rests primarily on his poetic and dramatic output and only secondarily on his novels. Among many volumes of poetry, *Les Contemplations* and *La Légende des siècles* stand particularly high in critical esteem, and Hugo is sometimes identified as the greatest French poet. In the English-speaking world his best-known works are often the novels *Les Misérables* and *Notre-Dame de Paris* (sometimes translated into English as *The Hunchback of Notre-Dame*).

Hume, David

David Hume (April 26, 1711 – August 25, 1776) was an 18th-century Scottish philosopher, economist, and historian, considered among the most important figures in the history of Western philosophy and the Scottish Enlightenment. He first gained recognition and respect as a historian, but interest in Hume's work in academia has in recent years centered on his philosophical writing. His *History of England* was the standard work on English history for sixty or seventy years until Macaulay's.

Huxley, Aldous

Aldous Leonard Huxley (July 26, 1984 – November 22, 1963) was an English writer and one of the most prominent members of the famous Huxley family. He spent the latter part of his life in the United States, living in Los Angeles from 1937 until his death in 1963. Best known for his novels and wide-ranging output of essays, he also published short stories, poetry, travel writing, and film stories and scripts. Through his novels and essays Huxley functioned as an examiner and sometimes critic of social mores, norms and ideals. Huxley was a humanist but was also interested towards the end of his life in spiritual subjects such as parapsychology and philosophical mysticism. By the end of his life Huxley was considered, in some academic circles, a leader of modern thought and an intellectual of the highest rank.

Huxley, Thomas Henry

Thomas Henry Huxley PC, FRS (4 May 1825 Ealing – 29 June 1895 Eastbourne, Sussex) was an English biologist, known as "Dawin's Bulldog" for his advocacy of Charles Darwin's theory of evolution.

Ingersoll, Robert G.

Colonel **Robert Green Ingersoll** (August 11, 1833 – July 21, 1899) was a Civil War veteran, American political leader, and orator during the Golden Age of Free Thought, noted for his broad range of culture and his defense of agnosticism.

Jackson, Stonewall

Thomas Jonathan "Stonewall" Jackson (January 21, 1824 – May 10, 1863) was a Confederate general during the American Civil War, and probably the most revered Confederate commander after General Robert E. Lee. He is most famous for his audacious Valley Campaign of 1862 and as a corps commander in the Army of Northern Virginia under Robert E. Lee. A Confederate picket accidentally shot him at the Battle of Chancellorsville on May 2nd, 1863, which the general survived, albeit with the loss of an arm to amputation. However, he died of complications of pneumonia eight days later, on May 10th, 1863.

Military historians consider Jackson to be one of the most gifted tactical commanders in United States history. His Valley Campaign and his envelopment of the Union Army right wing at Chancellorsville are studied worldwide even today as examples of innovative and bold leadership. He excelled as well at the First Battle of Bull Run (where he received his famous nickname "Stonewall"), Second Bull Run, Antietam, and Fredericksburg. Jackson was not universally successful as a commander, however, as displayed by his weak and confused efforts during the Seven

Days Battles around Richmond in 1862. His death was a severe setback for the Confederacy, affecting not only its military prospects, but the morale of its army and the general public; as Jackson lay dying, General Robert E. Lee sent a message to Jackson through Chaplain Lacy, saying "Give General Jackson my affectionate regards, and say to him: he has lost his left arm but I my right.."

James, William

William James (January] 11, 1842 – August 26, 1910) was a pioneering American psychologist and philosopher. He wrote influential books on the young science of psychology, educational psychology, psychology of religious experience and mysticism, and the philosophy of pragmatism. He was the brother of novelist Henry James and of diarist Alice James.

Jefferson, Thomas

Thomas Jefferson (April 13, 1743 – July 4, 1826) was the third President of the United States (1801 – 1809), the principal author of the Declaration of Independence (1776), and one of the most influential Founding Fathers for his promotion of the ideals of Republicanism in the United States. Major events during his presidency include the Louisiana Purchase (1803) and the Lewis and Clark Expedition (1804 – 1806).

As a political philosopher, Jefferson was a man of the Enlightenment and knew many intellectual leaders in Britain and France. He idealized the independent yeoman farmer as exemplar of republican virtues, distrusted cities and financiers, and favored states' rights and a strictly limited federal government. Jefferson supported the separation of church and state and was the author of the Virginia Statute for Religious Freedom (1779, 1786). He was the eponym of Jeffersonian democracy and the co-founder and leader of the Democratic-Republican Party, which dominated American politics for a quarter-century and was the precursor of the modern-day Democratic Party. Jefferson served as the wartime Governor of Virginia (1779 – 1781), first United States Secretary of State (1789 – 1793) and second Vice President (1797 – 1801).

Jesus

Jesus (7- 2 BC/BCE to 26 – 36 AD/CE), also known as **Jesus of Nazareth**, was a 1st century Jewish leader who is the central figure of Christianity, and is also an important figure in several other religions. He is also called **Jesus Christ**, where "Christ" is a title derived from the Greek (*Christós*), meaning the "Anointed One", which corresponds to the Hebrew-derived "Messiah". The name "Jesus" is an Anglicization of the Greek (*Iēsous*), itself a Hellenization of the Hebrew (*Yehoshua*) or Hebrew-Aramaic (*Yeshua*), meaning "YHWH rescues".

The main sources of information regarding Jesus' life and teachings are the four canonical Gospels of the New Testament: Matthew, Mark, Luke, and John. Most scholars in the fields of history and biblical studies agree that Jesus was a Galilean Jew, was regarded as a teacher and healer, was baptized by John the Baptist, and was crucified in Jerusalem on orders of the Roman Governor Pontius Pilate under the accusation of sedition against the Roman Empire. Few critical scholars believe that all ancient texts on Jesus' life are either completely accurate or completely inaccurate.

Johnson, Lyndon B.

Lyndon Baines Johnson (August 27, 1908 – January 22, 1973), often referred to as **LBJ**, was the thirty-sixth President of the United States (1963 – 1969). Johnson served a long career in the U.S. Congress, and in 1960 was selected by then-Presidential candidate John F. Kennedy to be his running-mate. Johnson became the thirty-seventh Vice President, and in 1963, he succeeded to the presidency following Kennedy's assassination. He was a major leader of the Democratic Party and as President was responsible for designing the Great Society, comprising liberal legislation including civil rights laws. Medicare (health care for the elderly), Medicaid (health care for the poor), aid to education, and a "War on Poverty". Simultaneously, he escalated the American involvement in the Vietnam War, from 16,000 American soldiers in 1963 to 550,000 in early 1968.

He was elected President in his own right in a landslide victory in 1964, but his popularity steadily declined after 1966 and his reelection bid in 1968 collapsed as a result of turmoil in his party. He withdrew from the race to concentrate on peacemaking. Johnson was renowned for his domineering (or dominating) personality and the "Johnson treatment", his arm-twisting of powerful politicians.

Johnson suffered a massive heart attack in 1973, the third in his lifetime. He died on January 22, 1973.

Johnson, Samuel

Samuel Johnson LL.D. MA (September 18, 1709 – 13 December 1784), often referred to simply as **Dr Johnson**, is one of England's best known literary figures: an essayist, biographer, lexicographer and a critic of English Literature. He was also a great wit and prose stylist, well known for his *aphorisms*. Dr Johnson is the most quoted English writer after Shakespeare and had been described as one of the outstanding figures of 18th-century England.

Joubert, Joseph

Joseph Joubert (born May 7, 1754 in Montignac, Périgord and died May 4, 1824 in Villeneuve-sur-Yonne) was a French moralist and essayist, remembered today largely for his *Pensées* published posthumously.

From age 14 Joubert attended a religious college in Toulouse, where he later taught until 1776. In 1778 he went to Paris where he met D'Alembert and Diderot, among others, and later became friends with young writer and diplomat Chateaubriand.

He alternated between living in Paris with his friends and life in the privacy of the countryside in Villeneuve-sur-Yonne. He was appointed inspector-general of the University under Napoleon.

Somewhat of the Epicurean school of philosophy, Joubert enjoyed even his own suffering as he believed sickness gave subtlety to the soul.

Joubert's works have been translated into numerous languages, into English by Paul Auster, among others.

Joyce, James

James Augustine Aloysius Joyce (2 February 1882 – 13 January 1941) was an Irish expatriate writer, widely considered to be one of the most influential writers of the 20th century. He is best known for his landmark novel *Ulysses* (1922) and its highly controversial successor *Finnegans Wake* (1939), as well as the short story collection *Dubliners* (1914) and the semi-autobiographical novel *A Portrait of the Artist as a Young Man* (1916).

Kant, Immanuel

Immanuel Kant (22 April 1724 – 12 February 1804) was an 18th-century German philosopher from the Prussian city of Königsberg (now Kaliningrad, Russia). He is regarded as one of the most influential thinkers of modern Europe and of the late Enlightenment.

Kaufman, George S.

George Kaufman (November 16, 1889 – June 2, 1961) was an American playwright, theatre director and producer, humorist, and drama critic.

His Broadway debut was in 1918 with the now-forgotten *Someone in the House*, written with Larry Evans and W. C. Percival. This play was panned, and it had the further handicap of opening on Broadway during a flu epidemic, when theatre attendance in New York City diminished drastically because the public were warned to avoid crowds. Kaufman sardonically advised his play's producers to print advertisements with this message: "Avoid crowds: see *Someone in the House*."

It would be quite a long time before Kaufman had another flop. In every Broadway season from 1921 through 1958, there was a play written or directed by Kaufman. Since Kaufman's death in 1961, every decade has featured at least a couple of revivals of his work. There have also been productions based on Kaufman properties, such as the 1981 musical version of *Merrily We Roll Along*, adapted by George Furth and Stephen Sondheim.

Kaufman was known as "The Great Collaborator" because he

wrote very few plays alone. His most successful solo script was *The Butter and Egg Man* in 1925. With others, Kaufman was prolific: with Marc Connelly he wrote *Merton of the Movies*, *Dulcy*, and *Beggar on Horseback*; with Ring Lardner he wrote *June Moon*.

Keillor, Garrison

Garrison Keillor (born **Gary Edward Keillor** on August 7, 1942 In Anoka, Minnesota) is an American author, storyteller, humorist, columnist, musician, satirist, and radio personality.

He is best known as host of the Minnesota Public Radio show *A Prairie Home Companion* (also known as *Garrison Keillor's Radio Show* on Britain's BBC 7, as well as on Australia's ABC and in Ireland).

Kennedy, Florynce

Florynce Kennedy (February 11, 1916 – December 22, 2000), was a lawyer, activist, civil rights advocate, and feminist.

Her activism is divided into two parts: feminism and civil rights. In feminism, she often traveled with writer Gloria Steinem, talking to women in a speaking tour. If a man asked the pair if they were lesbians – a stereotype of feminists at the time – Flo would famously answer, "Are you my alternative?". In 1971 she founded the Feminist Party, which nominated Shirley Chisholm for president. She also helped found the Women's Political Caucus and the National Organization for Women.

She is also known for her pro-choice activism on abortion, writing a book called *Abortion Rap*, and stating that "If men could get pregnant, abortion would be a sacrament."

Kennedy, John F.

John Fitzgerald Kennedy (May 29, 1917 – November 22, 1963) was the thirty-fifth President of the United States, serving from 1961 until his assassination in 1963.

After Kennedy's military service as commander of the USS *PT-109* during World War II in the South Pacific, his aspirations turned political. Kennedy represented the state of Massachusetts in the U.S. House of Representatives from 1947 to 1953 as a Democrat, and in the U.S. Senate from 1953 until 1961. Kennedy defeated former Vice President and Republican candidate Richard Nixon in the 1960 U.S. presidential election, one of the closest in American history. To date, he is the only practicing Roman Catholic to be elected President and the only President to have won a Pulitzer Prize. Events during his administration include the Bay of Pigs Invasion, the Cuban Missile Crisis, the building of the Berlin Wall, the Space Race, the American Civil Rights Movement and early events of the Vietnam War.

Kennedy was assassinated on November 22, 1963, in Dallas, Texas. Lee Harvey Oswald was charged with the crime, but was murdered two days later by Jack Ruby before he could be put on trial. The Warren Commission concluded that Oswald had acted alone in killing the president; however, the House Select Committee on Assassinations declared in 1979 that there was more likely a conspiracy that included Oswald. The entire subject remains controversial, with multiple theories about the assassination still being debated. The event proved to be a poignant moment in U.S. history because of its impact on the nation and the ensuing political repercussions. Many regard President Kennedy as an icon of American hopes and aspirations; he continues to rank highly in public opinion ratings of former U.S. presidents.

Kennedy, Rose Fitzgerald

Rose Fitzgerald Kennedy (July 22, 1890 – January 22, 1995) was the wife of Joseph Kennedy and the mother of President John Fitzgerald Kennedy.

Keynes, John Maynard

John Maynard Keynes, 1st Baron Keynes, CB (5 June 1883 – 21 April 1946) was a British economist whose ideas, called Keynesian economics, had a major impact on modern economic and political theory as well as on many governments fiscal policies. He advocated interventionist government policy, by which the government would use fiscal and monetary measures to mitigate the adverse effects of economic recessions, depressions and booms. He is one of the fathers of modern theoretical macroeconomics.

Khayyám, Omar

Ghiyās od-Dīn Abul-Fatah Omār ibn Ibrāhīm Khayyām Nishābūrī or **Omar Khayyam** (Nishapur, Persia,May 18, 1048 – December 4, 1131) was a Persian poet, mathematician, philosopher and astronomer who lived in Persia. His name is also given as **Omar al-Khayyami.**

He is best known for his poetry, and outside Iran, for the quatrains (*rubaiyaas*) in *Rubaiyat of Omar Khayyam*, popularized through Edward Fitzgerald's re-created translation. His substantial mathematical contributions include his *Treatise on Demonstration of Problems of Algebra*, which gives a geometric method for solving cubic equations by intersecting a hyperbola with a circle. He also contributed to calendar reform and may have proposed a heliocentric theory well before Copernicus.

Khrushchev, Nikita

Nikita Sergeyevich Khrushchev (April 17, 1894 – September 11, 1971); served as First Secretary of the Communist Party of the Soviet Union from 1953 to 1964, following the death of Joseph Stalin, and Chairman of the Council of Ministers from 1958 to 1964. Khrushchev's party colleagues removed him from power in 1964, replacing him with Leonid Brezhnev. He spent the last seven years of his life under the close supervision of the KGB.

Kierkegaard, Soren

Soren Aabye Kierkegaard (5 May 1813 – 11 November 1855) was a prolific 19th century Danish philosopher and theologian. Kierkegaard strongly criticized both the Hegelianism of his time, and what he saw as the empty formalities of the Danish church. Much of his work deals with religious problems such as the nature of faith, the institution of the Christian Church, Christian ethics and theology, and the emotions and feelings of individuals when faced with life choices. His early work was written under various pseudonyms who present their own distinctive viewpoints in a complex dialogue. Kierkegaard left the task of discovering the meaning of the works to the reader, because "the task must be made difficult, for only the difficult inspires the noble-hearted". Subsequently, many have interpreted Kierkegaard as an existentialist, neo-orthodoxist, postmodernist, humanist, individualist, etc. Crossing the boundaries of philosophy, theology, psychology, and literature, Kierkegaard came to be regarded as a highly significant and influential figure in contemporary thought.

King, Frank (cartoonist)

Frank King (April 9, 1883 – June 24, 1969) was an American cartoonist most famous for the comic strip *Gasoline Alley.*

Born in Cashton, Wisconsin, King grew up in Tomah, Wisconsin and attended the Chicago Academy of Fine Arts.

He broke into professional cartoonist at the *Minneapolis Times* in 1901 and moved through the decade to *Chicago's American*, the *Chicago Examiner*, and finally, in 1910, the *Chicago Tribune.*

King created several recurring strips, including *Tough Teddy*, *The Boy Animal Trainer*, *Here Comes Motorcycle Mike*, *Hi Hopper*, and, his first successful full-page comic, *Bobby Make-Believe* in 1915. King produced a black and white cartoon page, since 1914 named *The Rectangle*, featuring a variety of cartoons and serial features.

Gasoline Alley emerged from a corner of this page, first titled *Sunday morning in Gasoline Alley*, in 1918. A great success, the strip would become the first to portray the aging process of characters, and be regarded as the strip became comics' first soap opera. Although King retired from drawing *Gasoline Alley* in 1951, the strip is still running as of 2009.

King, Jr., Martin Luther

Martin Luther King, Jr.(January 15, 1929 – April 4, 1968), was one of the main leaders of the American civil rights movement. A Baptist minister by training, King became a civil rights activist early in his career, leading the Montgomery Bus Boycott and helping to found the Southern Christian Leadership Conference. His efforts led to the 1963 March on Washington, where King delivered his "I Have a Dream" speech, raising public consciousness of the civil rights movement and establishing King as one of the greatest orators in American history. In 1964, King became the youngest person to receive the Nobel Peace Prize for his efforts to end segregation and racial discrimination through civil disobedience and other non-violent means.

King was assassinated on April 4, 1968, in Memphis, Tennessee. He was posthumously awarded the Presidential Medal of Freedom by President Jimmy Carter in 1977. Martin Luther King Day was established as a national holiday in the United States in 1986. In 2004, King was posthumously awarded a Congressional Gold Medal.

Kipling, Rudyard

Joseph Rudyard Kipling (December 30, 1865 – January 18, 1936) was an English author and poet, born in Bombay, India, and best known for his works *The Jungle Book* (1894), *The Second Jungle Book* (1895), *Just So Stories* (1902), and Pu*ck of Pook's Hill* (1906); his novel, *Kim* (1901); his poems, including *Mandalay* (1890), *Gunga Din* (1890), and "If –"(1910); and his many short stories, including "The Man Who Would Be King" (1888) and the collections *Life's Handicap* (1891), *The Day's Work* (1898), and *Plain Tales from the Hills* (1888). He is regarded as a major "innovator" in the art of the short story"; his children's books are enduring classics of children's literature; and his best work speaks to a versatile and luminous narrative gift.

Kissinger, Henry

Henry Alfred Kissinger (born **Heinz Alfred Kissinger** on May 27, 1923) is a German-born American politician, and 1973 Nobel Peace Prize laureate. He served as National Security Advisor and later concurrently as Secretary of State in the Richard Nixon administration. Kissinger emerged unscathed from the Watergate scandal and maintained his powerful position when Gerald Ford became President.

A proponent of *Realpolitik*, Kissinger played a dominant role in United States foreign policy between 1969 and 1977. During this period, he pioneered the policy of *détente* to publicly show the US as showing kindness to Soviets while it secretly warred with other countries.

During his time in the Nixon and Ford administrations he cut a flamboyant figure, appearing at social occasions with many celebrities. His foreign policy record made him enemies among the anti-war left and among the anti-Communist right alike.

Kraus, Karl

Karl Kraus (April 28, 1874 – June 12, 1936) was an eminent Austrian writer and journalist, known as a satirist, essayist, aphorist, playwright and poet. He is generally considered one of the foremost German-language satirists of the 20th century, especially known for his witty criticism of the press, German culture, and German and Austrian politics.

Lauder, Estée

Estée Lauder (July 1, 1908 – April 24, 2004) was the co-founder, with her husband Joseph Lauder, of Estée Lauder Companies, a pioneering cosmetics company. She was born **Josephine Esther Mentzer** in Corona, Queens, New York, the daughter of Hungarian Jewish immigrants. She was the only woman on *Time* magazine's 1998 list of the 20 most influential business geniuses of the 20th century. She was the recipient of the Presidential Medal of Freedom.

She married Joseph Lauter in 1930. They had two sons. Estée divorced Joseph in 1939, and re-married him in 1942. The couple remained married thereafter until his death in 1982. The Lauter family changed their surname to "Lauder" in the late 1930s. Her older son, Leonard Lauder, was chief executive of Estée Lauder and is now chairman of the board. Her younger son, Ronald Lauder, is a prominent philanthropist, a Republican political appointee in the Reagan administration, and developer of property in Berlin, among other endeavors.

Lebowitz, Fran

Frances Ann "Fran" Lebowitz (b. October 27, 1950) is an American author. Born in Morristown, New Jersey, Lebowitz is best known for her sardonic social commentary on American life through her New York sensibilities. Some reviewers have called her a modern day Dorothy Parker.

After being expelled from high school and receiving a GED, Lebowitz worked many odd jobs before being hired by Andy Warhol as a columnist for *Interview*. This was followed by a stint at *Mademoiselle*. Her first book was a collection of essays titled *Metropolitan Life*, released in 1978, followed by *Social Studies* in 1981, both of which are collected (with a new introductory essay) in *The Fran Lebowitz Reader*.

For more than twenty years she has been famous in part for not writing *Exterior Signs of Wealth*, a long-overdue novel purportedly about rich people who want to be artists, and artists who want to be rich. Recently she has made recurring appearances as Judge Janice Goldberg on the television drama *Law & Order*.

Lee, Gypsy Rose

Gypsy Rose Lee (also known as **Rose Louise Hovick** and **Louise Hovick**)(B. February 9, 1911/1914 – April 26, 1970) was an American actress, burlesque entertainer, and writer whose 1957 memoir, which included a scathing portrait of her domineering mother, was made into the stage musical and film *Gypsy*.

Leno, Jay

James Douglas Muir "Jay" Leno (April 28, 1950) is an Emmy Award-winning American comedian and television host, who succeeded Johnny Carson as host of *The Tonight Show* in 1992, and as of 2009 has served as host for roughly half the amount of time that Carson served.

Levant, Oscar

Oscar Levant (December 27, 1906 – August 14, 1972) was an American pianist, composer, author, comedian, and actor. He was more famous for his mordant character and witticisms, on the radio and in movies and television, than for his music.

Levenson, Sam

Sam Levenson (December 28, 1911 – August 27, 1980) was an American humorist, writer, television host and journalist.

Sam Levenson was a Spanish teacher before writing the best-selling *Sex and the Single Child* (1969). In *One Era And Out The Other* (1973), *You Can Say That Again, Sam!* (1975), and *Everything But Money* (1966). He hosted the game show *Two for the Money* in 1956 (taking over for Herb Shriner) and the "Sam Levenson Show" from 1959 to 1964. Over a span of more than a decade, he appeared on *Toast of the Town* aka *The Ed Sullivan Show* 21 times, in addition to frequently serving as a substitute host on CBS's Arthur Godfrey Time. He was a guest host on *The Price is Right* and was a panelist on many other television programs such as *Password* and *What's My Line*. Levenson also had a cameo in the film *A Face in the Crowd*. He also appeared multiple times on *The Tonight Show with Johnny Carson* throughout the 1970s. Levenson also wrote the well-known poem "Time Tested Beauty Tips" for his grandchild, which has become falsely attributed to Audrey Hepburn.

Lincoln, Abraham

Abraham Lincoln (February 12, 1809 – April 15, 1865) was the Sixteenth President of the United States, serving from March 4, 1861 until his assassination. As an outspoken opponent of the expansion of slavery in the United States, Lincoln won the Republican Party nomination in 1860 and was elected president later that year. During his term, he helped preserve the United States by leading the defeat of the secessionist Confederate States of American in the American Civil War. He introduced measures that resulted in the abolition of slavery, issuing his Emancipation Proclamation in 1863 and promoting the passage of the Thirteenth Amendment to the Constitution in 1865.

Locke, John

John Locke, (August 29, 1632 – October 28, 1704) was an English philosopher. Locke is considered the first of the British Empiricists, but is equally important to social contract theory. His ideas had enormous influence on the development of epistemology and political philosophy, and he is widely regarded as one of the most influential Enlightenment thinkers and contributors to liberal theory. His writings influenced Voltaire and Rousseau, many Scottish Enlightenment thinkers, as well as the American revolutionaries. This influence is reflected in the American Declaration of Independence.

Locke's theory of mind is often cited as the origin for modern conceptions of identity and "the self", figuring prominently in the later works of philosophers such as David Hume, Jean-Jacques Rousseau and Immanuel Kant. Locke was the first philosopher to define the self through a continuity of "consciousness". He also postulated that the mind was a "blank slate" or "tabula rasa"; that is, contrary to Cartesian or Christian philosophy, Locke maintained that people are born without innate ideas.

Long, Huey

Huey Pierce Long, Jr. (August 30, 1893 – September 10, 1935) nicknamed **The Kingfish**, was an American politician from the U.S. state of Louisiana. A Democrat, he was noted for his radical populist policies. He served as Governor of Louisiana from 1928 to 1932 and as a U.S. senator from 1932 to 1935. Though a backer of Franklin D. Roosevelt in the 1932 presidential election, Long split with Roosevelt in June 1933 and allegedly planned to mount his own presidential bid.

Long created the Share Our Wealth program in 1934, with the motto "Every Man a King", proposing new wealth redistribution measures and the form of a net asset tax on large corporations and individuals of great wealth to curb poverty and crime resulting from the Great Depression. He was an ardent critic of the Federal Reserve System.

Charismatic and immensely popular for his social reform programs and willingness to take forceful action, Long was accused by his opponents of dictatorial tendencies for his near-total control of the state government. At the height of his popularity, the colorful and flamboyant Long was shot on September 8, 1935, at the Louisiana State Capital in Baton Rouge; he died two days later at the age of 42. His last words were reportedly, "God, don't let me die. I have so much left to do.":

Longfellow, Henry Wadsworth

Henry Wadsworth Longfellow (February 27, 1807 – March 24, 1882) was an American poet whose works include "Paul Revere's Ride", "A Psalm of Life", "The Song of Hiawatha", "Evangeline", and "Christmas Bells". He also wrote the first American translation of Dante Alighieri's "Divine Comedy" and was one of the five members of the group known as the Fireside Poets,. Longfellow was born and raised in the region of Portland, Maine. He attended university at an early age at Bowdoin College in Brunswick, Maine. After several journeys overseas, Longfellow settled for the last forty-five years of his life in Cambridge, Massachusetts.

Loren, Sophia

Sophia Loren (born September 20, 1934) is a motion picture and stage, Academy Award-winning actress and sex symbol. She is widely considered to be the most popular Italian actress of her time

Louis, Joe

Joseph Louis Barrow (may 13, 1914 – April 12, 1981), best known As **Joe Louis** and nicknamed **The Brown Bomber**, a native of Detroit, Michigan, is considered to be one of the greatest heavyweight boxing champions that ever lived. He held the title for over 11 years, recording 25 successful defenses of the title. In 2003, *Ring Magazine* rated Joe Louis No. 1 on the list of 100 greatest punchers of all time. In 2005, Louis was named the greatest heavyweight of all time by the International Boxing Research Organization., He participated in 27 heavyweights championship fights, a record which still stands.

Lowell, James Russell

James Russell Lowell (b. 22 February 1819, Cambridge, Massachusetts – d. 12 August 1891, Cambridge, Massachusetts) was an American Romantic poet, critic, satirist, diplomat, and abolitionist.

Luther, Martin

Martin Luther (November 10, 1483 – February 18, 1546) was a German monk, theologian, and Protestant Reformer. He is often considered the founder of Protestantism.

Luther's theology challenged the authority of the papacy by holding that the Bible is the sole source of religious authority and that all baptized Christians are a general priesthood. According to Luther, salvation was attainable only by faith in Jesus as the Messiah, a faith unmediated by the church. These ideas helped to inspire the Protestant Reformation and changed the course of Western civilization.

Luther's translation of the Bible into the German vernacular, making it more accessible to ordinary people, had a tremendous impact on the church and on German culture. The translation also furthered the development of a standard version of the German language, added several principles to the art of translation, and influenced the translation of the English King James Bible. His hymns inspired the development of congregational singing within Christianity. His marriage to Katharina von Bora set a model for the practice of clerical marriage within Protestantism.

Macaulay, Thomas Babington

Thomas Babington Macaulay, 1st Baron Macaulay, PC (25 October 1800 – 28 December 1859) was a nineteenth-century English poet, historian and Whig politician and Member of Parliament for Edinburgh. He wrote extensively as an essayist and reviewer, and on British history.

The son of Zachary Macaulay, a Scottish Highlander who became a colonial governor and abolitionist, Thomas was born in Leicestershire, England, and educated at Trinity College, Cambridge. Macaulay was noted as a child prodigy. As a toddler, gazing out the window from his cot at the chimneys of a local factory, he is reputed to have put the question to his mother: "Does the smoke from those chimneys come from the fires of hell?" Whilst at Cambridge he wrote much poetry and won several prizes. In 1825 he published a prominent essay on Milton in the Edinburgh Review. In 1826 he was called to the bar but showed more interest in a political than a legal career.

Macauley, Ed

Charles Edward "Ed" Macauley (born March 22, 1928 in St. Louis, Missouri) is a former professional basketball player.

Macauley spent his prep school days at St. Louis University High School, then went on to Saint Louis University, where his team won the NIT championship in 1948. He was named the AP Player of the Year in 1949.

Macauley played in the NBA with the St. Louis Bombers, Boston Celtics, and St. Louis Hawks. Macauley was named MVP of the first NBA All-Star Game (he played in the first seven), and was named to the NBA's All-NBA First Team three consecutive seasons. He was named to the All-NBA second team once, in 1953 – 54 – the same season he led the league in field goal percentage. Macauley's trade (with Cliff Hagan) to St. Louis brought Bill Russell to the Celtics. Macauley scored 11,234 points in ten NBA seasons and was inducted into the Basketball Hall of Fame in 1960. He also has a star on the St. Louis Walk of Fame.

Machiavelli, Niccolò

Niccolò di Bernardo dei Machiavelli (May 3, 1469 – June 21, 1527) was an Italian diplomat, political philosopher, musician, poet, and playwright. He is a figure of the Italian Renaissance and a central figure of its political component, most widely known for his treatises on realist political theory (*The Prince*) on the one hand and republicanism (*Discourses on Livy*) on the other. These two written works – plus his *History of Florence* commissioned by the Medici family – were published posthumously in 1531. After the ousting and execution of Savonarola, the Great Council elected Machiavelli as the second chancellor of the Republic of Florence in June of 1498.

MacIver, Robert Morrison

Robert Morrison MacIver (April 17, 1882 – June 15, 1970) was a U.S. (Scottish-born) sociologist. Born in North Beach Street, Stornoway, Isle of Lewis, he graduated from the Universities of Edinburgh and Oxford. MacIver was a University Lecturer at the

University of Aberdeen. He left Aberdeen for a post in Toronto in 1915, and remained there – doing wartime administrative work as well as teaching political philosophy, until moving to Barnard College of the University of Columbia in 1927. He was Lieber Professor there, 1929 – 1950. In his – rather long – period of formal education he had never made any formal, academically supervised study of sociology, his distinguished work in sociology and in critical discussion of crucial issues of the interpretation of research data, and issues of the state, society and community, were distinguished on his acumen, his philosophical understanding, and extensive study of the major pioneering works of Durkheim, Toennies, Max and Alfred Weber, George Simmel et al., in the British Museum Library, London, while resident as a student in Oxford.

Magrane, Joe

Joseph David Magrane (born July 2, 1964 in DesMoines, Iowa) was a Major League Baseball pitcher and is currently color commentary broadcaster for the Tampa Bay Devil Rays, teamed with play-by-play announcer Dewayne Staats since 1998.

Staats and Magrane are signed to be the Devil Rays' television team through the 2008 season.

During his rookie season he helped the Cardinals win the 1987 NL Pennant. He also led the National League in Hit Batsmen.

He led the National League in ERA (2.18) in 1988.

He finished 4th in voting for the 1989 NL MVP for having an 18-9 Win-Loss record, 34 Games, 33 Games Started, 9 Complete Games, 3 Shutouts, 1 Game Finished, 234, 2/3 Innings, 219 Hits Allowed, 81 Runs Allowed, 76 Earned Runs Allowed, 5 Home Runs Allowed, 72 Walks, 127 Strikeouts, 14 Wild Pitches, 971 Batters Faced, 7 Intentional Walks, 5 Balks and a 2.91 ERA.

An injured elbow in 1990 cost him almost all of the next two seasons and most of his effectiveness, and Magrane never really regained his early form. He did win 11 games between the St. Louis and California ball clubs in 1993, but could not muster more than 2 wins or 74 innings pitched in any other season until his retirement in 1996 at the relatively early age of 32.

Mailer, Norman

Norman Kingsley Mailer (January 31, 1923 – November 10, 2007) was an American novelist, journalist, playwright, screenwriter, and film director.

Along with Truman Capote, Joan Didion, and Tom Wolfe, Mailer is considered an innovator of creative nonfiction, a genre sometimes called New Journalism, but which covers the essay to the nonfiction novel. He was awarded the Pulitzer Prize twice and the National Book Award once. In 1955, Mailer, together with Ed Fancher and Dan Wolf, first published *The Village Voice*, which began as an arts-and politics-oriented weekly newspaper initially distributed in Greenwich Village. In 2005, he won the Medal for Distinguished Contribution to American Letters from The National Book Foundation.

Mantle, Mickey

Mickey Charles Mantle (October 20, 1931 – August 13, 1995) was an American baseball player who was inducted into the National Baseball Hall of Fame in 1974.

He played his entire 18-year major-league professional career for the New York Yankees, winning 3 American League MVP titles and playing for 16 All-Star teams. Mantle played on 12 pennant winners and 7 World Championship clubs. He still holds the records for most World Series home runs (18), RBIs (40), runs (42), walks (43), extra-base hits (26), and total bases (123).

Marquis, Don

Don Marquis (July 29, 1878 Walnut, Illinois – December 29, 1937 New York City) was an American humorist, journalist, and author. He was variously a novelist, poet, cartoonist, newspaper columnist, and playwright. He is best remembered for creating the characters "Archy" and "Mehitable", supposed authors of humorous verse.

On August 23, 1943, the United States Navy christened a Liberty ship, the USS Don Marquis (IX-215), in his memory.

Martial

Marcus Valerious Martialis, know in English as **Martial**, was a Latin poet from Hispania (the Iberian Peninsula) best known for his twelve books of Epigrams, published in Rome between AD 86 and 103, during the reigns of the emperors Domitian, Nerva and Trajan. In these short, witty poems he cheerfully satirises city life and the scandalous activities of his acquaintances, and romanticizes his provincial upbringing. He wrote a total of 1,561 – 1,235 of which are in elegiac couplets. He is considered the creator of the modern epigram.

Martin, Dean

Dean Martin (born **Dino Paul Crocetti**, June 7, 1917 – December 25, 1995) was an American singer, film actor, and comedian. He was one of the most famous music artists in the 1950s and 1960s. His hit singles included the songs "Memories Are Made Of This', "That's Amore", "Everybody Loves Somebody", "Mambo Italiano", "Sway", "Volare" and "Ain't That a Kick in the Head". He was a major star in all four areas of show business: concert stage, recordings, motion pictures, and television.

Marx, Groucho

Julius Henry "Groucho" Marx (October 2, 1890 – August 19, 1977), was an American comedian and film star. He is famed as a master of wit. He made 15 feature films with his siblings, the Marx Brothers, and also had a successful solo career, most notably as the host of the radio and television game show, *You Bet Your Life*. He had a distinctive image, which included a heavy greasepaint moustache and eyebrows and glasses.

Maugham, W. Somerset

William Somerset Maugham, CH (January 25, 1874 – December 16, 1965) was an English playwright, novelist, and short story writer. He was one of the most popular authors of his era, and reputedly the highest paid of his profession during the 1930s.

Meir, Golda

Golda Meir born **Goldie Mabovitch**, May 3, 1898 – December 8, 1978, known as **Golda Myerson** from 1917 – 1956) was the fourth prime minister of the State of Israel. After serving as the Minister of Labour and Foreign Minister, Golda Meir became Prime Minister of Israel on March 17, 1969. She was described as the "Iron Lady" of Israeli politics years before the epithet became associated with British prime minister, Margaret Thatcher. David Ben-Gurion used to call her "the only man in the Cabinet ". Meir was Israel's first woman prime minister and the third woman in the world to hold this office.

Menander

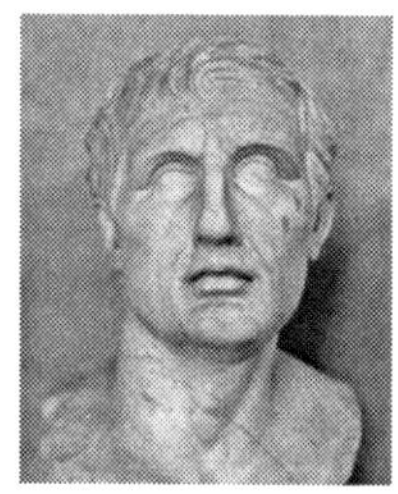

Menander (ca. 342 – 291 BC), Greek dramatist, the chief representative of the New Comedy, was born in Athens. He was the son of well-to-do parents; his father Diopeithes is identified by some with the Athenian general and governor of the Thracian Chersonese known from the speech of Demosthenes *De Chersoneso*. He presumable derived his taste for the comic drama from his uncle Alexis.

He was the friend, associate, and perhaps pupil of Theophrastus, and was on intimate terms with Demetrius of Phalerum. He also enjoyed the patronage of Ptolemy Soter, the son of Lagus, who invited him to his court.

Menander was the author of more than a hundred comedies, but only won the prize at Lenaia eight times. His rival in dramatic art (and in the affections of Glycera) was Philemon, who appears to have been more popular. Menander, however, believed himself to be the better dramatist, and, according to Aulus Gellius, used to ask Philemon: "Don't you feel ashamed whenever you gain a victory over me?"

Mencken, H. L.

Henry Louis (H. L.) Mencken (September 12, 1880, Baltimore – January 29, 1956, Baltimore, Maryland), was an American journalist, essayist, magazine editor, satirist, acerbic critic of

American life and culture, and a student of American English. Known as the "Sage of Baltimore", he is regarded as one of the most influential American writers and prose stylists of the first half of the 20th century.

Mencken is perhaps best remembered today for *The American Language*, a multi-volume study of how the English language is spoken in the United States and his satirical reporting on the Scopes trial, which is credited for naming the "Monkey" trial.

Montesquioeu, Charles de Secondat, baron de

Charles-Louis de Secondat, baron de La Brède et de Montesquieu (January 18, 1689 in Bordeaux – February 10, 1755), was a French social commentator and political thinker who lived during the Era of the Enlightenment. He is famous for his articulation of the theory of separation of powers, taken for granted in modern discussions of government and implemented in many constitutions throughout the world. He was largely responsible for the popularization of the terms feudalism and Byzantine Empire.

Moore, Roger

Sir Roger George Moore KBE (born 14 October 1927) is an English actor. He may be best known for portraying two British action heroes, Simon Templar in the television series *The Saint* from 1962 to 1969, and James Bond in seven films from 1973 to 1985. He has been a UNICEF ambassador since 1991.

Mull, Martin

Martin Mull (born August 18, 1943) is an American actor who has starred in his own TV sitcom and acted in prominent films. He is also a comedian, painter and recording artist.

Munro, Hector Hugh

Hector Hugh Munro (December 18, 1870 – November 14, 1916) better known by the pen name **Saki**, was a British writer, whose witty and sometimes macabre stories satirized Edwardian society and culture. He is considered a master of the short story and is often compared to O. Henry and Dorothy Parker. His tales feature delicately drawn characters and finely judged narratives. "The Open Window" may be his most famous, with a closing line ("Romance at short notice was her speciality") that has entered the lexicon.

In addition to his short stories (which were first published in newspapers, as was the custom of the time, and then collected into several volumes) he also wrote a full-length play, *The Watched Pot*, in collaboration with Charles Maude; two one-act plays: a historical study, *The Rise of the Russian Empire*, the only book published under his own name; a short novel, *The Unbearable Bassington*; the episodic *The Westminster Alice* (a Parliamentary parody of *Alice in Wonderland*), and *When William Came*, subtitled *A Story of London Under the Hohenzollerns*, an early alternative history. He was influenced by Oscar Wilde, Lewis Carrroll, and Kipling, and himself influenced A. A. Milne, Noël Coward, and P. G. Wodehouse.

Namath, Joe

Joseph William Namath (born May 31, 1943, Beaver Falls, Pennsylvania), also known as **Broadway Joe**, was an American football quarterback for the University of Alabama under legendary coach Paul "Bear" Bryant from 1962 – 64, and in the American Football League and National Football League during the 1960s and '70s. Namath played for the New York Jets for most of his professional career, finishing his career with the Los Angeles Rams. He was later elected to the Hall of Fame.

Nash, Ogden

Frederic Ogden Nash (August 19, 1902 – May 19, 1971) was an American poet best known for writing pithy and funny light verse.

Nathan, George Jean

George Jean Nathan (February 14, 1882 – April 8, 1958) was an American drama critic and editor. Nathan was born in Fort Wayne, Indiana. He graduated from Cornell University in 1904, where he was a member of the Quill and Dagger society.

Noted for the erudition and cynicism of his reviews, Nathan was an early champion of Eugene O'Neill. Together with H.L. Mencken, he co-edited the magazine *The Smart Set* from 1914 and co-founded The *American Mercury* in 1924. He was also a founder and an editor (1932 – 35) of the *American Spectator*, and after 1943 he wrote a syndicated column for the *New York Journal-American.*

Over the years, Nathan's criticisms were published in *Mr. George Jean Nathan Presents* (1917), *The Critic and the Drama* (1922), *The Testament of a Critic* (1931), *Since Ibsen* (1933), *Passing Judgments* (1935), *The World of George jean Nathan* (1952), and *The Magic Mirror* (1960). Nathan's philosophy of criticism is laid out in *Autobiography of an Attitude* (1925).

Nepos, Cornelius

Cornelius Nepos (c. 100 – 24 BC) was a Roman biographer. Supposedly he was born at Hostilia, a village in Cisalpine Gaul not far from Verona. His Gallic origin is attested by Ausonius,, and Pliny the Elder calls him *Padi accola* ('a dweller on the River Po, *Natural History* III.22). He was a friend of Catullus, who dedicates his poems to him, Cicero and Titus Pomponius Atticus. Eusebius places him in the fourth year of the reign of Augustus, which is supposed to be when he began to attract critical acclaim by his writing. Pliny the Elder notes he died in the reign of Augustus (*Natural History* IX.39, X.23).

Nettles, Graig

Graig Nettles (born August 20, 1944, in San Diego, California) (nicknamed **Puff**) is a former Major League Baseball third baseman and left-handed batter who played for the Minnesota Twins (1967 – 69), Cleveland Indians (1970 – 72), New York Yankees (1973 – 83), San Diego Padres (1984 – 86), Atlanta Braves (1987) and Montreal Expos (1988). He played collegiate baseball with the Aztecs of San Diego State University.

Nettles, known as Puff to fans and teammates, was one of the best defensive third basemen of all time, and despite his relatively low career batting average, he was an excellent offensive contributor, setting an American League record for career home runs by a third baseman.

Niebuhr, Reinhold

Karl Paul Reinhold Niebuhr (June 21, 1892 – June 1, 1971) was a Protestant theologian best know for his study of the task of relating the Christian faith to the reality of modern politics and diplomacy. He is a crucial contributor to modern just war thinking.

Nietzsche, Friedrich

Friedrich Wilhelm Nietzsche (October 15, 1844 – August 25, 1900) was a German philosopher. He wrote critiques of religion, morality, contemporary culture, philosophy, and science, using a distinctive style and displaying a fondness for aphorism. Nietzsche's influence remains substantial within and beyond philosophy, notably in existentialism and postmodernism. His style, and radical questioning of the value and objectivity of truth, raise considerable problems of interpretation, generating an extensive secondary literature in both continental and analytic philosophy. Nonetheless, his key ideas include interpreting tragedy as an affirmation of life, an eternal recurrence that has fallen into numerous interpretations, a reversal of Platonism, and a repudiation of Christianity as it was in the 19th century.

Nixon, Richard

Richard Milhous Nixon (January 9, 1913 – April 22, 1994) was the thirty-seventh President of the United States serving from 1969 until his resignation in 1974. Prior to being elected President, Nixon served as the thirty-sixth Vice President of the United States in the administration of Dwight D. Eisenhower from 1953 to 1961. Nixon is the only person to be elected twice to the offices of the presidency and the vice presidency, and is the only president to have resigned the office. During the Second World War, he served as a Navy lieutenant commander in the Pacific, before being elected to the Congress, and later serving as Vice President. After an unsuccessful presidential run in 1960, Nixon was elected in 1968.

Under President Nixon, the United States followed a foreign policy marked by détente with the Soviet Union and by the opening of diplomatic relations with the People's Republic of

China. Domestically, his administration faced resistance to the Vietnam War. As a result of the Watergate scandal, Nixon resigned the presidency in the face of likely impeachment by the United States House of Representatives and conviction by the Senate. His successor, Gerald Ford, issued a controversial pardon for any federal crimes Nixon may have committed.

Nixon suffered a stroke on April 18, 1994 and died four days later at the age of 81.

Onassis, Aristotle

Aristotelis Sokratis (also **Ari**) **Onassis** (January 15, 1906 – March 15, 1975) was the most famous shipping magnate of the 20th century.

Onassis was born in Smyrna, Ottoman Empire (now Izmir, Turkey) to a middle-class Greek family. At the time of his birth, Smyrna had a very significant and prosperous Greek population. After being briefly occupied by Greece (1919 – 1922) in the aftermath of the allied victory in World War I, the city was re-captured by Turkey; the Onassis family holdings were lost, causing them to move to Greece as refugees. In 1923, Aristotle Onassis left his country to go to Argentina with allegedly only $63. After difficult beginnings, he revived the family's tobacco business. In 1925, he received Argentinian and Greek citizenships. After engaging in many different entrepreneurial activities with determination and passion for success, he finally managed to become a world-class businessman making his first million by the age of 25, owning commercial ships, tankers and whalers. In 1954, the FBI investigated Onassis for fraud against the U.S. government. He was charged with violating the citizenship provision of the shipping laws which require that all ships displaying the U.S. flag be owned by U.S. citizens. Onassis entered a guilty plea and paid $7 million. He founded Olympic Airways (today Olympic Airlines), the Greek national carrier, in 1957.

Orben, Robert

Robert Orben (born March 4, 1927) is an American magician and professional comedy writer. He is also an author of books for magicians. He wrote a book called "Speaker's Handbook of Humor".

Robert Orben published his first gag book at the age of 18 in 1946, when he was working in Stuart Robson Jr.'s (stage manager for Florenz Ziegfeld) conjuror's shop in New York. Professional magicians would use his gags to add humor to their acts; comedians also came into magic stores, for props and books, as there were no comedy stores or resources as such at that time.

When Robert Orben wrote his first gag book, *Encyclopedia of Patter*, it proved very popular, and he started publishing more books of gags, complete with sketches, ad libs, bits of business and routines. Titles included *Patter Parade*, *Laugh Package*, *Sight Bits*, and *Screamline Comedy*.

O'Rourke, P. J.

Patrick Jake O'Rourke (born November 14, 1947 in Toledo, Ohio) is an American political satirist, journalist, and writer. O'Rourke is the H. L. Mencken Research Fellow at the Cato Institute and is a regular correspondent for *The Atlantic Monthly*, *The American Spectator*, and *The Weekly Standard*, and frequent panelist on National Public Radio's game show *Wait Wait...Don't Tell Me!* He is perhaps best known in the United Kingdom as the face of a long-running series of television advertisements for British Airways in the 1990s.

He is the author of 13 books, most recently *On The Wealth of Nations*, a commentary on Adam Smith's *An Inquiry into the Nature and Causes of the Wealth of Nations* (and the first in *The Atlantic Monthly's* "Books That Changed The World" series). According to a *60 Minutes* profile, he is also the most quoted living man in the *The Penguin Dictionary of Modern Humorous Quotations*.

Orwell, George

Eric Arthur Blair (25 June 1903 – 21 January 1950), known by the pen name **George Orwell**, was an English author and journalist. Noted as a novelist and critic as well as a political and cultural commentator, Orwell is among the most widely admired English-language essayists of the 20th century. He is best known for two novels critical of totalitarianism in general, and Stalinism in particular: *Animal Farm* and *Nineteen Eighty-Four*. Both were written and published towards the end of his life.

Ovid

Publius Ovidius Naso (March 20, 43 BC – 17 AD) was a Roman poet known to the English-speaking world as **Ovid** who wrote on many topics, including love, abandoned women and mythological transformations. Ranked alongside Virgil and Horace as one of the three canonical poets of Latin literature, Ovid was generally considered a great master of the elegiac couplet. His poetry, much imitated during Late Antiquity and the Middle Ages, had a decisive influence on European art and literature for centuries.

Paine, Thomas

Thomas Paine (Thetford, England, 29 January 1737 – June 1809, New York City, U.S.) was an English pamphleteer, revolutionary, radical, classical liberal and intellectual. Born in Great Britain, he lived and worked there until his late thirties, when he migrated to the American colonies just in time to take part in the American Revolution. His main contribution was as the author of the powerful, widely read pamphlet, *Common Sense* (1776), advocating independence for the American Colonies from the Kingdom of Great Britain, and of *The American Crisis*, supporting the Revolution.

Later, Paine was a great influence on the French Revolution. He wrote the *Rights of Man* (1791) as a guide to the ideas of the Enlightenment. Despite an inability to speak French, he was elected to the French National Assembly in 1792. Regarded as an ally of the Girondists, he was seen with increasing disfavour by the Montagnards and in particular by Robespierre.

Paine was arrested in Paris and imprisoned in December 1793; he was released in 1794. He became notorious with his book, *The Age of Reason* (1793 – 94), which advocated deism and took issue with Christian doctrines. While in France, he also wrote a pamphlet titled *Agrarian Justice* (1795), which discussed the origins of property and introduced a concept that is similar to a guaranteed minimum income.

Paine remained in France during the early Napoleonic era, but condemned Napoleon's moves towards dictatorship, calling him "the completest charlatan that ever existed". Paine remained in France until 1802, when he returned to America on an invitation from Thomas Jefferson, who had been elected president.

Paine died at 59 Grove Street in Greenwich Village, New York City, on the morning of June 8, 1809. He was 72.

Park, Brad

Douglas Bradford (Brad) Park (born July 6, 1948 in Toronto, Ontario) was an NHL ice hockey player in the National Hockey League (NHL) and is a member of the Hockey Hall of Fame. He played for the New York Rangers, Boston Bruins and Detroit Red Wings.

Park was drafted by the New York Rangers in the first round (2nd overall) in the 1966 NHL Amateur Draft and, after a brief stint with the minor-league Buffalo Bisons of the AHL, began playing for the Rangers in 1968. He quickly became the Rangers' best defenceman and drew comparisons with the great Bobby Orr. His offensive skill, stickhandling and pugnacity attracted much attention from fans.

Park was made the assistant captain of the Rangers and briefly served as their captain. In 1972 Park led his team to the Stanley Cup finals but lost to Orr and the Boston Bruins. That same year he was the runner-up for the Norris Trophy and was named MVP in the 1972 Summit Series.

Parker, Dorothy

Dorothy Parker (August 22, 1893 – June 7, 1967) was an American writer and poet, best known for her caustic wit, wisecracks, and sharp eye for 20th century urban foibles.

From a conflicted and unhappy childhood, Parker rose to acclaim, both for her literary output in such venues as *The New Yorker* and as a founding member of the Algonquin Round Table, a group she would later disdain. Following the breakup of that circle, Parker traveled to Hollywood to pursue screenwriting. Her successes there, including two Academy Award nominations, would eventually be curtailed, as her involvement in left-wing politics would lead to a place on the infamous Hollywood blacklist.

Parker survived three marriages (two to the same man) and several suicide attempts, but grew increasingly dependent on alcohol. Although she would come to dismiss her own talents and deplore her reputation as a "wisecracker", her literary output and her sparkling wit have endured long past her death.

Parton, Dolly

Dolly Rebecca Parton (born January 19, 1946) is a Grammy Award-winning country music singer/songwriter, composer, author, actress and philanthropist. She remains one of the most successful female country artists in history, with 25 number-one singles (a record for a female country artist) and 41 top-10 country albums (a record for any country artist).

Peale, Norman Vincent

Dr. Norman Vincent Peale (May 31, 1898 – December 24, 1993) was a Protestant preacher and author (most notably of *The Power of Positive Thinking*) and a progenitor of the theory of "positive thinking".

Peter, Laurence J.

Dr. Laurence J. Peter (September 16, 1919 – January 12, 1990) was an educator and "hierarchiologist" , best known to the general public for the formulation of the Peter Principle.

He was born in Vancouver, British Columbia, and began his career as a teacher in 1941. He received the degree of Doctor of Education from Washington State University in 1963.

He became widely famous in 1968, on the publication of The Peter Principle, in which he states: "In a hierarchy every employee tends to rise to his level of incompetence."

Phaedrus

Phaedrus (c. 15 BC – c. AD 50), Roman fabulist, was probably a Thracian slave, born in Pydna of Macedonia (Roman province) and lived in the reigns of Augustus, Tiberius, Gaius and Claudius. He is recognized as the first writer to latinize entire books of fables, using the iambic metre Greek prose of the Aesop tales.

Picasso, Pablo

Pablo Ruiz Picasso (October 25, 1881 – April 8, 1973), often referred to simply as **Picassso**, was a Spanish painter and sculptor. His full name is **Pablo Diego José Francisco de Paula Juan Nepomuceno María de los Remedious Cipriano de la Santísima Trinidad Clito Ruiz y Picasso**. One of the most recognized figures in 20th century art, he is best known as the co-founder, along with Georges Braque, of cubism.

Plato

Plato (Greek: *plátōn,* "wide, broad-browed")(424/423 BC – 348/347 BC), was a Classical Greek philosopher. Together with is teacher, Socrates, and his student, Aristotle, Plato helped to lay the philosophical foundations of Western culture. Plato was also a mathematician, writer of philosophical dialogues, and founder of the academy in Athens, the first institution of higher learning in the western world. Plato was originally a student of Socrates, and was as much influenced by his thinking as by what he saw as his teacher's unjust death.

Plato's brilliance as a writer and thinker can be witnessed by reading his Socratic dialogues. Some of the dialogues, letters, and other works that are ascribed to him are considered spurious. Interestingly, although there is little question that Plato lectured at the Academy that he founded, the pedagogical function of his dialogues, if any, is not known with certainty. The dialogues have since Plato's time been used to teach a range of subjects, mostly including philosophy, logic, rhetoric, mathematics, and other subjects about which he wrote.

Plautus, Titus Maccius

Titus Maccius Plautus (c. 254 – 184 BCE), commonly know as **Plautus**, was a Roman playwright His comedies are among the earliest surviving intact works in Latin literature. He is also one of the earliest pioneers of musical theater. The word **Plautine** is used to refer to Plautus's works or works similar to or influenced by his.

Pliny the Younger

Gaius or **Caius Plinius Caecilius Decundus**, born Gaisu or Caius Plinius Caecilius (61/63 – ca. 113), better know as **Pliny the Younger**, was a lawyer, a remarkable writer, an author and a natural philosopher of Ancient Rome.

Poe, Edgar Allan

Edgar Allan Poe (January 19, 1809 – October 7, 1849) was an American poet, short-story writer, editor, and literary critic, and is considered part of the American Romantic Movement. Best known for his tales of mystery and the macabre, Poe was one of the earliest American practitioners of the short story and invented the detective-fiction genre. He is credited with contributing to the emerging genre of science fiction. He was the first well-known American writer to try to earn a living through writing alone, resulting in a financially difficult life and career.

Pope, Alexander

Alexander Pope (21 May 1688 – 30 May 1744) is generally regarded as the greatest English poet of the early eighteenth century, best known for his satirical verse and for his translation of Homer. He is the third most frequently quoted writer in the English language, after Shakespeare and Tennyson. Pope was a master of the heroic couplet.

Pope John XXIII

Pope John XXIII (Latin: *Ioannes PP.XXIII*; Italian: *Giovanni XXIII*), born **Angelo Giuseppe Roncalli** (November 25, 1881 – June 3, 1963), known as **Blessed John XXIII** since his beatification, was elected as the 261st Pope of the Roman Catholic Church and sovereign of Vatican City on October 28, 1958. He called the Second Vatican Council (1962 – 1965) but did not live to see it to completion, dying on June 3, 1963, two months after the completion of his final encyclical, *Pacem in Terris*. He was beatified on September 3, 2000, along with Pope Pius IX, the first popes since Pope St. Pius X to receive this honor. His feast day is October 11 in the Catholic Church, the day that Vatican II's first session opened. He is also commemorated on June 3 by the Evangelical Lutheran Church in America and on June 4 by the Anglican Church of Canada.

In Italy he is remembered with the affectionate appellative of "Il Papa Buono" ("The Good Pope").

Presley, Elvis

Elvis Aaron Presley (January 8, 1935 – August 16, 1977), was an American singer, musician and actor. He is a cultural icon, often known as "**The King of Rock 'n' Roll**", or simply "**The King**".

Presley began his career as one of the first performers of rockabilly, an uptempo fusion of country and rhythm and blues with a strong back beat. His novel versions of existing songs, mixing "black" and "white" sounds, made him popular – and controversial – as did his uninhibited stage and television performances. He recorded songs in the rock and roll genre, with tracks like "Hound Dog" and "Jailhouse Rock" later embodying the style. Presley had a versatile voice and had unusually wide success encompassing other genres, including gospel, blues, ballads and pop. To date, he is the only performer to have been inducted into four music halls of fame.

In the 1960s, Presley made the majority of his thirty-three movies – mainly poorly reviewed musicals. In 1968, he returned to live music in a television special and thereafter performed across the U.S., notably in Las Vegas. Throughout his career, he set records for concert attendance, television ratings and recordings sales. He is one of the best-selling and most influential artists in the history of popular music. Health problems plagued Presley in later life which, coupled with a punishing tour schedule and addiction to prescription medication, led to his premature death at age 42.

Priestley, J. B.

John Boynton Priestley, OM (born 13 September 1894, Bradford, West Riding of Yorkshire, died 14 August 1984, Warwickshire) was an English writer and broadcaster.

By the age of 30 he had established a reputation as a humorous writer and critic. His 1927 novel *Benighted* was adapted into the James Whale film *The Old Dark House* in 1932. His first major success came with a novel, *The Good Companions* (1929) which earned him the James Tait Black Memorial Prize for fiction and made him a national figure. His next novel *Angel Pavement* (1930) further established him as a successful novelist.

Pryor, Richard

Richard Franklin Lennox Thomas Pryor III (December 1, 1940 – December 10, 2005) was an American comedian, actor, and writer.

Pryor was a storyteller known for unflinching examinations of racism and customs in modern life, and was well known for his frequent use of colorful language, vulgarities, and racial epithets such as "nigger", "Honky", "cracker", and "motherfucker". He reached a broad audience with his trenchant observations, although public opinion of his act was often divided. He is commonly regarded as the most important stand up comedian of his time: Jerry Seinfeld called Pryor "The Picasso of our profession:, Whoopi Goldberg cited him as her biggest influence, stating "The major influence was Richard – I want to say those things he's saying." Bob Newhart has called Pryor "the seminal comedian of the last 50 years".

His body of work includes such concert movies and recordings as *Richard Pryor: Live and Smokin'* (1971), *That Nigger's Crazy* (1974), *...Is It Something I Said?* (1975), *Bicentennial Nigger* (1976), *Richard Pryor: Live in Concert* (1979), *Richard Pryor: Live on the Sunset Strip* (1982) and *Richard Pryor: Here and Now*. He also starred in numerous films as an actor, usually in comedies such as *Silver Streak*, but occasionally in dramatic roles, such as Paul Schrader's film *Blue Collar* and epic roles like Gus Gorman from *Superman III* (1983). He also collaborated on many projects with actor Gene Wilder. He won an Emmy |Award in 1973, and five Grammy Awards in 1974, 1975, 1976, 1981, and 1982. In 1974, he also won two American Academy of Humor awards and the Writers Guild of America Award. In 2004, Pryor was voted the greatest stand-up act of all time by Comedy Central.

Puzo, Mario

Mario Gianluigi Puzo (October 15, 1920 – july 2, 1999) was an Italian-American author known for his novels about the Mafia, especially *The Godfather* (1969).

Puzo was born into a poor family of Neapolitan immigrants living in the hell's Kitchen neighborhood of New York City. Many of his books draw heavily on this heritage. After graduating form the City College of New York, he joined the United States Army Air Forces in World War II. Due to poor eyesight, the military did not let him undertake combat duties but made him a public relations officer stationed in Germany. After the war, he wrote his first book, *The Dark Arena*, which came out in 1955.

His most famous work, *The Godfather*, was first published in 1969 after he had heard anecdotes about Mafia organizations during his time in pulp journalism. The book was later developed into a trilogy of films (*The Godfather*, *The Godfather Part II* and *The Godfather Part III*) directed by Francis Ford Coppola.

Puzo wrote the first draft of the script for the 1974 disaster film *Earthquake*, which he was unable to continue working on due to his commitment to *The Godfather: Part II*. Puzo also co-wrote Richard Donner's *Superman: The Movie* and the original draft for *Superman II*.

Quintilian, Marcus Fabius

Marcus Fabius Quintilianus (ca. 35 – ca. 100) was a Roman rhetorician from Hispania, widely referred to in medieval schools of rhetoric and in Renaissance writing. In English translation, he is usually referred to as **Quintilian**, although the alternate spellings of **Quintillian** and **Quinctilian** are occasionally seen, the latter in older texts.

Quintillian was born ca. 35 in Calagurris (now Calahorra, La

Rioja) in Hispania. His father, a well-educated man, sent him to Rome to study rhetoric early in the reign of Nero.

Rawlings, Marjorie Kinnan

Marjorie Kinnan Rawlings (August 8, 1896 – December 14, 1953) was an American author who lived in rural Florida and wrote novels with rural themes and settings. Her best known work, *The Yearling*, about a boy who adopts an orphaned fawn, won a Pulitzer Prize for fiction in 1939 and was later made into a movie, also known as *The Yearling*. The book was written long before the concept of young-adult fiction, but is now commonly included in teen-reading lists.

Renoir, Pierre-Auguste

Pierre-Auguste Renoir (February 25, 1841 – December 3, 1919) was a French artist who was a leading painter in the development of the Impressionist style. As a celebrator of beauty, and especially feminine sensuality, it has been said that "Renoir is the final representative of a tradition which runs directly from Rubens to Watteau".

Repplier, Agnes

Agnes Repplier (April 1, 1855 – November 15, 1950) was an American essayist born in Philadelphia, Pennsylvania. Her essays are esteemed for their scholarship and wit.

Reston, James

James Barrett Reston (November 3, 1909 – December 6, 1995) (nicknamed "**Scotty**") was a prominent American journalist whose career spanned the mid 1930s to the early 1990s. Associated for many years with *The New York Times*, he became perhaps the most powerful, influential, and widely-read journalist of his era.

Robinson, Sugar Ray

Sugar Ray Robinson (born **Walker Smith Jr.**, May 3, 1921 – April 12, 1989) was a professional boxer. Frequently cited as the greatest boxer of all time, Robinson's performances at the welterweight and middleweight divisions prompted sportswriters to create "pound for pound" rankings, where they compared fighters regardless of weight. He was inducted into the International Boxing Hall of Fame in 1990.

Robinson was 85-0 as an amateur with 69 of those victories coming by way of knockout, 40 in the first round. He turned professional in 1940 at the age of 19 and by 1951 had a professional record of 128-1-2 with 84 knockouts. Robinson held the world welterweight title from 1946 to 1951, and won the world middleweight title in the latter year. He retired in 1952, only to come back two and a half years later and regain the middleweight title in 1955. He then became the first boxer in history to win a divisional world championship five times.

Rochefoucauld, François de La, (writer)

François VI, duc de La Rochefoucauld, le Prince de Marcillac (September 15, 1613 – March 17, 1680), was a noted French author of maxims and memoirs, as well as an example of the accomplished 17th-century nobleman. He was born in Paris in the Rue des Petits Champs, at a time when the royal court oscillated between aiding the nobility and threatening it. Until 1650, he bore the title of Prince de Marcillac.

Rockefeller, John D.

John Davidson Rockefeller, Sr. (July 8, 1839 – May 23, 1937) was an American industrialist and philanthropist. Rockefeller revolutionized the petroleum industry and defined the structure of modern philanthropy. In 1870, Rockefeller founded the Standard Oil Company and ran it until he retired in the late 1890s. He kept his stock and as gasoline grew in importance, his wealth soared and he became the world's richest man and first U.S. dollar billionaire, and is often regarded as the richest person in history. Standard Oil was convicted in Federal Court of monopolistic practices and broken up in 1911. Rockefeller spent the last 40 years of his life in retirement. His fortune was mainly used to create the modern systematic approach of targeted philanthropy with foundations that had a major effect on medicine, education, and scientific research. His foundations pioneered the development of medical research, and were instrumental in the eradication of hookworm and yellow fever. He was a devoted Northern Baptist and supported many church-based institutions throughout his life.

Rockefeller, Nelson

Nelson Aldrich Rockefeller (July 8, 1908 – January 26, 1979) was the forty-first Vice President of the United States, governor of New York, philanthropist, and businessman.

A leader of the liberal wing of the Republican Party, he was Governor of New York from 1959 to 1973, where he launched many construction and modernization projects. A descendant of one of the world's richest and best known families, he failed repeatedly in his attempts to become president, but he was appointed Vice President in 1974. He served from 1974 to 1977, and did not join the 1976 GOP national ticket with President Gerald Ford. He retired from politics when his term as Vice President was over.

Rodríguez, Juan "Chi-Chi"

Juan Antonio "Chi-Chi" Rodríguez (born October 23, 1935) is a Puerto Rican professional golfer. He was the first Puerto Rican to be inducted into the World Golf Hall of Fame.

Rodríguez was born in Rio Piedras, Puerto Rico into a poor family, one of six siblings. His father used to earn only $18 a week as a laborer and cattle handler. When Rodríguez was only seven years old, he would help the family by earning money as a water carrier on a sugar plantation. One day Juan wandered off, as many children his age do, but into a golf course. When he saw that the caddies were earning more money than him, he decided to become a caddy himself.

Rodríguez would take a branch from a guava tree and turn it into a golf club. Using a metal can as a "golf ball", he would practice what he had seen the "real" golfers do, teaching himself how to play golf. By the time he was nine years old, he was proficient at golf and in 1947 at the age of 12, he scored a remarkable 67.

In 1954, when Rodríguez was 19, he joined the Army. During his breaks, he would visit whichever golf course was nearby, where he continued to perfect his game.

Rodríguez turned professional in 1960. In 1963, at 28, Rodríguez won the Denver Open, which he considers as his favorite win. In total he won eight titles on the PGA Tour between 1963 and 1979. He played on the 1973 U.S. Ryder Cup team.

At first, Rodríguez used to put his hat over the hole whenever he made a birdie or eagle. After he heard that other golfers were complaining about his little act, he decided to try something new. Juan developed his signature "toreador dance", where he would make believe that the birdie was a "bull" and that his putter was a "sword" and he would terminate the "bull". Rodríguez represented Puerto Rico on 12 World Cup teams. In 1986, he won the Hispanic Recognition Award. In 1988, he was named Replica's Hispanic Man of the Year.

Rodríguez became eligible to play on the Senior PGA Tour (now known as the Champions Tour) in 1985 and did so for many years with great success, accumulating 22 tournament victories between 1986 and 1993. He was the first player on the Senior PGA Tour to win the same event in three consecutive years. He set a tour record with eight consecutive birdies en route to a win at the 1987 Silver Pages Classic.

In 1989, he was voted the Bob Jones Award, the highest honor given by the United States Golf Association in recognition of distinguished sportsmanship in golf. In 1991, he lost an 18-hole playoff to a legendary Jack Nicklaus in the U.S. Senior Open. In 1992, Juan "Chi-Chi" Rodríguez was inducted into the World Golf Hall of Fame, the first Puerto Rican so honored.

Rogers, Ginger

Ginger Rogers (born **Virginia Katherine McMath**, July 16, 1911 – April 25, 1995) was an Academy Award-winning American film and stage actress and singer. In a film career spanning fifty years she made a total of seventy-three films, and is now principally celebrated for her role as Fred Astaire's romantic interest and dancing partner in a series of ten Hollywood musical films that revolutionized the genre.

Rogers, Will

William Penn Adair "Will" Rogers (November 4, 1879 – August 15, 1935) was a Cherokee-American cowboy, comedian, humorist, social commentator, vaudeville performer and actor.

Known as Oklahoma's favorite son, Rogers was born to a prominent Indian Territory family and learned to ride horses and use a lariat so well that he was listed in the Guinness Book of World Records for throwing three ropes at once – one around the neck of a horse, another around the horse's rider, and a third around all four legs of the horse. He ultimately traveled around the world three times, made movies (50 silent films and 21 "talkies"), wrote more than 4,000 nationally-syndicated newspaper columns, and became a world-famous figure.

By the mid-1930s, Rogers was adored by the American people , and was the top-paid movie star in Hollywood at the time. On an around-the-world trip with aviator Wiley Post, Rogers died when their small airplane crashed near Barrow, Alaska Territory in 1935.

Roosevelt, Franklin D.

Franklin Delano Roosevelt (January 30, 1882 – April 12, 1945), often referred to by his initials **FDR**, was the thirty-second President of the United States. Elected to four terms in office, he served from 1933 to 1945, and is the only U.S. president to have served more than two terms. He was a central figure of the 20th century during a time of worldwide economic crisis and world war.

During the Great Depression of the 1930s, Roosevelt created the New Deal to provide relief for the unemployed, recovery of the economy, and reform of the economic and banking systems. Although recovery of the economy was incomplete until almost 1940, many programs initiated in the Roosevelt administration continue to have instrumental roles in the nation's commerce, such as the FDIC, TVA, and the SEC. One of his most important legacies is the Social Security system.

Roosevelt won four presidential elections in a row, causing a realignment that political scientists call the Fifth Party System.

His aggressive use of an active federal government re-energized the Democratic Party, created a New Deal Coalition which dominated American politics until the late 1960s. He and his wife, Eleanor Roosevelt, remain touchstones for modern American liberalism. Conservatives vehemently fought back, but Roosevelt usually prevailed until he tried to pack the Supreme Court in 1937. Thereafter, the new Conservative coalition successfully ended New Deal expansion; during the war it closed most relief programs like the WPA and Civilian Conservation Corps, arguing that unemployment had disappeared.

After 1938, Roosevelt championed re-armament and led the nation away from isolationism as the world headed into World War II. He provided extensive support to Winston Churchill and the British war effort before the attack on Pearl Harbor pulled the U.S. into the fighting. During the war, Roosevelt, working closely with his aide Harry Hopkins, provided decisive leadership against Nazi Germany and made the United States the principal arms supplier and financier of the Allies who later, alongside the United States, defeated Germany, Italy and Japan. Roosevelt led the United States as it became the Arsenal of Democracy, putting 16 million American men into uniform.

Rostand, Jean

Jean Rostand (October 30, 1894 – September 4, 1977) was a French biologist and philosopher.

Active as an experimental biologist, Rostand became famous for his work as a science writer, as well as a philosopher and an activist. His scientific work covered a variety of biological fields such as amphibian embryology, parthenogenesis and teratogeny, while his literary output extended into popular science, history of science and philosophy.

Rousseau, Jean-Jacques

Jean-Jacques Rousseau, (June 28, 1712 – July 2, 1778) was a philosopher and composer of the Enlightenment whose political philosophy influenced the French Revolution, the development of both liberal and socialist theory, and the growth of nationalism. With his *Confessions* and other writings, he practically invented modern autobiography and encouraged a new focus on the building of subjectivity that would bear fruit in the work of thinkers as diverse as Hegel and Freud. His novel *Julie, ou la nouvelle Héloïse* was one of the best selling fictional works of the eighteenth century and was important to the development of romanticism. Rousseau also made important contributions to music both as a theorist and a composer.

Runyon, Damon

Damon Runyon (October 4, 1884 – December 10, 1946) was a newspaperman and writer.

He was best known for his short stories celebrating the world of Broadway in New York City that grew out of the Prohibition era. He spun humorous tales of gamblers, hustlers, actors and gangsters; few of whom go by "square" names, preferring instead to be known as "Nathan Detroit", "Big Jule", "Harry the Horse", "Good Time Charley", "Dave the Dude", and so on. These stories were written in a very distinctive vernacular style: a mixture of formal speech and colorful slang, almost always in present tense, and always devoid of contractions.

Russell, Bertrand

Bertrand Arthur William Russell, 3rd Earl Russell, OM, FRS, (18 May 1872 – 2 February 1970), was a Welsh philosopher, historian, logician, mathematician, advocate for social reform, pacifist, and prominent rationalist.

A prolific writer, he was a popularizer of philosophy and a commentator on a large variety of topics. Continuing a family tradition in political affairs; he was a prominent anti-war activist, championing free trade between nations and anti-imperialism. He also co-authored, with Alfred North Whitehead, Principia Mathematica, an attempt to ground Mathematics on the laws of Logic. The book has had a considerable influence on Analytic Philosophy.

Safire, William

William L. Safire (born December 17, 1929) is an American author, semi-retired columnist, and former journalist and presidential speechwriter.

He is perhaps best known as a long-time syndicated political columnist for *The New York Times* and a regular contributor to "On Language" in the *New York Times Magazine*, a column on popular etymology, new or unusual usages, and other language-related topics.

Saget, Bob

Robert Lane Saget (born May 17, 1956) is an American actor, stand-up comedian, writer, director, producer, and game show host. He is well known for his role as Danny Tanner in the ABC sitcom *Full House* from 1987 to 1995, host of *America's Funniest Home Videos* from 1989 to 1997. Currently he is the host of the NBC game show *1 vs. 100* as well as the narrator of the CBS comedy series *How I Met Your Mother*.

Saget is generally known for his clean-cut, family-friendly television persona from the hit shows *Full House* and *America's Funniest Home Videos*, which have been widely rerun in syndication for over a decade. In contrast, Saget is also known for using edgy humor in his stand-up comedy acts and movies.

Santayana, George

George Santayana (December 16, 1863, Madrid – September 26, 1952, Rome), was a philosopher, essayist, poet, and novelist.

A lifelong Spanish citizen, Santayana was raised and educated in the United States, wrote in English and is generally considered an American man of letters, even though, of his nearly 89 years, he spent only 39 in the U.S. He is perhaps best known as an aphorist, and for the oft-misquoted remark, "Those who cannot remember the past are condemned to repeat it", from *Reason in Common Sense*, the first volume of his *The Life of Reason*.

Sargent, John Singer

John Singer Sargent (January 12, 1856 – April 14, 1925) was the most successful portrait painter of his era, as well as a gifted landscape painter and watercolorist. Sargent was born in Florence, Italy to American parents. He studied in Italy and Germany, and then in Paris under Emile Auguste Carolus-Duran.

Schulz, Charles M.

Charles Monroe Schulz (November 26, 1922 – February 12, 2000) was a 20th-century American cartoonist best known worldwide for his *Peanuts* comic strip.

Scott-Maxwell, Florida

Florida Pier Scott-Maxwell (1883 – 1979) was a writer, playwright, and suffragist who took up a career in analytical psychology in 1933, studying under Carl Jung in both Scotland and England.

(From Penguin group (usa) online.)

Seneca the Elder

Lucius, or **Marcus, Annaeus Seneca**, known as **Seneca the Elder** and **Seneca the Rhetorician** (ca. 54 BC – ca. 39 AD) was a Roman rhetorician and writer, born of a well-to-do equestrian family of Cordoba, Hispania.

His *praenomen* is uncertain, but in any case Marcus is an arbitrary conjecture of Raphael of Volterra. During a lengthy stay on two occasions at Rome, Seneca attended the lectures of famous orators and rhetoricians, to prepare for an official career as an advocate. His 'ideal' orator was Cicero, and Seneca disapproved of the florid tendencies of the oratory of his time.

Shakespeare, William

William Shakespeare (baptized 26 April 1564 – 23 April 1616) was an English poet and playwright, widely regarded as the greatest writer in the English language and the world's pre-eminent dramatist. He is often called England's national poet and the "Bard of Avon" (or simply "The Bard"). His surviving works consist of 38 plays, 154 sonnets, two long narrative poems, and several other poems. His plays have been translated into every major living language and are performed more often than those of any other playwright.

Shakespeare produced most of his known work between 1590 and 1613. His early plays were mainly comedies and histories, genres he raised to the peak of sophistication and artistry by the end of the sixteenth century. Next he wrote mainly tragedies until about 1608, producing plays, such as *Hamlet*, *King Lear*, and *Macbeth*, considered some of the finest in the English language. In his last phase, he wrote tragicomedies and collaborated with other playwrights. Many of his plays were published in editions of varying quality and accuracy during his lifetime, and in 1623, two of his former theatrical colleagues published the First Folio, a collected edition of his dramatic works that included all but two of the plays now recognized as Shakespeare's.

Shaw, George Bernard

George Bernard Shaw (26 July 1856 – 2 November 1950) was a world-famous playwright. Born in Dublin, he moved to London at age twenty and lived in England for the remainder of his life. Shaw's first success was as a music and literary critic, but he was drawn to drama and authored more than sixty plays during his career. Typically his work is leavened by a delightful vein of comedy, but nearly all of it has serious undertones. His plays and prefaces pinpoint institutionalized defects in many aspects of Western culture and suggest reforms. Education, marriage, religion, government, health care, class privilege…All of these were targets, but his prime aim was to free the working class from the abusive exploitation that pervaded the Victorian era. Humor was Shaw's way of making his attacks on the establishment less distressing to his audiences.

Politically an ardent socialist, Shaw wrote many brochures and speeches for the Fabian Society and became an accomplished orator in furtherance of its causes. Those included gaining equal political rights for men and women, alleviating abuses of the working class, rescinding private ownership of productive land, and promoting healthful lifestyles.

Sheridan, Richard Brinsley

Richard Brinsley Sheridan (October 30, 1751 – July 7, 1816) was an Irish playwright and Whig statesman.

Smith, Sydney

Sydney Smith (June 3, 1771, Woodford, Essex, England – February 22, 1845 London), was an English writer and clergyman.

Socrates

Socrates (c. 470 BC – 399 BC), of the deme Alopece of Athens, was a Classical Greek philosopher. He is best known for the creation of Socratic irony and the Socratic Method, or elenchus. Specifically, Socrates is renowned for developing the practice of a philosophical type of pedagogy, in which the teacher asks questions of the student to elicit the best answer, and fundamental insight, on the part of the student.

Socrates is credited with exerting a powerful influence upon the founders of Western philosophy, most particularly Plato and Aristotle, and while Socrates' principal contribution to philosophy is in the field of ethics, he also made important and lasting contributions to the fields of epistemology and logic.

Sowell, Thomas

Thomas Sowell (born June 30, 1930), is an American economist, political writer, and commentator. While often described as a "black conservative", he prefers not to be labeled, and considers himself more libertarian than conservative. He often writes from an economically laissez-faire perspective. He is currently a senior fellow of the Hoover Institution at Stanford University. In 1990, he won the Francis Boyer Award, presented by the American Enterprise Institute. In 2002 he was awarded the National Humanities Medal for prolific scholarship melding history, economics, and political science.

Spinks, Leon

Leon Spinks (born July 11, 1953 in St. Louis, Missouri) is a former boxer. He had an overall record of 26 wins, 17 losses and 3 draws as a professional, with 14 knockout wins. While still an amateur, he also became a member of the United States Marine Corps. Spinks went from being heavyweight champion of the world to being homeless in little more than a decade.

He won the gold medal in the light heavyweight division during the 1976 Summer Olympics in Montreal, alongside brother Michael Spinks, who also won a gold medal in those games. Two years earlier, at the inaugural 1974 World Amateur Boxing Championships in Havana, Cuba, he captured the bronze medal.

Squire, J. C.

Sir John Squire (John Collings Squire) (April 2, 1884 – December 20, 1958) was a British poet, writer, historian, and influential literary editor of the post-World War I period. He also moved in society circles.

Stalin, Joseph

Joseph Vissarionovich Jugashvili (December 18, 1878 – March 5, 1953), better known by his adopted name, **Joseph Stalin** meaning "made of steel", was General Secretary of the Communist Party of the Soviet Union's Central Committee from 1922 until his death in 1953.

During that time, he established the eponymous regime, **Stalinism**. Although Stalin's formal position originally had little significant influence, his office being nominally one of several Central Committee Secretariats, Stalin's increasing control of the Party from 1928 onwards led to his becoming the *de facto* party leader and the dictator of his country, in full control of the Soviet Union and its people. His crash programs of industrialization and collectivization in the 1930s and his campaigns of political repression cost the lives of millions of people. However, it helped industrialize the Soviet union making it a great power by 1931. Only six years later, the Soviet Union had become the second largest industrial nation in the world.

During Stalin's reign, the Soviet Union played a major role in the defeat of Nazi Germany in the Second World War (1939 – 1945) (more commonly known in Russia and post-Soviet republics as the Great Patriotic War). Under Stalin's leadership, the Soviet Union went on to achieve recognition as one of just two superpowers in the post-war era, a status that lasted for nearly four decades after his death.

Stengel, Casey

Charles Dillon "Casey" Stengel (July 30, 1890 – September 29, 1975), nicknamed "The Old Professor", was an American baseball player and manager from the early 1910s into the 1960s. He was born in Kansas City, and was originally nicknamed "Dutch", a common nickname at that time for Americans of German ancestry. After his major league career started, he acquired the nickname "Casey", which originally came from the initials of his hometown ("K. C."), which evolved into "Casey", influenced by the wide popularity of the poem *Casey at the Bat*. In the 1950s, sportswriters dubbed him with yet another nickname, "The Old Professor", for his sharp wit and his ability to talk at length on anything baseball-related.

Stevenson, Adlai

Adlai Ewing Stevenson II (February 5, 1900 – July 14, 1965) was an American politician, noted for his intellectual demeanor and advocacy of liberal causes in the Democratic party. He served one term as governor of Illinois and ran, unsuccessfully, for president against Dwight D. Eisenhower in 1952 and 1956. He served as Ambassador to the United Nations from 1961 to 1965.

Stevenson, Robert Louis

Robert Louis (Balfour) Stevenson (November 13, 1850 – December 3, 1894), was a Scottish novelist, poet, and travel writer, and a leading representative of neo-romanticism in English literature. He was greatly admired by many authors, including Jorge Luis Borges, Ernest Hemingway, Rudyard Kipling and Vladimir Nabokov.

Most modernist writers dismissed him, however, because he was popular and did not write within their narrow definition of literature. It is only recently that critics have begun to look beyond Stevenson's popularity and allow him a place in the Western Canon.

He prepared for a law career but never practiced. He traveled frequently, partly in search of better climates for his weak lungs (possibly due to tuberculosis), which contributed to his death at age 44.

Stewart, James (actor)

James Maitland Stewart (20 May 1908 – 2 July 1997), popularly known as Jimmy Stewart especially in the United States, was an iconic, Academy Award-winning American film and stage actor, best known for his self-effacing screen persona. Over the course of his career, he starred in many films widely considered classics and was nominated for five Oscars, winning one in competition and one life achievement. He also had a noted military career, rising to the rank of Brigadier General in the United States Air Force.

Strachey, Lytton

Giles Lytton Stachey (March 1, 1880 – January 21, 1932) was a British writer and critic. He is best known for establishing a new form of biography in which psychological insight and sympathy are combined with irreverence and wit. His 1921 biography *Queen Victoria* was awarded the James Tait Black Memorial Prize.

Sutton, Don

Donald Howard Sutton (born April 2, 1945) is a former Major League Baseball player and current television sportscaster.

A right-handed pitcher, Sutton played for the Sioux Falls Packers as a minor leaguer, and entered the major league at the age of 21. Don Sutton's major league debut was on April 14, 1966. In the majors, he played 23 years for the Los Angeles Dodgers, Houston Astros, Milwaukee Brewers, Oakland Athletics, and California Angels. He won a total of 324 games, 58 of them shutouts and five of them one-hitters, and he is eighth on baseball's all time strikeout list with 3,574 K's. He also holds the major league record for number of consecutive losses to one team, having lost 13 straight games to the Chicago Cubs. A 4-time All-Star, Sutton was elected to the Baseball Hall of Fame in 1998.

Swift, Jonathan

Jonathan Swift (November 30, 1667 – October 19, 1745) was an Irish cleric, Dean of St. Patrick's, Dublin, satirist, essayist, political pamphleteer (first for Whigs than for Tories), and poet, famous for works like *Gulliver's Travels*, *A Modest Proposal*, *A Journal to Stella*, *The Drapier's Lettters*, *The Battle of the Books*, and *A Tale of a Tub*. Swift is probably the foremost prose satirist in the English language, and is less well known for his poetry. Swift published all of his works under pseudonyms – such as Lemuel Gulliver, Isaac Bickerstaff, M.B. Drapier – or anonymously. He is also known for being a master of two styles of satire; the Horatian and Juvenalian styles.

Syrus, Publilius

Publilius (less correctly Publius) **Syrus**, a Latin writer of maxims, flourished in the lst century BC. He was a native of Syria, and was brought as a slave to Italy, but by his wit and talent he won the favor of his master, who freed and educated him.

His mimes, in which he acted himself, had a great success in the provincial towns of Italy and at the games given by Caesar in 46 BC. Publilius was perhaps even more famous as an improviser, and received from Caesar himself the prize in a contest in which he vanquished all his competitors, including the celebrated Decimus Laberius.

All that remains of his works is a collection of *Sentences* (*Sententiae*), a series of moral maxims in iambic and trochaic verse. This collection must have been made at a very early date, since it was known to Aulus Gellius in the 2nd century AD. Each maxim is comprised of a single verse, and the verses are arranged in alphabetical order according to their initial letters. In the course of time the collection was interpolated with sentences drawn form other writers, especially from apocryphal writings of

Seneca; the number of genuine verses is about 700. They include many pithy sayings, such as the famous "*judex damnatur ubi nocens absolvitur*" ("The judge is condemned when the guilty is acquitted.") adopted as its motto by the *Edinburgh Review*).

Tacitus

Publius (or **Gaius**) **Cornelius Tacitus** (ca. 56 – ca. 117) was a senator and a historian of the of the Roman Empire. The surviving portions of his two major works – the *Annals* and the *Histories* – examine the reigns of the Roman Emperors Tiberius, Claudius, Nero and those that reigned in the Year of the Four Emperors. These two works span the history of the Roman Empire from the death of Augustus in 14 AD to (presumably) the death of emperor Domitian in 96 AD. There are significant lacunae in the surviving texts.

Talleyrand-Périgord, Charles Maurice de

Charles Maurice de Talleyrand-Périgord, 1st Sovereign Prince de **Bénévent** (February 2, 1754 – May 17, 1838), *the Prince of Diplomats*, was a French diplomat. He worked successfully form the regime of Louis XVI, through the French Revolution and then under Napoleon I, Louis XVIII and Louis-Philippe. Known since the turn of the 19th century simply by the name **Talleyrand**, he is widely regarded as on of the most versatile and influential diplomats in European history.

Teresa, Mother

Mother Teresa (Albanian: **Agnes Gonxha Bojaxhiu**; August 26, 1910 – September 5, 1997) was a Roman Catholic nun who founded the Missionaries of Charity in Kolkata (Calcutta), India in 1950. For over forty years she ministered to the poor, sick, orphaned, and dying, while guiding the Missionaries of Charity's expansion, first throughout India and then in other countries.

By the 1970s she had become internationally famed as a humanitarian and advocate for the poor and helpless, due in part to a documentary, and book, *Something Beautiful for God* by Malcolm Muggeridge. She won the Nobel Peace Prize in 1979 for her humanitarian work. Mother Teresa's Missionaries of Charity continued to expand, and at the time of her death it was operating 610 missions in 123 countries, including hospices and homes for people with HIV/AIDS, leprosy and tuberculosis, soup kitchens, children's and family counseling programs, orphanages, and schools.

Thomas, Dylan

Dylan Marlais Thomas (27 October 1914 – 9 November 1953) was a Welsh poet. He is regarded by many as one of the 20th century's most influential poets.

In addition to poetry, Thomas also wrote short stories and scripts for film and radio, with the latter frequently performed by Thomas himself. His public readings, particularly in America, won him great acclaim; his booming, at times ostentatious, voice with a subtle Welsh lilt, became almost as famous as his works. His best known works include "Under Milk Wood" and "Do not go gentle into that good night", a poem written in 1951 about his dying father.

Thoreau, Henry David

Henry David Thoreau (July 12, 1817 – May 6, 1862: born **David Henry Thoreau**) was an American author, naturalist, transcendentalist, tax resister, development critic, and philosopher who is best known for *Walden*, a reflection upon simple living in natural surroundings, and his essay, *Civil Disobedience*, an argument for individual resistance to civil government in moral opposition to an unjust state.

Thoreau's books, articles, essays, journals, and poetry total over 20 volumes. Among his lasting contributions were his writings on natural history and philosophy, where he anticipated the methods and findings of ecology and environmental history, two sources of modern day environmentalism.

Thurber, James

James Grover Thurber (December 8, 1894 – November 2, 1961) was a U.S. humorist and cartoonist. Thurber was best known for his contribution (both cartoon and short stories) to *The New Yorker* magazine.

Tolstoy, Leo

Count **Lev Nikolayevich Tolstoy** (September 9, 1828 – November 20, 1910) was a Russian writer – novelist, essayist, dramatist and philosopher as well as pacifist Christian anarchist and educational reformer. He was the most influential member of the aristocratic Tolstoy family.

As a fiction writer, Tolstoy is widely regarded as one of the greatest of all novelists, particularly noted for his masterpieces *War and Peace* and *Anna Karenina.* In their scope, breadth and realistic depiction of 19th-century Russian life, the two books stand at the peak of realist fiction. As a moral philosopher Tolstoy was notable for his ideas on nonviolent resistance through works such as *The Kingdom of God is Within You,* which in turn influenced such twentieth-century figures as Mohandas K. Gandhi and Martin Luther King, Jr.

Tomlin, Lily

Lily Tomlin (born September 1, 1939) is an Academy Award-nominated American actress, comedian, writer and producer. Tomlin's body of work, which has spanned over 40 years, has garnered her several Tony Awards and Emmy Awards, as well as a Grammy Award.

Tomlin was born **Mary Jean Tomlin** in Detroit, Michigan, daughter of Lillie Mae (née Ford), a housewife and nurse's aide who moved to Detroit from Paducah, Kentucky during the Great Depression, and Guy Tomlin, a factory worker. She is a 1957 graduate of Cass Technical High School. Tomlin attended Wayne State University, where her interest in the theater and performing arts began. After college, Tomlin began doing stand-up comedy in nightclubs in Detroit and later, in New York City. Her first television appearance was on *The Merv Griffin Show* in 1965.

In 1969, Tomlin joined the sketch comedy show *Laugh-In.* Her characters from the show have been associated with her throughout her career, including the gum-chewing, wisecracking, snorting telephone operator Ernestine, the bratty five-year old Edith Ann, rocking in her oversized chair, making rude noises, and telling stories about her baby brother and her dog, Buster, and the Tasteful Lady, who lives a gracious and naively entitled life in the upper class and shades of whom show up in Tomlin's film role in *All of Me*. Additional characters include Susie the Sorority Girl, who appeared on Tomlin's album *Modern Scream* and in her 1975 appearance on *Saturday Night Live*.

Truman, Harry S.

Harry S. Truman (May 8, 1884 – December 26, 1972) was the thirty-third President of the United States (1945 – 1953). As vice president, he succeeded to the office upon the death of Franklin D. Roosevelt.

During World War I he served as an artillery officer. After the war he became part of the political machine of Tom Pendergast and was elected a county judge in Missouri and eventually a United States Senator. In 1944, Roosevelt replaced Henry A. Wallace as vice president with Truman for Roosevelt's fourth term.

Tucker, Sophie

Sophie Tucker (January 13, 1884 – February 9, 1966) was a singer and comedian, one of the most popular entertainers in America during the first third of the 20th century.

She was born **Sonia Kalish** to a Jewish family in Tsarist Russia. Her family emigrated to the United States when she was an infant, and settled in Hartford, Connecticut. The family changed its name to Abuza, and her parents opened a restaurant.

Turner, Lana

Lana Turner (February 8, 1921 – June 29, 1995) was an Academy Award-nominated American film actress. On-screen, she was well-known for the glamour and sensuality she brought to almost all her movie roles. Off-screen, she led a stormy and colorful private life which included seven husbands, numerous lovers, and a famous murder scandal.

Twain, Mark

Samuel Langhorne Clemens (November 30, 1835 – April 21, 1910), better known by the pen name **Mark Twain**, was an American humanist, humorist, satirist, lecturer and writer. Twain is most noted for his novels *Adventures of Huckleberry Finn*, which has since been called the Great American Novel, and *The Adventures of Tom Sawyer*. He is also known for his quotations. During his lifetime, Twain became a friend to presidents, artists, leading industrialists and European royalty.

Twain enjoyed immense public popularity, and his keen wit and incisive satire earned him praise from both critics and peers. American author William Faulkner called Twain "the father of American literature".

Vidal, Gore

Eugene Luther Gore Vidal (born October 3, 1925) is an American author of novels, stage plays, screenplays, and essays, and the scion of a prominent political family. He is an outspoken critic of the American political Establishment, and a noted wit and social critic who wrote the ground-breaking *The City and the Pillar* (1948) that outraged mainstream critics as the first major American novel to feature unambiguous homosexuality.

Villa, Pancho

Doroteo Arango Arámbula (June 5, 1877 – July 23, 1923), better known as **Francisco** or **"Pancho" Villa**, was a Mexican Revolutionary general. As commander of the *División del Norte* (Division of the North), he was the veritable caudillo of the Northern Mexican state of Chihuahua, which, due to its size, mineral wealth and proximity to the United States, made him a major player in Revolutionary military and politics. His charisma and effectiveness gave him great popularity, particularly in the North, and he was provisional Governor of Chihuahua in 1913 and 1914. While his violence and ambition prevented him from being accepted into the "pantheon" of national heroes until some twenty years after his death, today his memory is honored by many Mexicans. In addition, numerous streets and neighborhoods in Mexico are named in honor of him. In 1916 he raided Columbus, New Mexico. This act provoked the unsuccessful Punitive Expedition commanded by General John J. Pershing, which failed to capture Villa after a year in pursuit.

Voltaire

François-Marie Arouet (21 November 1694 – 30 May 1778), better known by the pen name **Voltaire**, was a French Enlightenment writer, essayist, deist and philosopher known for his wit, philosophical sport, and defense of civil liberties, including freedom of religion and the right to a fair trial. He was an outspoken supporter of social reform despite strict censorship laws and harsh penalties for those who broke them.

A satirical polemicist, he frequently made use of his works to criticize Christian Church dogma and the French institutions of his day.

Many of Voltaire's works and ideas would influence important thinkers of both the American and French Revolutions, an honor that he would share with other political theorists such as John Locke and Thomas Hobbes.

Walpole, Horace, 4th Earl of Orford

Horace Walpole, 4th Earl of Orford (24 September 1717 – 2 March 1797), more commonly known as **Horace Walpole**, was politician, writer, architectural innovator and cousin of Lord Nelson. His *Letters* are highly readable, and give a vivid picture of the more intellectual part of the aristocracy of his period.

Walters, Barbara

Barbara Jill Walters (born September 25, 1929) is an American journalist, writer and media personality who has been a regular fixture on morning television shows (*Today* and *The View*), an evening news magazine (*20/20*), and on *The ABC Evening News* as the first female evening news anchor. Walters was first known as a popular TV morning news anchor for over 10 years on NBC's *Today*, where she worked with Hugh Downs and later hosts Frank McGee and Jim Hartz. Walters later spent 25 years as co-host of ABC's newsmagazine *20/20*. She was the first woman to co-anchor the network evening news, working with Harry Reasoner on *The ABC Evening News*.

Washington, George

George Washington (February 22, 1732 – December 14, 1799) was a central, critical figure in the founding of the United States, as well as the nation's first president (1789 – 1797), after leading the Continental Army to victory over the Kingdom of Great Britain in the American Revolutionary War (1775 – 1783).

Washington was seen as symbolizing the new nation and republicanism in practice. His devotion to civic virtue made him an exemplary figure among early American politicians. During Washington's funeral oration, Henry Lee said that of all Americans, he was "first in war, first in peace, and first in the hearts of his countrymen". While often underrated by scholars, still consistently Washington is ranked first or in the first three with Abraham Lincoln and Franklin D. Roosevelt, both of whom radically altered the Constitutional government envisioned by Washington and the Founders, as one of the top three U.S. Presidents.

Washington, Martha

Martha Dandridge Custis Washington (June 2, 1731 – May 22, 1802) was the wife of George Washington, the first president of the United States. Although the title was not coined until after her death, Martha Washington is considered to be the first First Lady of the United States. During her lifetime, she was simply known as "Lady Washington".

Watson, James D.

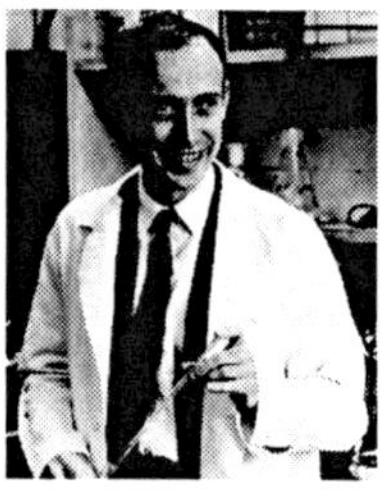

James Dewey Watson (born April 6, 1928) is an American molecular biologist, best known as one of the co-discoverers of the structure of DNA. Watson, Francis Crick, and Maurice Wilkins were awarded the 1962 Nobel Prize in Physiology or Medicine "for their discoveries concerning the molecular structure of nucleic acids and its significance for information transfer in living material".

Waugh, Evelyn

Arthur Evelyn St. John Waugh (October 28, 1903 – April 10, 1966) was an English writer, best known for such satirical novels as *Decline and Fall, Vile Bodies, Scoop, A Handful of Dust* and *The Loved One*, as well as for broader and more personal works, such as *Brideshead Revisited* and the *Sword of Honour* trilogy, that are influenced by his own experiences and his conservative and Catholic viewpoints. Many of Waugh's novels depict British aristocracy and high society, which he satirizes but to which, paradoxically, he was also strongly attracted. In addition, he wrote short stories, three biographies, and the first volume of an unfinished autobiography. His travel writings and his extensive diaries and correspondence have also been published.

Wells, Carolyn

Carolyn Wells (June 18, 1862 – March 26, 1942) was an American author and poet. After finishing school she worked as a librarian for the Rahway Library Association. Her first book, *At the Sign of the Sphinx* (1896), was a collection of charades. Her next publications were *The Jingle Book* and *The Story of Betty* (1899), followed by a book of verse entitled *Idle Idyls* (1900). After 1900, Wells wrote numerous novels and collections of poetry. Carolyn Wells wrote a total of more than 170 books.

Wells, H. G.

Herbert George Wells (September 21, 1866 – August 13, 1946), better known as **H. G. Wells**, was an English writer best known for such science fiction novels as *The Time Machine, The War of the Worlds, The Invisible Man, The First Men in the Moon* and *The Island of Doctor Moreau*. He was a prolific writer of both fiction and non-fiction, and produced works in many different genres, including contemporary novels, history, and social commentary. He was also an outspoken socialist. His later works become increasingly political and didactic, and only his early science fiction novels are widely read today. Wells and Jules Verne are each sometimes referred to as "The Father of Science Fiction"

West, Mae

Mae West (August 17, 1893 – November 22, 1980) was an American actress, playwright, screenwriter, and sex symbol.

Famous for her bawdy double entendres, West made a name for herself in vaudeville and on the stage in New York before moving to Hollywood to become a comedian, actress and writer in the motion picture industry.

One of the most controversial stars of her day, West encountered many problems including censorship.

When her cinematic career ended, she continued to perform on stage, in Las Vega, in the United Kingdom, on radio and television, and recorded Rock and Roll albums.

Wharton, Edith

Edith Wharton (January 24, 1862 – August 11, 1937) was an American novelist, short story writer, and designer.

Wharton was born **Edith Newbold Jones** to the wealthy New York family often associated with the phrase "Keeping up with the Joneses". She combined her insider's view of America's privileged classes with a brilliant, natural wit to write humorous and incisive novels and short stories. As such, she was well-acquainted with many of her era's literary and public figures, including Henry James and Theodore Roosevelt.

Wilde, Oscar

Oscar Fingal O'Flahertie Wills Wilde (October 16, 1854 – November 30, 1900) was an Irish playwright, novelist, poet, and author of short stories. Known for his barbed wit, he was one of the most successful playwrights of late Victorian London, and one of the greatest celebrities of his day. As the result of a famous trial, he suffered a dramatic downfall and was imprisoned for two years of hard labour after being convicted of the offence of "gross indecency".

Will, George

George Frederick Will (born May4, 1941) is a Pulitzer Prize-winning, conservative American newspaper columnist, journalist, and author.

Williams, Robin

Robin McLaurim Williams (born July 21, 1951) is an Academy Award-winning American actor and comedian who has done television, stage, and film work.

Wilson, Tom (cartoonist)

Tom Wilson (born August 1, 1931) is an American cartoonist. Born in Grant Town, Marion County, West Virginia, he is the creator of the comic strip Ziggy, and drew it from 1971 to 1987. After that it was continued by his son, Tom Wilson II.

Wilson, Woodrow

Thomas Woodrow Wilson (December 28, 1856 – February 3, 1924) was the twenty-eight President of the United States. A devout Presbyterian and leading "intellectual" of the Progressive Era, he served as president of Princeton University then became the reform governor of New Jersey in 1910. With Theodore Roosevelt and William Howard Taft dividing the Republican vote, Wilson was elected President as a Democrat in 1912. He proved highly successful in leading a Democratic Congress to pass major legislation including the Federal Trade Commission, the Clayton Antitrust Act, the Underwood Tariff, the Federal Farm Loan Act and most notably the Federal Reserve System.

Narrowly re-elected in 1916, his second term centered on World War I. He tried to maintain U.S. neutrality, but when Germany began unrestricted submarine warfare he wrote several admonishing notes to Germany. Subsequently he asked Congress to declare war on the Central Powers. He focused on diplomacy and financial considerations, leaving the waging of the war primarily in the hands of the military establishment.

On the home front he began the first effected draft in 1917, raised billions through Liberty loans, imposed an income tax, set up the War Industries Board, promoted labor union growth, supervised agriculture and food production through the Lever Act, took over control of the railroads, and suppressed anti-war movements. He paid surprisingly little attention to military affairs, but provided the funding and food supplies that helped the Americans in the war and hastened Allied victory in 1918.

Winchell, Walter

Walter Winchell (April 7, 1897 – February 20, 1972), an American newspaper and radio commentator, invented the gossip column at the *New York Evening Graphic*. He broke the journalistic taboo against exposing the private lives of public figures, permanently altering the shape of journalism and celebrity. He was a top gossip reporter, whose newspaper column and radio show could make or break a celebrity.

Windsor, Duke of

The peerage title **Duke of Windsor** was created in the Peerage of the United Kingdom in 1937 for "The Prince Edward, formerly King of the United Kingdom, as well as each of the other Commonwealth realms. Edward had abdicated on 11 December 1936 so that he could marry the American divorcee Wallis Simpson, who became the **Duchess of Windsor**. At the time of the abdication there was much controversy as to what the ex-King should be referred to – other possibilities were the Dukedoms of Cambridge or Connaught (although neither was likely because the Marquessate of Cambridge and the Dukedom of Connaught were both extant at the time). One theory is that it was Prime Minister Stanley Baldwin's idea to give him the title Duke of Windsor. Another is that it was the new King George VI who brought up the idea of a title just after the abdication instrument was signed, and suggested using "the family name" (recounted in the Duke's memoir *A King's Story*).

Winfrey, Oprah

Oprah Gail Winfrey (born January 29, 1954) is the American multiple-Emmy Award winning host of *The Oprah Winfrey Show*, the highest-rated talk show in television history. She is also an influential book critic, an Academy Award-nominated actress, and a magazine publisher. She has been ranked the richest African American of the 20th century, the most philanthropic African American of all time, and the world's only black billionaire for three straight years. She is also according to some assessments, the most influential woman in the world.

Winters, Jonathan

Jonathan Harshman Winters III (born November 11, 1925) is an American comedian and actor.

After attending private boarding school at Culver Military Academy in Culver, Indiana, Winters enlisted in the Marines at age 17 and served in the South Pacific during World War II. After his discharge he studied cartooning at Dayton Art Institute, where he met Eileen Schauder, whom he married in 1948. He began comedy routines and acting while studying at Kenyon College in Gambier, Ohio. He was also a local radio personality at WIZE in Springfield, Ohio.

Beginning as a stand-up comic with a madcap wildness, Winters recorded many classic comedy albums. Probably the best known of his characters from this period is Maudie Frickert, the seemingly sweet old lady with the barbed tongue. He was a favorite of Jack Paar and appeared frequently on his television programs. In addition, he would often appear on the *Tonight Show* with Johnny Carson, usually in the guise of some character. Carson often did not know what Winters had planned and usually had to tease out the character's back story through the course of the interview.

Winters, Shelley

Shelley Winters (August 18, 1920 – January 14, 2006) was an American actress who won Academy Awards for her supporting roles in *The Diary of Anne Frank* and *A Patch of Blue*, and a

Golden Globe Award for her role in *The Poseidon Adventure*. She appeared in dozens of films as well as on stage and television.

Wodehouse, P. G.

Sir Pelham Grenville Wodehouse, KBE (15 October 1881 – 14 February 1975) was a comic writer who had enjoyed enormous popular success for more than seventy years. Despite all the political and social upheavals that occurred during his life, much of which was spent in France and the United States, Wodehouse's main canvas remained that of prewar English upper-class society, reflecting his birth, education, and youthful writing career.

An acknowledged master of English prose, Wodehouse was admired both by contemporaries like Hilaire Belloc, Evelyn Waugh and Rudyard Kipling as well as by modern writers like Douglas Adams, Salman Rushdie and Terry Pratchett. Sean O'Casey famously called him "English literature's performing flea", a description that Wodehouse used as the title of a collection of his letters to a friend, Bill Townend.

Best known today for the Jeeves and Blandings Castle novels and short stories, Wodehouse was also a talented playwright and lyricist who was part author and writer of fifteen plays and 250 lyrics for some thirty musical comedies. He worked with Cole Porter on the musical *Anything Goes* (1934) and frequently collaborated with Jerome Kern and Guy Bolton. He wrote the lyrics for the hit song "Bill" in Kern's *Show Boat* (1927), wrote the lyrics for the Gershwin – Romberg musical *Rosalie* (1928), and collaborated with Rudolph Friml on a musical version of *The Three Musketeers* (1928).

Wolfe, Tom

Thomas Kennerly Wolfe (born March 2, 1931 in Richmond, Virginia), known as **Tom Wolfe**, is a best-selling American author and journalist. He is one of the founders of the New Journalism movement of the 1960s and 1970s.

Wordsworth, William

William Wordsworth (April 7, 1770 – April 23, 1850) was a major English romantic poet who, with Samuel Taylor Coleridge, helped launch the Romantic Age in English literature with their 1798 joint publication, *Lyrical Ballads*.

Wordsworth's masterpiece is generally considered to be *The Prelude*, an autobiographical poem of his early years which the poet revised and expanded a number of times. The work was posthumously titled and published, prior to which it was generally known as the poem "to Coleridge". Wordsworth was England's Poet Laureate from 1843 until his death in 1850.

Wouk, Herman

Herman Wouk (born may 27, 1915) is a best selling American author with a number of notable novels to his credit, including *The Caine Mutiny*, *The Winds of War*, and *War and Remembrance*.

Wright, Frank Lloyd

Frank Lloyd Wright (June 8, 1867 – April 9, 1959) was one of the world's most prominent and influential architects.

He developed a series of highly individual styles, influenced the design of buildings all over the world, and to this day remains America's most famous architect.

Wright was also well known in his lifetime. His colorful personal life frequently made headlines, most notably for the failure of his first two marriages and for the 1914 fire and murders at his Taliesin studio.

Youngman, Henny

Henry "Henny" Youngman (March 16, 1906 – February 24, 1998) was a British-born American comedian and violinist famous for "one-liners", short, simple jokes usually delivered rapid-fire. His best known (and often misattributed) one-liner was "Take my wife – please".

Index of Quotations by Author

ABOUT THE AUTHOR

Bradford G. Wheler is the former CEO, President and Co-owner of Allan Electric Company. He sold the company to a New York Stock Exchange list utility company back when the stock market was hot. Brad retired after staying on as President during a transition period.

Brad's life long love of history, art, books and the humor in man's nature lead to this book and the founding of BookCollaborative.com.

His community involvements include being a Trustee of Cazenovia College, a member of the Board of Directors of the Greater Cazenovia Area Chamber of Commerce, and Chairman of the Board of Directors and Alumni Association President of Sigma Phi Society at Cornell University in Ithaca, NY.

Brad holds a BS and ME in Civil and Environmental Engineering from Cornell University in Ithaca, NY. He has a MBA degree from Fordham University in New York, NY and is a Licensed Professional Engineer in New York and several other states. He is also a graduate of the Manlius Pebble Hill school.

Brad lives with his wife Julie and their golden retriever Quincy in Cazenovia, NY

LaVergne, TN USA
10 September 2009
157387LV00004B/4/P

9 780982 253809

maîtres chanteurs

maîtres chanteurs

textes Guilhem Lesaffre
photographies Alain Jouffray son Fernand Deroussen

EpA

6 Introduction

14 Sur les arbres

54 Dans les buissons

96 Autres perchoirs

148 Annexes

introduction

Comment le chant vient aux oiseaux

Ci-dessus : bruant fou.
À droite : pouillot de Bonelli.

Ils crient et ils chantent

Dans leur très grande majorité, les oiseaux s'expriment vocalement, sous forme de cris ou de chants.

Les expressions vocales des oiseaux ont toutes, ou presque, une fonction sociale. Il s'agit de communiquer avec des congénères ou avec des représentants d'autres espèces, afin de transmettre des informations relatives aux émotions, aux réactions, aux intentions, à la perception du milieu : cohésion de la famille ou du groupe, peur, agressivité, satisfaction, mise en garde, découverte d'une source de nourriture...

Les cris, en général brefs et peu musicaux (mais il existe quantité d'exceptions !), émis par le mâle comme par la femelle, sont surtout associés à deux ou trois fonctions essentielles : signaler – à un partenaire, à un jeune, à un congénère – sa présence ou un danger, repousser un rival ou un intrus.

Le chant, normalement plus long que les cris, et souvent plus agréable à entendre, a pour double fonction de base la séduction d'une partenaire et la tenue à l'écart de rivaux éventuels. Il est en général l'apanage du mâle mais il existe des espèces dont la femelle chante, d'autres chez qui le mâle et la femelle chantent ensemble (soit simultanément, soit successivement) avec une telle précision que l'on a l'impression d'entendre un seul chant.

Pour le profane, qui se contente d'apprécier leurs vocalises d'un point de vue musical, le chant des oiseaux doit être mélodieux pour mériter ce nom. Selon de telles normes, le merle ou le rouge-gorge chantent mais les pépiements du moineau ne sont que des cris ou, pis, du bruit. Pour l'ornithologue, en revanche, la notion de chant possède une valeur plus étendue et s'applique tant à des oiseaux au répertoire limité ou à la virtuosité très médiocre qu'à des espèces plus douées.

Schématiquement, les membres de l'ordre des passereaux (oiseaux souvent de petite taille, comme la grive ou la fauvette, représentant environ la moitié des espèces existant actuellement) sont considérés comme les oiseaux chanteurs par excellence, même si certains d'entre eux, comme les corbeaux, sont loin

d'être des virtuoses... Parmi les oiseaux des autres ordres, on trouve une petite proportion de « chanteurs » à la voix agréable (limicoles tels les chevaliers ou les courlis, rapaces nocturnes, pigeons et tourterelles...) et un grand nombre de groupes beaucoup moins bien lotis (grèbes, canards, rapaces, mouettes...).

Outre les chants et les cris, certains oiseaux ont recours à d'autres moyens d'expression sonore. Ainsi, la cigogne blanche « craquette » en claquant du bec. Lors du piqué, les plumes des côtés de la queue de la bécassine des marais vibrent en un étonnant chevrotement. Les pics tambourinent sur les arbres à l'aide de leur bec robuste. Le paon fait bruisser les plumes de sa roue...

Ci-dessus : accenteur mouchet.
À droite : fauvette à tête noire.

Mais comment chantent-ils ?

De l'air et un syrinx, voilà tout ce dont un oiseau a besoin pour chanter. Contrairement à nous, qui émettons des sons à l'aide de notre larynx – donc de notre gorge –, les oiseaux disposent pour cela d'un organe particulier, le syrinx (mot parfois utilisé au féminin, par référence à l'instrument de musique antique), situé à la confluence entre les deux bronches et la trachée – donc à hauteur du thorax, si bien qu'un oiseau chante en somme avec sa poitrine. Le syrinx est constitué de membranes qui vibrent au passage de l'air expiré, selon des fréquences liées à leur degré d'ouverture. La tension des membranes est déterminée par des muscles dont le nombre et la structure induisent la qualité des productions vocales. Un faucon, par exemple, ne possède qu'une seule paire de ces muscles tandis qu'un passereau en compte sept.

Le fait que la membrane de chacune des deux bronches puisse vibrer indépendamment de l'autre entraîne des particularités étonnantes. Un oiseau peut ainsi émettre deux mélodies simultanées, ou bien chanter en faisant vibrer successivement une membrane puis l'autre, dans une continuité apparente. Enfin, certains chanteurs privilégient un côté, ce qui fait d'eux des « gauchers » ou des « droitiers » de la voix !

On précisera au passage que si les capacités en matière de chant sont en grande partie innées, figurant dans les gènes, elles font également l'objet d'un apprentissage, dans des proportions variables. Les jeunes oiseaux s'imprègnent des productions des adultes des alentours. Il existe ainsi des variations en fonction des prédispositions héréditaires et de la qualité des acquisitions.

On rencontre donc, chez certaines espèces (surtout parmi celles au chant assez élaboré), de bons chanteurs, inventifs, inspirés, captivants, et d'autres moins enthousiasmants…

Timbres, motifs et strophes

Comme tous les sons, les chants d'oiseaux sont caractérisés par leur hauteur, leur intensité, leur timbre, leur durée, leur rythme et leur organisation mélodique.

La hauteur est en relation avec la fréquence de la vibration considérée. Elle s'exprime en kHz (kiloHerz). L'intensité correspond à l'amplitude de la vibration. Le timbre est fonction de vibrations combinées, souvent harmoniques, c'est-à-dire analogues mais à des fréquences différentes.

La décomposition du chant permet d'en comprendre la structure. La plus petite unité, correspondant à une note, est appelée élément ou, par référence à la linguistique, phonème. Plusieurs éléments réunis forment un motif ou syllabe. La strophe ou phrase (signalons à cette occasion que, par commodité, ce dernier terme a parfois été utilisé dans l'ouvrage dans son sens légèrement plus étendu) est composée d'éléments ou de motifs, séparés par des intervalles ou silences. Enfin, des strophes se succédant de façon cohérente forment une séquence.

Il convient de réaliser que ces éléments sont souvent fort brefs. Un élément, c'est un dixième de seconde, un motif, à peine plus d'une demi-seconde parfois, une pause

moins d'un dixième de seconde et une strophe peut ne durer que deux secondes. Certaines de ces subtilités ne sont pas perceptibles pour l'oreille humaine, mais le sont parfaitement pour celle des oiseaux, dont le pouvoir de résolution – c'est-à-dire de distinction entre deux sons – est en moyenne dix fois plus élevé que chez l'homme. Quelques millièmes de seconde de silence suffisent à un oiseau pour saisir le passage au son suivant. Les ornithologues, voici quelques années, paliaient le manque de performance de l'oreille humaine en écoutant, au ralenti, à la vitesse de 33 tours à la minute des disques 45 tours de chants d'oiseaux, afin de comprendre la structure fine des émissions vocales étudiées.

Où et quand chantent les oiseaux ?

Selon les espèces, les oiseaux se placent bien en vue pour chanter ou se dissimulent. Se poster en évidence sur un perchoir dominant (voire en plein ciel) offre l'avantage d'augmenter la portée du chant, mais présente l'inconvénient de signaler l'oiseau aux prédateurs éventuels. Les oiseaux se montrent volontiers routiniers, utilisant des postes de chant favoris, bien situés par rapport à leur territoire.

Contrairement à une idée établie, les oiseaux ne chantent pas seulement au printemps, même si cette saison est évidemment celle des grands concerts naturels. Certaines des espèces sédentaires ou qui ne se livrent pas à d'importantes migrations peuvent chanter presque toute l'année. Une belle journée d'hiver sans vent est ainsi souvent l'occasion d'entendre de nombreux chants. Enfin, l'automne est régulièrement une période de reprise des chants, notamment pour les oiseaux qui établissent un territoire pour l'hiver.

La plupart des oiseaux chantent de jour, mais beaucoup commencent à le faire alors que le jour n'est pas levé ou cessent de le faire alors que le soleil déjà est couché depuis un moment. De rares espèces – dont le célèbre rossignol – chantent autant ou presque de nuit que de jour.

L'apogée des chants se situe tôt le matin, un peu avant et juste après le lever du soleil. Une reprise, parfois bien fournie, a lieu dans la soirée.

Un temps calme et un ciel assez dégagé sont de bons facteurs de stimulation des chants (et offrent les meilleures conditions pour les écouter). Un vent fort ou une pluie soutenue, sans parler de la combinaison des deux, découragent les maîtres chanteurs…

Ci-contre : hypolaïs polyglotte.

sur les **arbres**

Accenteur mouchet

Prunella modularis

Dans les villes où il vit, c'est l'un des premiers oiseaux, sinon le premier, à annoncer le retour du printemps. Perché sur une antenne de télévision ou un pot de cheminée, il délivre sa joyeuse ritournelle aigrelette dévidée sans vrai souci d'organisation. Ce n'est certes pas un grand virtuose mais son chant est évocateur d'un tournant dans l'année. À la campagne aussi, l'accenteur donne de la voix.

Quittant le sol qu'il affectionne en temps normal, et où il se faufile discrètement sous les buissons ou non loin d'eux, il gagne le sommet d'un arbre ou d'une haie. C'est de là qu'il se fait entendre à plusieurs reprises dans la journée, abandonnant pour un moment ses petites occupations routinières, et notamment la recherche de nourriture. Cette quête scrupuleuse est exigeante en temps car la modestie des portions, graines menues ou invertébrés minuscules, doit être compensée par leur quantité.

Qu'il chante ou se taise, l'accenteur mouchet mérite d'être examiné avec attention. C'est à cette seule condition que l'on peut découvrir et apprécier les attraits d'un plumage apparemment bien sobre mais présentant en fait de délicats détails semblant avoir été apposés à la pointe d'un pinceau fin.

cd piste 01

Taille : 14 cm

Répartition géographique simplifiée : presque toute l'Europe

Milieux fréquentés : campagne, bois, parcs et jardins

Période de présence : sédentaire au Sud, hôte d'été au Nord

Degré d'abondance : très commun

Postes de chant : arbres, haies, bâtiments

Période de chant : dès février et jusqu'en été (peut chanter toute l'année ou presque)

Observation : très facile

Chardonneret élégant

Carduelis carduelis

Légèreté, gaieté, agrément : ces trois mots pourraient suffire à vanter les qualités du chant du chardonneret élégant. Élégant, il l'est à coup sûr avec son carnavalesque masque vermillon, ses ailes ornées de jaune d'or et son bec aigu, si pratique pour extraire les plus petites graines de leur réceptacle. Mais sa beauté se double d'un plaisant talent de chanteur. Souvent perché en évidence, le chardonneret se lance dans de petits concerts au rythme pressé. Ces successions désordonnées de notes sautillantes, dansantes, sont une célébration des vertus de l'improvisation. Même si l'on finit par reconnaître des motifs qui reviennent avec plus ou moins de régularité, c'est bien l'invention qui s'adjuge la part du lion.

Revers de la médaille, le chardonneret paye encore trop souvent de sa liberté son talent de chanteur. Autrefois en Europe – en Belgique ou en Espagne par exemple –, et aujourd'hui encore en Afrique du Nord, ce passereau est capturé à grande échelle pour finir dans une cage terriblement exiguë, suspendue à une fenêtre.

La voix du chardonneret est plaisante même lorsqu'il ne chante pas. Ses cris cliquetants ou cristallins évoquent la bonne humeur, la joie de vivre. Comme l'espèce est rarement solitaire, les cris de plusieurs individus se mêlent volontiers, et les petites bandes font entendre de bruyants chœurs enjoués.

cd piste 02

Taille : 13 cm

Répartition géographique simplifiée : presque toute l'Europe

Milieux fréquentés : campagne, parcs et jardins (jusqu'en ville)

Période de présence : toute l'année

Degré d'abondance : très commun

Postes de chant : arbres, haies, buissons

Période de chant : surtout avril à juillet

Observation : très facile

Fauvette à tête noire

Sylvia atricapilla

Cette fauvette possède un double atout : elle est l'un de nos chanteurs les plus accomplis et on peut la rencontrer en de très nombreuses régions dans des milieux assez variés, si bien qu'il est aisé d'en profiter. Pour beaucoup, le printemps n'est pas tout à fait le printemps tant que la première fauvette à tête noire ne s'est pas fait entendre... Retrouver son chant flûté, suave, merveilleusement inventif, est l'un des petits bonheurs réservés aux naturalistes et à tous ceux qui savent prêter l'oreille. Les meilleures conditions pour profiter du chant de cette virtuose sont réunies tôt le matin, en un lieu calme, un peu encaissé – comme un vallon, une gorge – où le son est amplifié par la résonance. C'est alors un délicieux plaisir pour l'oreille.

Aucune fauvette à tête noire ne chante exactement comme sa voisine, aucune, non plus, ne chante deux fois tout à fait de la même manière. Pour autant, il est possible de relever chez chacune d'elles tel ou tel motif qui revient fréquemment, notamment en guise de conclusion. Ces motifs se retrouvent à l'échelle régionale et permettent d'établir des distinctions entre plusieurs populations de l'espèce. Certaines fauvettes à tête noire sortent du lot, soit par le caractère particulièrement inventif de leur production, soit par leur maîtrise des imitations de la voix d'autres passereaux.

cd piste 03 (la fauvette des jardins, piste 4, est illustrée p. 155)

Taille : 14 cm

Répartition géographique simplifiée : presque toute l'Europe

Milieux fréquentés : bois et forêts, campagne, parcs et jardins (jusqu'en ville)

Période de présence : surtout mars-avril à octobre-novembre (peut hiverner)

Degré d'abondance : très commune

Postes de chant : arbres, fourrés, haies

Période de chant : surtout avril à juillet

Observation : assez facile à facile

Particularités : quelques imitations ; certains chanteurs sont d'excellents imitateurs

Grimpereau des bois
Grimpereau des jardins

Certhia familiaris, Certhia brachydactyla

À l'instar des pouillots ou des roitelets, voici deux espèces si proches par l'aspect qu'on les appelle « jumelles ». Leur plumage ne comporte que d'infimes variations du même modèle de base et leur morphologie diffère de manière amusante : le grimpereau des jardins possède un bec long et des ongles courts tandis que le grimpereau des bois dispose d'un bec plus court et d'ongles plus longs !

S'ajoutent à ces subtiles disparités des préférences écologiques quelque peu dissemblables qui peuvent guider l'observateur sans apporter toujours de réponse définitive. Enfin, il est des régions où l'une des espèces existe à l'exclusion de l'autre… normalement. Le comportement des grimpereaux, toujours occupés à escalader les troncs par à-coups nerveux en se confondant avec l'écorce, ne facilitant pas leur identification visuelle spécifique, il est heureux que l'on puisse se rabattre sur leur voix.

Le chant permet en effet de les distinguer, atout précieux là où les deux cousins sont amenés à cohabiter. On comparera la voix fluette et la phrase simple du grimpereau des jardins (page ci-contre) à la voix plus pleine et à la mélodie plus complexe du grimpereau des bois (double page suivante). La confusion est rendue impossible…

cd pistes 05 et 06

Taille : 12 cm

Répartition géographique simplifiée : grimpereau des jardins : surtout Centre et Sud de l'Europe ; grimpereau des bois : surtout Est et Nord de l'Europe

Milieux fréquentés : bois et forêts

Période de présence : toute l'année

Degré d'abondance : communs

Poste de chant : arbres (surtout le tronc)

Période de chant : grimpereau des jardins : presque toute l'année (surtout février à juin) ; grimpereau des bois : février à juin

Observation : facile

Grive musicienne

Turdus philomelos

Elle n'a certes pas volé son nom français – ni d'ailleurs son nom scientifique de *philomelos*, « amie du chant » – tant sa voix est musicale et variée.

La grive musicienne est l'un des premiers oiseaux à saluer le retour du printemps. Elle le fait avec tant de hâte qu'elle s'y prend alors que l'hiver est encore là ! Commençant à chanter tôt, dès le lever du soleil, elle se fait aussi entendre dans la journée et jusqu'en fin de soirée. Aucune grive ne chante comme sa voisine et l'on peut parvenir, avec un peu de pratique et d'attention, à reconnaître les différents virtuoses, dans un jardin ou lors d'une promenade régulière en forêt. Chez chaque chanteuse, en effet, certains motifs reviennent de loin en loin, sans véritable stratégie. Ce sont ces refrains qui peuvent être considérés comme la signature vocale de telle ou telle grive musicienne.

Autre détail permettant l'identification individuelle : les imitations. Il est assez fréquent que cette grive glisse dans sa production l'imitation d'un son ou d'une phrase volés à une autre espèce. Finalement, la grive musicienne a tout pour plaire… Seule ombre au tableau : ses concerts peuvent parfois durer de longs moments, au point qu'ils risquent de devenir irritants pour une oreille sensible, surtout tôt le matin !

cd piste 07

Taille : 21 cm

Répartition géographique simplifiée : presque toute l'Europe

Milieux fréquentés : bois et forêts, parcs et jardins (jusqu'en ville)

Période de présence : toute l'année en Europe moyenne

Degré d'abondance : très commune

Poste de chant : arbres

Période de chant : dès janvier/février et jusqu'en juin (parfois aussi à l'automne)

Observation : facile à très facile

Particularités : quelques imitations

Loriot d'Europe

Oriolus oriolus

Certains ont tout. Ainsi le loriot ne se contente-t-il pas d'être l'un des plus beaux oiseaux qu'il soit possible de rencontrer en Europe, puisqu'il est aussi l'un de ceux qui possèdent la voix la plus agréable. Pourtant, si le chant s'entend facilement, l'oiseau au plumage jaune vif ne se laisse pas aisément observer. En dépit de son éclatante couleur, il reste le plus souvent invisible au milieu des hautes frondaisons où l'ombre et la lumière se marient en un réseau composite et protecteur. La patience finit cependant par être récompensée et l'on parvient quand même à repérer le loriot au moment où il quitte un bosquet pour gagner le suivant. Des rencontres fortuites ont parfois lieu lors des migrations et l'on peut avoir la chance de tomber sur un voyageur doré en terrain découvert... Quant à espérer voir la femelle, c'est encore une autre histoire car son plumage verdâtre joue un rôle efficace en matière de camouflage !

Le chant du loriot ne brille pas par son inventivité mais plutôt par la qualité de son timbre. C'est la suavité d'un nectar, c'est le mélange du flûté et du liquide. C'est la belle saison et c'est en somme un peu d'Afrique chez nous tant le « didelio » fait songer à la voix pleine et mélodieuse de certains oiseaux tropicaux.

cd piste 08

Taille : 24 cm

Répartition géographique simplifiée : toute l'Europe, sauf la quasi-totalité des Îles britanniques et de la Scandinavie

Milieux fréquentés : bois, peupleraies, parcs

Période de présence : avril à août

Degré d'abondance : assez commun

Poste de chant : arbres (dissimulé dans le feuillage)

Période de chant : mai et juin

Observation : difficile à très difficile

Particularité : intercale souvent des cris grinçants entre les phrases chantées

On voudrait croire que rien n'est plus doux que la flûte du merle ;
et qui dépasserait l'ambitieux loriot, sur la plus haute branche de l'arbre
le plus haut perché ?

Alain, Le Rossignol, *Propos*, Bibliothèque de la Pléiade, Nrf, 1965.

Merle noir

Turdus merula

Même les moins doués des merles noirs parviennent à tirer très honorablement leur épingle du jeu, laissant loin derrière eux les chanteurs de bien d'autres espèces. Quant aux meilleurs interprètes, ils caracolent sans peine dans le peloton de tête des oiseaux virtuoses. Inspiré, un merle noir peut être écouté de longs moments sans jamais lasser.

Chaque production surprend tant par son inventivité que par la richesse du timbre. Les silences glissés entre les phrases contribuent à mettre celles-ci en valeur : le bec jaune d'or s'entrouvre et la cascade musicale s'écoule ; il se referme et l'air semble encore résonner des notes flûtées. L'on se prend à attendre avec intérêt l'émission vocale suivante en se demandant ce que le merveilleux chanteur va pouvoir encore ajouter au concert qu'il offre si généreusement.

Les meilleurs moments pour profiter de la performance de l'oiseau noir sont l'aube et le crépuscule quand les oiseaux locaux ne donnent pas encore de la voix ou se sont déjà tus, de préférence au premier printemps, lorsque les migrateurs ne sont pas encore revenus et que le « paysage sonore » n'est pas encore trop encombré.

cd piste 09

Taille : 25 cm

Répartition géographique simplifiée : toute l'Europe

Milieux fréquentés : bois et forêts, campagne, parcs et jardins (y compris en ville)

Période de présence : toute l'année dans la plupart de l'Europe

Degré d'abondance : très commun

Postes de chant : arbres, haies, bâtiments

Période de chant : presque toute l'année, surtout de mars à juin

Observation : très facile

Particularité : la différence de niveau peut être marquée entre les bons chanteurs et ceux qui le sont moins.

Le ciel est bleu, le soleil brille :

Le merle chante, il s'égosille…

Le vent se met à souffler :

Le merle s'est envolé.

Jean-Luc Moreau, Le Merle, *L'Arbre perché*, Éditions ouvrières, 1980.

Mésange bleue

Parus caeruleus

Des trilles nerveux viennent de retentir dans le parc. La mésange bleue trahit ainsi son inquiétude à l'approche d'un prédateur. Un coup d'œil circulaire permet de localiser l'origine de l'alarme : un épervier file dans le ciel, provoquant l'envol des grives migratrices qui avaient trouvé refuge au sommet des grands arbres. Toujours sur le qui-vive et souvent perchée en hauteur, la mésange bleue repère fréquemment les dangers potentiels avant d'autres oiseaux. Elle les signale aussitôt par ses cris qui ne manquent pas d'attirer l'attention.

Dès les balbutiements du printemps, alors que les premiers migrateurs ne sont pas encore de retour, le chant de la mésange bleue anime jardin, bois ou bocage. L'oiseau n'est pas un virtuose mais la vivacité et l'entrain de ses phrases vibrées forcent la sympathie. Il ne faut pas longtemps pour repérer le petit chanteur. Bien en vue dans les branchages encore nus, il interrompt un instant sa progression, s'égosille et volette sans plus attendre vers un nouveau poste de chant. Il ne cesse pas pour autant de chercher sa nourriture, de petites proies invertébrées cachées dans les bourgeons et sur l'écorce.

Connaître son répertoire n'est pas l'assurance absolue de conclure à sa présence car sa grande cousine la mésange charbonnière l'imite parfois fort bien...

cd piste 10

Taille : 11 cm

Répartition géographique simplifiée : toute l'Europe

Milieux fréquentés : bois et forêts, campagne, parcs et jardins (y compris en ville)

Période de présence : toute l'année

Degré d'abondance : très commune

Postes de chant : arbres, fourrés, haies

Période de chant : toute l'année, surtout de janvier/février à juin

Observation : très facile

Mésange charbonnière

Parus major

L'entrain et la variété sont les atouts majeurs du chant de la mésange charbonnière. S'y ajoute à l'occasion la pureté du son. L'hiver n'est pas encore tout à fait terminé et l'on entend déjà, pour peu que le soleil soit généreux, les premières vocalises de cette élégante mésange jaune cravatée de noir. Sans jamais interrompre très longtemps l'active quête de nourriture qui l'emmène d'un arbre à l'autre, la charbonnière émet les motifs cristallins typiques qui entrent dans la composition de son répertoire étendu.

Chacune a ses préférences et revient avec plus ou moins de régularité à des formules établies qui sont un peu sa signature vocale et permettent à l'observateur attentif de les reconnaître. Mais à côté de cela, c'est la porte ouverte à l'improvisation, à la fantaisie débridée. La mésange charbonnière ne se contente d'ailleurs pas de ses productions propres puisqu'elle sait à merveille imiter ses cousines, qu'il s'agisse de la mésange bleue ou des mésanges nonnette ou noire.

Enfin, aux agréables motifs qui évoquent immanquablement la transparence de l'air du premier printemps, la mésange charbonnière ne se prive pas d'ajouter des sons grinçants, nerveux, qui lui font perdre plusieurs places dans le hit-parade ornitho-musical…

cd piste 11

Taille : 14 cm

Répartition géographique simplifiée : toute l'Europe

Milieux fréquentés : bois, forêts, campagne, parcs et jardins (y compris en ville)

Période de présence : toute l'année

Degré d'abondance : très commune

Postes de chant : arbres, fourrés, haies

Période de chant : presque toute l'année (rare en été) mais surtout de février à mai

Observation : très facile

Particularité : imitations, notamment d'autres mésanges

Pinson des arbres

Fringilla coelebs

Par une journée de fin d'hiver ou de début de printemps, selon les régions et les années, on est surpris par le premier chant du pinson des arbres : déjà ! Il s'agit souvent d'une ébauche, d'une version incomplète ou maladroite de ce que sera le chant une fois les beaux jours plus nettement revenus. Pourtant, tout hésitante qu'elle soit, cette première phrase est réjouissante.

Bientôt, les fruitiers vont se couvrir de fleurs et tout va recommencer... Les jours suivants, la production du pinson s'améliore et l'audacieux pionnier est bientôt accompagné d'un ou deux congénères. En quelques semaines, tous les pinsons du coin apporteront leur contribution au concert avec un bel entrain. Le mot n'est pas trop fort car le pinson des arbres est un as de la répétition, un champion de l'endurance. Mieux vaut apprécier sa ritournelle descendante car il peut la servir plusieurs centaines de fois par heure quand il est en forme ! Il est peu douteux que cette générosité, associée au ton du chant, soit à l'origine de l'expression « gai comme un pinson ».

La trame générale de l'émission est à peu près constante au sein de l'espèce mais des variations régionales et individuelles viennent apporter une originalité plus ou moins marquée, intéressante à noter.

cd piste 12

Taille : 15 cm

Répartition géographique simplifiée : toute l'Europe

Milieux fréquentés : bois et forêts, campagne, parcs et jardins (y compris en ville)

Période de présence : toute l'année (absent de Scandinavie et de l'Est de l'Europe en hiver)

Degré d'abondance : très commun

Postes de chant : arbres, haies, bâtiments

Période de chant : février/mars à juillet

Observation : très facile

Particularité : existence de « dialectes » régionaux

Maintenant le voilà perché et immobile ; le bec ouvert, la gorge enflée, il lance sa chanson de printemps, qui n'est ni variée ni longue [...]. C'est plutôt langage que musique ; mais la voix est forte, éclatante, riche, pleine de vie et de gaieté.

Alain, Le Pinson, *Propos*, Bibliothèque de la Pléiade, Nrf, 1965.

Pouillot véloce
Pouillot fitis

Phylloscopus collybita, Phylloscopus trochilus

Que de satisfactions le pouillot véloce a-t-il procurées, sans le savoir, à tous ceux qui aiment observer les oiseaux et les entendre chanter au printemps ! Son chant est en effet l'un des plus simples à identifier et à mémoriser, même si des variations peuvent exister d'un soliste à l'autre (d'autres particularités se rencontrent chez cette espèce, que l'on découvrira dans la fiche ci-dessous).

Le nom poétique de « compteur d'écus » qu'il a autrefois reçu à la campagne lui va comme un gant. Il n'est pas difficile d'imaginer des pièces tombant dans une escarcelle déjà bien garnie lorsque l'on entend l'oiselet égrener ses notes métalliques soigneusement détachées, comme pour faciliter le décompte d'une fortune virtuelle. Le pouillot véloce (photo du haut) se met à chanter à son retour précoce, alors que son cousin, le pouillot fitis, qui revient de migration quelque temps après, tarde à se faire entendre. Autant les deux espèces se ressemblent, à quelques détails près, autant leurs chants sont différents. Chez le fitis, pas de monotone succession de notes mais une plaisante mélodie flûtée à la tonalité vaguement mélancolique. De quoi ne pas confondre ces délicats passereaux occupés en permanence à chasser les menus insectes dans les feuillages.

cd pistes 13 et 14

Taille : 10 à 12 cm

Répartition géographique simplifiée : pouillot véloce, presque toute l'Europe ; pouillot fitis, surtout Nord de l'Europe

Milieux fréquentés : milieux boisés, fourrés, parcs, jardins

Période de présence : pouillot véloce, mars à octobre (peut hiverner à l'ouest et au sud) ; pouillot fitis, avril à septembre

Degré d'abondance : très communs

Postes de chant : arbres, fourrés

Période de chant : pouillot véloce, mars à juillet ; pouillot fitis, avril à juin

Observation : facile à très facile

Particularités : la sous-espèce sibérienne *tristis*, qui se rencontre parfois en Europe occidentale lors des migrations, possède un chant original (« mélange » de véloce et de fitis) qui permet de l'identifier. Le pouillot véloce du Pays basque et d'Espagne se reconnaît à son chant différent ; il est maintenant considéré par certains comme une espèce à part entière sous le nom de Pouillot ibérique *Phylloscopus ibericus*.

Pouillot de Bonelli

Phylloscopus bonelli

Évoquer ce petit oiseau blanc et vert, c'est se transporter par la pensée au flanc d'un vallon rocailleux tapissé de plantes odorantes, où les pins peinent à tamiser la lumière blanche qui baigne un paysage à la Cézanne. Les cigales stridulent sans trêve dans la chaleur mais on parvient cependant à percevoir de temps à autre un trille bref, métallique, qui pourrait bien être produit par un gros insecte.

Des recherches actives – elles peuvent parfois se prolonger au point de provoquer quelque agacement, tant le passereau recherché se fond dans son milieu, à la fois par ses teintes mais aussi en raison de sa petitesse – permettent toutefois de finir par localiser l'auteur de ces brèves phrases répétées sans régularité. Un pouillot de Bonelli évolue tout là-haut, dans le houppier des conifères.

Avec méthode, exhibant son dessous pâle, il cherche insectes, larves et araignées qui croyaient avoir trouvé un refuge idéal au cœur des bouquets d'aiguilles. Son menu bec fin est l'outil idéal pour cette quête méticuleuse que l'oiselet interrompt seulement pour un rapide brin d'entretien du plumage ou pour lancer sa petite phrase sans prétention, sorte de battement pressé qu'il est intéressant de comparer à la production vocale du bruant zizi.

cd piste 15

Taille : 11 cm

Répartition géographique simplifiée : Sud de l'Europe

Milieux fréquentés : milieux boisés, de feuillus ou de conifères

Période de présence : avril à juillet/août

Degré d'abondance : assez commun

Poste de chant : arbres

Période de chant : avril à juin

Observation : assez difficile à difficile

Roitelet à triple bandeau
Roitelet huppé

Regulus ignicapillus, Regulus regulus

Deux miniatures. Deux petits bijoux qu'il faut absolument voir à l'œil nu, de près, pour pouvoir prendre conscience de leur taille minuscule et de leur apparente fragilité. Les deux roitelets se ressemblent beaucoup et, pour accentuer la confusion, se mêlent parfois en petites bandes, notamment en hiver. Les femelles et les jeunes sont, pour l'essentiel, semblables mais les mâles se reconnaissent plus facilement… pour peu qu'on les voie bien. Et c'est là que se pose le problème car il est finalement assez rare qu'on puisse les observer dans de bonnes conditions.

Ce sont souvent de toutes petites boules de plumes à contre-jour, dissimulées au sommet des arbres – souvent des grands conifères. Les cris des deux espèces sont en outre analogues pour le non-spécialiste. Il reste heureusement le chant pour favoriser l'identification de nos roitelets. Celui du roitelet à triple bandeau (photo du bas) est une simple série accélérée de notes aiguës et fines tandis que le chant du roitelet huppé est composé de notes également accélérées, chacune plus dansante que la précédente, et dont la série s'achève sur un agréable petit motif gazouillé. C'est l'occasion d'un excellent exercice de comparaison…

cd pistes 16 et 17

Taille : 9 cm

Répartition géographique simplifiée : roitelet huppé, presque toute l'Europe ; roitelet à triple bandeau, manque en Scandinavie et (sauf en hiver) dans les Îles britanniques

Milieux fréquentés : bois, jardins, marais, villes

Période de présence : roitelet huppé, toute l'année ; roitelet à triple bandeau, toute l'année (seulement en été dans le Centre et l'Est de l'Europe)

Degré d'abondance : communs à très communs

Postes de chant : arbres, fourrés, haies

Période de chant : roitelet huppé, presque toute l'année mais surtout de février/mars à juin ; roitelet à triple bandeau, surtout de mars à juillet

Observation : assez difficile à difficile

Rouge-gorge familier

Erithacus rubecula

Pour qui connaît un tant soit peu le rouge-gorge (les ornithologues ne glissent pas de trait d'union dans son nom...), son chant évoque aussi bien la gaieté du printemps que la mélancolie de l'automne. Cette dualité paradoxale en apparence tient tout simplement au fait que le chanteur à plastron rouge chante à une première période de l'année, celle où il lui faut délimiter un territoire de nidification et y attirer une femelle. Voilà pour le printemps. Une fois les nichées élevées, c'est le grand silence estival. Les rouges-gorges paraissent avoir disparu.

Dissimulés à couvert, retirés au cœur des feuillages, ils changent de plumage. C'est l'époque de la mue où les oiseaux aiment à se cacher car ils sont conscients de leur vulnérabilité accrue. La mue terminée, chaque rouge-gorge peut à nouveau se montrer au grand jour et clamer à haute voix ses droits sur le petit domaine où il passera l'hiver. L'espèce, à cette saison, présente une originalité parfaitement respectueuse de la parité entre sexes puisque les femelles, tout comme les mâles, chantent pour défendre les frontières du territoire qu'elles conserveront durant toute la mauvaise saison.

cd piste 18

Taille : 13 cm

Répartition géographique simplifiée : toute l'Europe

Milieux fréquentés : bois et forêts, campagne, parcs et jardins (y compris en ville)

Période de présence : toute l'année

Degré d'abondance : très commun

Postes de chant : arbres, fourrés, haies, bâtiments

Période de chant : presque toute l'année (sauf juillet/août) mais surtout de février à juin

Observation : très facile

Rouge-queue à front blanc

Phoenicurus phoenicurus

Certains chants d'oiseaux évoquent la gaieté, d'autres ont une coloration mélancolique. La brève mélodie du rouge-queue à front blanc appartient sans conteste à la seconde catégorie. Cela est d'autant plus vrai si on l'entend par un matin de lumière voilée, après une averse, au cœur d'un massif forestier où les vieux chênes « porte-graines » épargnés par le bûcheron dominent un sous-bois dégagé.

Ce type de milieu est cependant loin d'être le seul où rencontrer ce passereau au plumage joliment coloré – c'est l'un de nos plus beaux passereaux – qui mérite d'être observé dans de bonnes conditions. De retour d'Afrique où il est allé passer l'hiver au-delà du Sahara, ce grand migrateur s'installe aussi dans les pinèdes ou les parcs aux vieux arbres façonnés par les ans. Il fréquente également les jardins, même dépourvus d'arbres offrant des cavités car son nid peut prendre place dans un simple trou de mur.

Où qu'il ait choisi de vivre durant la belle saison, le rouge-queue à front blanc répète avec application sa petite phrase depuis ses postes favoris. C'est lorsqu'il se pose sur l'un d'eux en déployant la queue qu'il est possible d'en voir la belle teinte orangée.

cd piste 19

Taille : 14 cm

Répartition géographique simplifiée : toute l'Europe

Milieux fréquentés : milieux boisés, parcs et jardins (y compris en ville)

Période de présence : avril à octobre

Degré d'abondance : assez commun

Postes de chant : arbres, bâtiments, antennes de télévision

Période de chant : avril à juin

Observation : assez à très facile

Sittelle torchepot

Sitta europaea

En début de printemps, alors que les migrateurs ne sont pas encore de retour du Sud de l'Europe ou d'Afrique, certaines parcelles de forêt seraient bien silencieuses si la sittelle torchepot n'assurait pas l'animation sonore des futaies où les grands chênes dominent un sous-bois plus ou moins étoffé. Elle semble prendre sa tâche à cœur, multipliant les interventions et mettant à profit la richesse de son répertoire. Tantôt des coups de sifflet étirés, tantôt des successions de cris composant une sorte de morse original, tantôt enfin des trilles toniques qui peuvent rappeler à s'y méprendre certaines sonneries de téléphone...

À sa volubilité expansive, la sittelle ajoute un tempérament d'un grand dynamisme. Toujours en mouvement, elle escalade un tronc, vole jusqu'au suivant qu'elle descend, tête en bas avant de filer jusqu'à une grosse branche. Progressant par saccades, fermement agrippée à l'écorce grâce à ses doigts robustes et à ses ongles aigus et arqués, la sittelle examine les anfractuosités, les fissures, pour y débusquer insectes et araignées. Lorsqu'un mâle s'efforce d'attirer une femelle, il tempère un instant son activité et, installé sur une haute branche, lance sans se lasser ses puissants coups de sifflet, audibles de fort loin.

cd piste 20

Taille : 13 cm

Répartition géographique simplifiée : presque toute l'Europe

Milieux fréquentés : bois et forêts, parcs et jardins (y compris en ville)

Période de présence : toute l'année

Degré d'abondance : commune

Poste de chant : arbres

Période de chant : presque toute l'année (sauf en plein été), mais surtout de février à mai/juin

Observation : très facile

Verdier d'Europe

Carduelis chloris

Les ailes un peu tombantes révélant ainsi leurs plages jaunes, un solide bec rosé pointant vers le haut, le verdier débite, sans se lasser, son répertoire à l'intention d'une femelle dont il cherche à se faire remarquer. Les notes dansantes, souvent répétées en courtes séries, sont séparées à intervalles irréguliers par des bourdonnements métalliques étirés typiques de ce passereau granivore. Ses qualités de chanteur, réelles sans toutefois atteindre le niveau de celles de son cousin le chardonneret, ont par le passé valu au verdier d'être capturé et mis en cage. Il était parfois croisé avec le canari pour donner des hybrides nommés, de façon imagée, « mulets ». Ces pratiques ont heureusement disparu et le verdier peut désormais jouir de sa liberté sans restrictions.

Peu farouche, répandu, et nullement avare de sa voix, il ajoute à cela – comme s'il lui fallait se faire encore plus remarquer – l'habitude de s'égosiller lors d'un vol nuptial qui l'entraîne pour plusieurs dizaines de secondes dans un circuit capricieux à grands coups d'ailes curieusement ralentis. Le verdier prend alors des allures d'énorme papillon, à moins qu'il ne fasse songer à l'un de ces oiseaux mécaniques de métal et de plastique que des battements d'ailes saccadés emportent dans les airs.

cd piste 21

Taille : 15 cm

Répartition géographique simplifiée : toute l'Europe

Milieux fréquentés : campagne, parcs et jardins (y compris en ville)

Période de présence : toute l'année

Degré d'abondance : très commun

Postes de chant : arbres, haies

Période de chant : surtout de février à juillet

Observation : très facile

Particularité : chante posé ou en vol

dans les buissons

Bruant jaune

Emberiza citrinella

Un battement assez métallique, en général aussitôt suivi d'un son aigu, étiré, légèrement bourdonnant. Sous le soleil de midi dont des troupes de petits cumulus presque figés ne parviennent pas à tempérer l'ardeur, ce chant est l'un des seuls à se faire entendre dans la plaine par une belle journée de juin. Tout autour, les amples champs de blé sont à peine entravés par quelques boqueteaux rescapés et des lambeaux de haies oubliés par miracle. Il n'en faut pas plus au bruant jaune pour s'établir.

Posé sur son poteau de clôture ou au bout de sa branche morte favorite, il revendique ses droits de propriétaire. En bon bruant, il redresse la tête à chaque strophe. Bec bien ouvert, pointé vers le ciel, il semble vouloir améliorer la portée de sa chansonnette. Jaune, il l'est décidément. C'est bien ce que l'on voit de lui, même de très loin, notamment lorsqu'il chante en bombant le torse. Sa tête et sa poitrine sont d'une belle couleur vive que l'on jurerait empruntée aux boutons-d'or qui parsèment l'herbe le long du chemin. Sur ce fond clair, l'œil, noir et rond comme un grain de mûre, ressort bien, donnant à l'oiseau une expression vaguement étonnée. Jugeant avoir assez donné de la voix, le bruant d'or se laisse tomber au sol et le silence se fait pour quelques instants...

cd piste 22

Taille : 16 cm

Répartition géographique simplifiée : presque toute l'Europe

Milieux fréquentés : campagne cultivée, landes

Période de présence : toute l'année

Degré d'abondance : commun

Postes de chant : arbustes, haies, arbres, piquets de clôture

Période de chant : dès février, mais surtout d'avril à juillet

Observation : très facile

Au printemps l'Oiseau naît et chante :
N'avez-vous pas ouï sa voix ?...
Elle est pure, simple et touchante,
La voix de l'Oiseau – dans les bois !

Gérard de Nerval, Dans les bois ! *Annales romantiques*, 1835.

Bruant ortolan

Emberiza hortulana

Le bruant ortolan se passerait certainement volontiers de sa réputation gastronomique... Sous le prétexte que les quelques grammes de chair qu'il représente sont succulents, sa population a été mise à mal par des siècles de piégeage – dès l'époque romaine. Si l'on ajoute à cela le redoutable impact de la modification de certains des milieux qu'il affectionne, il est permis de se demander pour combien de temps encore il sera possible d'entendre son chant dans certaines régions d'Europe occidentale... Ce n'est pas que l'ortolan soit un modèle de virtuosité mais il est néanmoins plaisant par sa tonalité et se révèle intéressant par les variations qui peuvent exister d'un chanteur à l'autre et d'une région à l'autre.

Dans bien des cas, la ressemblance avec la phrase du bruant jaune est frappante. Même amorce en battement et même motif étiré, dans la foulée. Toutefois, la voix de l'ortolan est plus grave, plus pleine, bref, plus musicale. Elle résonne dans des milieux fort variés, sous des latitudes éloignées. Pour tel observateur, elle fait partie de l'ambiance sonore de la garrigue piquée de genévriers, pour tel autre, elle est associée au vignoble catalan, tandis que pour un troisième, elle rappelle un voyage en Scandinavie. Un éclectisme dont il faut souhaiter qu'il parvienne à se maintenir.

cd piste 23

Taille : 16 cm

Répartition géographique simplifiée : presque toute l'Europe (manque dans les Îles britanniques et en Norvège)

Milieux fréquentés : campagne ouverte avec arbres épars, vignes, cultures en terrasses, garrigue

Période de présence : avril à septembre/octobre

Degré d'abondance : souvent rare et localisé

Postes de chant : arbustes, arbres, fils aériens

Période de chant : surtout mai et juin

Observation : facile

Bruant proyer

Miliaria calandra

Avec les vocalises de l'alouette des champs, le modeste chant du bruant proyer constitue l'essentiel de l'ambiance sonore des grandes plaines sans obstacles vouées à la culture des céréales. Mais alors que l'alouette pourrait aisément prétendre au rang de diva, le proyer doit se contenter du rôle ingrat d'accompagnateur zélé. Le zèle est une qualité qu'il faut lui reconnaître car il ne se lasse pas de reproduire sa petite phrase aiguë. Jamais d'invention mais une constance remarquable. Perché sur une plante clandestine épargnée par les produits phytosanitaires, ou encore sur un fil aérien – le progrès a parfois du bon... –, le passereau dodu se rengorge, redresse la tête et laisse échapper sa brève chanson, le bec bien ouvert.

On l'a comparée à juste titre au roulement accéléré d'une perle dans une coupelle ou encore à celui d'un ultime cachou dans une boîte métallique. Il y a de cela, et la vibration de ce battement sonore rappelle celle des ondes de chaleur s'élevant fébrilement au-dessus des champs qui fuient jusqu'à l'horizon. Sa consciencieuse prestation achevée, le bruant replet abandonne son perchoir, ailes vibrantes et pattes pendantes, habitude qui trahit son identité, même de loin.

cd piste 24

Taille : 18 cm

Répartition géographique simplifiée : toute l'Europe, sauf la Scandinavie

Milieu fréquenté : campagne cultivée

Période de présence : selon les régions, présent toute l'année ou seulement à la belle saison

Degré d'abondance : localement commun

Postes de chant : plantes hautes, buissons, haies, fils aériens

Période de chant : de février à juillet/août

Observation : très facile

Les Bruants, perchés sur l'extrême bouquet de feuilles de l'arbrisseau, renversent la tête en arrière, dans une pose extatique.

Jacques Delamain, *Pourquoi les oiseaux chantent*, Stock, 1928.

Bruant zizi

Emberiza cirlus

Avec lui, il ne faut pas s'attendre à des merveilles. Le bruant zizi s'en tient scrupuleusement à sa petite phrase, sorte de trille ou de battement régulier, bref, plutôt métallique. Si les variations sont quasiment inexistantes chez un même mâle, la personnalité musicale de chacun des représentants de l'espèce est très délicate – sinon impossible – à saisir. Bref, la fantaisie n'est pas la caractéristique de ce passereau.

Perché en hauteur, il relève un peu la tête et accompagne sa sommaire production sonore d'une vibration de la queue, synchronisée avec l'émission des notes. Ce mouvement spasmodique de la queue peut être considéré comme une traduction visuelle de l'effort représenté par le chant. Placide, le bruant zizi répète sa modeste ritournelle en marquant de petites pauses.

Pour simple qu'il soit, le chant du bruant zizi est sonore et marque bien l'oreille. Il suffit en tous cas à écarter les rivaux éventuels et à intéresser les femelles. Ces dernières sont porteuses d'un sobre plumage rayé à dominante brunâtre qui constitue, au sol, un camouflage efficace. Bien plus remarquable, le mâle, en dépit des dessins et des teintes qu'il arbore, notamment à la tête, reste assez difficile à repérer lorsqu'il arpente le sol, en quête des petites graines dont il se nourrit.

cd piste 25

Taille : 16 cm

Répartition géographique simplifiée : Sud et Ouest de l'Europe (au sud d'une ligne Calais-Istanbul)

Milieux fréquentés : campagne, lisières et clairières, parcs et jardins

Période de présence : toute l'année

Degré d'abondance : assez commun (parfois localisé)

Postes de chant : arbustes, haies, arbres, poteaux et fils aériens

Période de chant : toute l'année mais surtout de février/mars à août

Observation : très facile

Cisticole des joncs

Cisticola juncidis

Il serait pour le moins difficile de prétendre que ce minuscule oiselet a été sélectionné ici pour les qualités de son chant… Sa production se limite en effet à un seule et unique son, inlassablement répété. Encore ce son n'est-il pas mélodieux le moins du monde. Métallique, sec, il ferait plutôt songer à un bruit mécanique. Pourtant, la cisticole mérite sa place aux côtés des chanteurs accomplis. Son secret ? Elle compense la médiocrité de ses performances vocales par un comportement original. Sans craindre de se dépenser, cette miniature chante en volant. À quelques mètres de hauteur, elle décrit un grand circuit à la trajectoire onduleuse. Battant des ailes, elle prend de l'altitude ; les fermant, elle en perd aussitôt. Chaque feston est ponctué d'une note cliquetante et le manège se prolonge ainsi, parfois pendant plusieurs minutes. Il n'est pas très facile de localiser le petit chanteur en plein ciel, au point qu'il reste parfois invisible en dépit de la constance de sa production…

En pleine saison de reproduction, la cisticole consacre une part importante de son temps au chant, au point que, dans les régions où elle abonde, ses cliquetis métronomiques peuvent finir par devenir quelque peu lancinants ! Plus positivement, ils sont également synonymes de chaleur, de soleil, de ciel bleu et de vacances dans le Midi…

cd piste 26

Taille : 10 cm

Répartition géographique simplifiée : de la Bretagne à la Grèce, souvent le long des côtes

Milieux fréquentés : champs, prairies et friches, souvent secs

Période de présence : toute l'année

Degré d'abondance : assez commune à commune mais localisée

Postes de chant : en dehors du chant aérien, végétation palustre, buissons, fils aériens, arbres

Période de chant : toute l'année

Observation : facile… une fois l'oiseau repéré

Particularité : chante surtout en vol

Fauvette grisette

Sylvia communis

Il n'est guère difficile d'entendre au printemps les vocalises explosives de la fauvette grisette. Dès son retour d'Afrique, crânement posée au sommet d'un rameau d'églantier dépassant d'une grosse haie, elle débite avec prodigalité ses courtes phrases tressautantes. Prompte à changer de perchoir, elle se dissimule parfois davantage pour s'exprimer tout en surveillant les alentours à l'abri du feuillage. Il lui arrive de ne pas s'en tenir à de brèves interventions et de prolonger quelque peu sa petite chanson. Quelle qu'en soit la longueur, celle-ci est le plus souvent assez peu mélodieuse, même si elle n'est pas désagréable à entendre.

Ce qui frappe le plus, c'est son aspect tonique, comme si l'oiseau était perpétuellement survolté. Cette exubérance se manifeste aussi à intervalles irréguliers lorsque la grisette s'élève soudain verticalement en chantant avec excitation, se maintient sur place quelques secondes en proie à une amusante danse de Saint-Guy, avant de chuter comme une pierre vers un perchoir. Une telle vitalité rend parfois son observation quelque peu ardue mais on finit heureusement, en général, par profiter d'un moment où elle se décide à rester en place un peu plus longtemps…

cd piste 27

Taille : 14 cm

Répartition géographique simplifiée : presque toute l'Europe

Milieux fréquentés : campagne avec haies, friches broussailleuses, jeunes plantations

Période de présence : avril à septembre

Degré d'abondance : commune

Postes de chant : arbustes, haies, buissons

Période de chant : surtout fin avril à juin

Observation : facile

Particularité : vol chanté assez fréquent

Sa brève phrase volubile ne produit pas beaucoup d'impression : elle n'a rien de très mélodieux, tant elle est brusque et nerveuse, bredouillée à la hâte.

Paul Géroudet, *Les Passereaux*, t. II, coll. Les Beautés de la Nature, Delachaux et Niestlé, 1953.

Fauvette mélanocéphale

Sylvia melanocephala

Il faut parfois avoir les nerfs solides et ne pas se montrer trop impatient lorsque l'on cherche à apercevoir la fauvette mélanocéphale... Ce passereau typique du maquis est en effet – comme les autres fauvettes méditerranéennes – un artiste chevronné du camouflage. S'il a décidé de demeurer invisible, il n'y a rien à faire ! Ses cris secs, graves et rêches, émis avec une grande prodigalité, semblent n'être faits que pour accroître la frustration de l'observateur en signalant l'endroit où l'oiseau reste diaboliquement à couvert. L'obstination finit cependant en général par payer, car cette fauvette consent parfois à se montrer coopérative en s'exposant au bout d'une branchette dégagée. L'on ne regrette alors pas d'avoir consacré du temps à débusquer cet oiseau à l'élégant plumage, certes peu coloré, mais donc la capuche noir pur tranche sur la gorge neigeuse et sert d'écrin velouté au grenat vif de l'œil.

Tout aussi peu discret que ses cris, le chant de la fauvette mélanocéphale est une succession de phrases vigoureuses séparées de brèves pauses. Le débit accéléré donne l'impression que l'oiseau est appelé ailleurs à des tâches urgentes et se hâte d'en finir avec ses vocalisations. De loin en loin, le chanteur, gagné par l'excitation, se lance dans un court vol chanté, à l'instar de la fauvette grisette.

cd piste 28

Taille : 13,5 cm

Répartition géographique simplifiée : extrême Sud de l'Europe (en France, façade méditerranéenne)

Milieux fréquentés : maquis, bois clairs, garrigue haute, parcs et jardins

Période de présence : toute l'année

Degré d'abondance : assez commune

Poste de chant : buissons

Période de chant : mars à juillet

Observation : assez difficile à facile

Particularité : vol chanté occasionnel

Fauvette passerinette

Sylvia cantillans

Pour surprendre la fauvette passerinette, mieux vaut se lever tôt... Plus tard dans la journée, ses milieux d'élection rappellent furieusement l'Afrique où elle se retire prudemment en hiver. La chaleur est alors partout et le grésillement insistant des cigales semble l'augmenter encore.

Difficile, dans ces conditions, de rechercher le délicat passereau agréablement coloré qui excelle à se dissimuler dans la végétation brûlée de lumière et se montre en outre un peu moins enclin à s'exprimer vocalement. Si donc l'on prend la précaution de se mettre en quête lorsque le soleil ne fait pas encore preuve d'agressivité, il est possible d'espérer une rencontre avec la passerinette, parfois seulement furtive. Pourtant, bien souvent, il faut se contenter de l'entendre. Son chant enjoué est un bel exemple de souffle endurant. Débité de manière précipitée, il se prolonge si bien que l'on rate parfois les très brèves interruptions que s'accorde le chanteur. C'est un mélange de sons un peu grinçants et de notes plus musicales, ponctué de sifflements. Cette alternance donne au total un chant plaisant, qui n'est pas sans rappeler celui de la fauvette mélanocéphale.

cd piste 29

Taille : 12,5 cm

Répartition géographique simplifiée : extrême Sud de l'Europe (en France, Midi méditerranéen)

Milieux fréquentés : bois clairs, garrigue haute, maquis

Période de présence : avril à septembre/octobre

Degré d'abondance : localement assez commune

Postes de chant : buissons, arbustes, arbres

Période de chant : avril à juin

Observation : assez difficile

Tout le ciel neuf est en azur
Et, limpide au long du vieux mur,
La rivière fait sa toilette,
Vole fauvette,
Jetant mainte perle au buisson [...]

Albert Samain, Chanson, *Poèmes pour la grande amie*, Mercure de France.

Fauvette pitchou

Sylvia undata

Catapulté par un invisible ressort, un petit oiseau à longue queue jaillit parfois en chantant avec vivacité au-dessus de la lande où les ajoncs sont piquetés d'une profusion de petites fleurs jaunes au surprenant parfum de… noix de coco. Au comble de l'excitation, la fauvette pitchou échappe ainsi pour quelques secondes à l'inextricable et épineux fouillis végétal où elle a choisi de vivre. Son vol nuptial tressautant, au cours duquel elle semble attachée à un fil, est l'occasion de l'observer fugitivement.

Le reste du temps, grise et menue comme une souris, elle excelle à se faufiler dans la végétation, se contentant de se percher en évidence quelques secondes de temps à autre, juste le temps de lancer son petit chant grinçant. C'est peu pour admirer son plumage joliment nuancé et son œil rouge vif, sans oublier les minuscules taches blanches constellant sa gorge hirsute. La modeste phrase grésillante et nerveuse peut échapper à l'oreille si d'autres oiseaux se manifestent en même temps. Toutefois, comme elle est répétée avec une certaine régularité, on finit par la remarquer. Et puis, de toute façon, il n'est pas possible de manquer le chant aérien auquel se livre l'espèce.

cd piste 30

Taille : 13,5 cm

Répartition géographique simplifiée : Sud-Ouest de l'Europe (en France, surtout façades atlantique et méditerranéenne)

Milieux fréquentés : landes broussailleuses, maquis bas, garrigue

Période de présence : toute l'année

Degré d'abondance : localisée

Poste de chant : buissons

Période de chant : février à octobre

Observation : difficile à très difficile

Particularité : vol chanté assez fréquent

Gorgebleue à miroir

Luscinia svecica

Les marais salants offrent à l'œil leur quadrillage de canaux, rigoles et fossés enchâssant le miroitement des nappes d'eau de mer captive aux teintes variées. C'est là qu'il faut s'installer, non loin de bouquets ou de haies de tamaris échevelés par la brise océane, si l'on veut assister au concert des gorgebleues. La patience est vite récompensée par ces élégants petits oiseaux.

Généreux, ils ne se contentent pas d'arborer un éclatant plastron bleu vif souligné d'une bande tricolore mais sont aussi de captivants virtuoses. Chacun des chanteurs, après un prélude de sons détachés, compose un étonnant chapelet de notes souvent musicales, parfois plus discordantes, de bribes harmonieuses, de cris, d'envolées flûtées et, surtout, d'imitations d'autres espèces. Il y a là du rossignol, de l'alouette, de la fauvette, du moineau, du chardonneret et même du grillon !

Comme si cela ne suffisait pas à satisfaire l'observateur, la gorgebleue abandonne de temps à autre son perchoir. Décrivant alors en vol un bref circuit, elle continue à chanter dans les airs avant de regagner un poste stratégique où elle se pose doucement, ailes et queue étalées.

cd piste 31

Taille : 13,5 cm

Répartition géographique simplifiée : surtout Nord de l'Europe (en France, côte atlantique)

Milieux fréquentés : en Europe du Nord, saulaies et bois de trembles ; ailleurs, zones humides avec buissons, roseaux, quelques arbres

Période de présence : de mars à septembre

Degré d'abondance : localisée

Postes de chant : buissons, arbustes, arbres

Période de chant : avril à juin

Observation : assez facile

Particularité : chante posée ou en vol

Hypolaïs polyglotte

Hippolais polyglotta

Quelle exubérance ! L'hypolaïs polyglotte ne saurait se contenter d'une vie paisible. Elle consacre une bonne partie de son existence à des déplacements éreintants et périlleux entre l'Afrique où elle passe la mauvaise saison, et l'Europe qu'elle investit pour s'y reproduire. À peine arrivée de migration, elle se lance dans des improvisations survoltées au débit haché. Commençant le plus souvent par quelques pépiements de moineau excellemment imités, elle enchaîne ensuite avec nervosité, débitant sa chansonnette durant un bon moment. Ce torrent de notes pressées n'est pas désagréable à écouter mais n'atteint toutefois pas un niveau musical digne d'éloges.

Certains mâles, cependant, sont plus inspirés que d'autres. Leur chant assez musical par moments peut comporter une forte proportion d'imitations d'autres espèces, ce qui constitue un attrait supplémentaire : le terme polyglotte se trouve alors justifié. Il n'en reste pas moins que l'imitatrice patentée est bien la cousine de la polyglotte, l'hypolaïs ictérine, à l'aspect trompeusement identique mais dont le chant est bien plus mélodieux et tonique. Sa production inventive, audible de jour comme de nuit, est présentée dans le disque joint au présent ouvrage.

cd pistes 32 (Hypolaïs polyglotte) et 33 (Hypolaïs ictérine)

Taille : 12,5 cm

Répartition géographique simplifiée : Sud-Ouest de l'Europe

Milieux fréquentés : milieux boisés avec clairières, jeunes plantations, fourrés, friches avec buissons

Période de présence : fin avril à septembre

Degré d'abondance : commune

Postes de chant : arbustes, arbres, haies

Période de chant : surtout mai et juin

Observation : facile

Linotte mélodieuse

Carduelis cannabina

Il est des chants d'oiseaux sucrés et veloutés comme une framboise... Celui de la linotte mélodieuse – et Dieu sait si elle l'est ! – est de ceux-là. Poursuivant l'analogie, on remarquera que la linotte, à son front et sur la poitrine porte comme des traces de petits fruits rouges écrasés... Troublante coïncidence ! Ce passereau menu au plumage délicatement nuancé ne cherche pas à imposer sa voix, dirait-on. Posée dans la lande au sommet d'un ajonc fleuri, elle babille avec obstination sur un ton qui évoque la gaieté, l'insouciance : ne parle-t-on pas, d'ailleurs, de « tête de linotte » ?

Il faut se hâter de profiter de ces agréables vocalises car il est rare que le chanteur reste en place très longtemps. Tenaillé par une bougeotte irrépressible, il s'interrompt brusquement pour filer, d'un vol onduleux, retrouver des congénères éparpillés çà et là. À moins que son départ n'ait été causé par une inquiétude, réelle ou sans fondement. Alarme hystérique d'un merle, bruit soudain dans le voisinage ou apparition d'un épervier, tout est facteur de trouble et conduit à l'arrêt du petit concert privé. Fort heureusement, il ne tardera pas à reprendre aussitôt l'alerte passée.

cd piste 34

Taille : 13 cm

Répartition géographique simplifiée : presque toute l'Europe

Milieux fréquentés : campagne, jardins, landes et friches broussailleuses

Période de présence : toute l'année

Degré d'abondance : commune

Postes de chant : buissons, arbustes, haies, arbres

Période de chant : de février à juillet

Observation : très facile

Particularité : peut chanter en volant

Pie-grièche écorcheur
Pie-grièche à tête rousse

Lanius collurio, Lanius senator

Cas de figure intéressant : l'élève et son maître. C'est à ce type de relation que l'on ne peut s'empêcher de songer en écoutant les chants des pies-grièches écorcheur et à tête rousse. Les productions des deux cousines ont un indéniable air de famille. Le même modèle de départ paraît avoir servi pour l'une et l'autre. Même débit prolongé, même principe dans la succession de sons différents, enfin, même alternance de gazouillis plaisants et de motifs grinçants, beaucoup moins harmonieux. Mais là où l'écorcheur se contente de la discrétion, presque de la timidité, et semble brider son talent d'improvisatrice, la pie-grièche à tête rousse se laisse aller. Elle donne de la voix et fait apprécier son inventivité confondante. Certes, elle ne recule pas devant les sons rauques ou chuintants mais, en compensation, quelle collection de notes musicales, de sons agréables !

Les meilleurs mâles surprennent toujours par la variété et la qualité de leur chant. L'inconvénient est que ces pies-grièches ne se produisent que peu de temps. Une fois revenues sur leurs terres au terme de la migration de printemps, elles se taisent après avoir fait ce qu'il fallait pour s'imposer. Par chance, même silencieuses, elles demeurent splendides et passionnantes à observer.

cd pistes 35 et 36

Taille : 16 à 19 cm

Répartition géographique simplifiée : pie-grièche écorcheur, presque toute l'Europe ; pie-grièche à tête rousse, Sud de l'Europe

Milieux fréquentés : pie-grièche écorcheur, campagne avec grosses haies, landes et friches avec buissons et petits arbres épars ; pie-grièche à tête rousse, paysages mêlant bois clairs et cultures, zones dégagées avec arbustes épars, vergers

Période de présence : de mai à août/septembre

Degré d'abondance : localisée (pie-grièchc à tête rousse) à assez commune (pie-grièche écorcheur)

Postes de chant : arbustes, buissons, haies, petits arbres

Période de chant : surtout mai et juin

Observation : assez facile mais ces espèces chantent avec parcimonie

Particularité : imitations fréquentes

Rossignol philomèle

Luscinia megarhynchos

Les nuits précédentes ont été consacrées au voyage de retour depuis le cœur de l'Afrique. Le rossignol philomèle est maintenant parvenu à destination, retrouvant les fourrés où il va pouvoir laisser libre cours à son prodigieux talent de chanteur. Contrairement à ce que l'on croit souvent, il ne donne pas ses récitals seulement la nuit. C'est cependant bien alors que l'on peut apprécier dans les meilleures conditions ses superbes qualités vocales. Le chant du rossignol semble apporter une profondeur particulière à l'obscurité et, comme en retour, la nuit le magnifie. Glissé entre les phrases, le silence nocturne paraît destiné à en exacerber la beauté. Autant le chant du merle peut être suave, autant celui du rossignol est explosif, tonique, pour tout dire : « sauvage » ! Une énergie essentielle, fondamentale, s'en dégage. Cette énergie est évidente quand on a la chance de surprendre le rossignol en pleine action. Le corps est secoué de spasmes au rythme des phrases, la mandibule inférieure tremble au fil des notes, les plumes hérissées de la gorge vibrent en cadence. Tant de dépense physique se traduit par une émission d'une étonnante puissance.

De manière typique, le rossignol commence régulièrement par un fin sifflement répété, d'intensité croissante, débouchant sur des notes éclatantes en série rapide. L'invention est au rendez-vous et rend ardue la description de la production vocale, d'autant que le rossignol aime chanter durant de longs moments, ignorant à quel point il comble ses admirateurs.

cd piste 37

Taille : 16 cm

Répartition géographique simplifiée : manque en Scandinavie et dans la majorité des Îles britanniques

Milieux fréquentés : bois et forêts, campagne avec grosses haies

Période de présence : d'avril à septembre

Degré d'abondance : commun

Postes de chant : arbustes, fourrés, arbres

Période de chant : avril à juin

Observation : difficile à très difficile

Particularité : chante de nuit comme de jour

Rousserolle effarvatte

Acrocephalus scirpaceus

Au printemps, il ne saurait y avoir de marais couvert de roseaux digne de ce nom, sans son impétueux concert de rousserolles effarvattes. Bien dissimulés au milieu du fouillis serré des hautes tiges grêles, ces passereaux élancés aux teintes en harmonie avec leur milieu palustre donnent l'impression de participer à une compétition vocale. Il n'est vraiment pas facile de parvenir à en distinguer un, mais lorsque c'est le cas, il est amusant de suivre les palpitations de sa gorge aux plumes hérissées. La rousserolle effarvatte offre un répertoire composé d'un incroyable mélange de sons rêches, râpeux, grinçants, froissés. Il est rare que des notes moins discordantes se glissent dans le long discours proposé par chaque chanteur.

Pourtant, malgré des caractéristiques en apparence peu favorables, le chant de l'effarvatte n'est pas désagréable car il est plutôt doux. Associé aux coassements des grenouilles, il fait partie de l'ambiance sonore des zones humides où les panaches plumeux des phragmites ondulent sous le vent. Ces plantes sont presque indispensables à la rousserolle effarvatte car c'est en général entre leurs tiges que son nid, délicate nacelle tissée, est adroitement arrimé. Cette situation la protège des prédateurs mais pas du parasitisme du coucou gris qui vient souvent y déposer son œuf, plus gros mais d'aspect analogue.

cd piste 38

Taille : 13 cm

Répartition géographique simplifiée : majeure partie de l'Europe

Milieu fréquenté : roselières

Période de présence : d'avril à octobre

Degré d'abondance : localement commune

Poste de chant : roseaux

Période de chant : dès avril et surtout de mai à début juillet

Observation : assez difficile

Rousserolle turdoïde

Acrocephalus arundinaceus

Les phragmitaies, ces étendues de roseaux associées aux zones humides, hébergent plusieurs espèces de petits passereaux qui trouvent là nourriture et abri. Ces oiseaux, souvent des migrateurs dont beaucoup reviennent d'Afrique, animent de leurs chants les roselières durant la belle saison. Les rousserolles effarvattes et les phragmites des joncs notamment, mais aussi les bruants des roseaux, sont en général les mieux représentés. Toutefois, dans certaines régions où les phragmitaies ont été épargnées par le « progrès » et couvrent encore des surfaces respectables, il est possible d'entendre un autre chanteur, à la voix tonitruante. Nullement mélodieux, le chant de la rousserolle turdoïde, en impose cependant par sa vigueur, son côté « sauvage et primitif ». L'oiseau, bien plus gros que sa cousine la rousserolle effarvatte, est également beaucoup moins discret qu'elle.

La turdoïde, en effet, n'hésite pas à se poster presque au sommet d'un grand phragmite, sous le panache de la plante. Solidement campée, tête levée, bec dressé, gorge hirsute et vibrante, elle lance avec force ses grattements râpeux, ses coups de crécelle explosifs, ses raclements plus ou moins graves, repris et répétés en combinaisons variées. Il n'est pas rare que ce chant dynamique domine l'ambiance sonore du marais, à moins que les batraciens soient particulièrement en forme...

cd piste 39

Taille : 16-20 cm

Répartition géographique simplifiée : toute l'Europe sauf la majorité des Îles britanniques et de la Scandinavie

Milieu fréquenté : grandes roselières denses

Période de présence : de fin avril à septembre

Degré d'abondance : peu commune, localisée

Poste de chant : roseaux

Période de chant : de fin avril à fin juillet

Observation : assez facile

C'est lui faire beaucoup d'honneur ; d'autres appellations locales, telles que Carasse ou Karaki, donnent une idée plus juste d'un talent vocal plus marqué par la vigueur que par la qualité des sons.

Jacques Delamain, *Portraits d'oiseaux* (Nouvelle série), Librairie Stock, 1952.

Rousserolle verderolle

Acrocephalus palustris

Dans la petite vallée où quelques vénérables peupliers dominent de riches prairies humides et des fossés que se disputent la reine-des-prés et la consoude, plusieurs oiseaux semblent s'être donné rendez-vous. Dans le même secteur, on entend le babil du chardonneret, l'alarme de l'hirondelle rustique, les litanies de la grive musicienne ou encore les notes flûtées de la fauvette à tête noire. Curieusement, ces oiseaux, et bien d'autres encore, s'époumonent les uns après les autres, sans jamais empiéter sur la production du voisin. Tout aussi bizarrement, l'ensemble de ces sons semble bien provenir précisément du même endroit...

Avec un peu de patience et le sens de l'observation, on finit par découvrir le pot aux roses : un seul oiseau est responsable de ce petit concert improvisé. Une rousserolle verderolle, installée à couvert dans la végétation profuse, enchaîne ses imitations en faisant preuve d'une merveilleuse inventivité. Il n'est pas envisageable de se lasser d'écouter cette artiste qui a atteint la perfection en matière de contrefaçon. Les meilleurs chanteurs ont un répertoire d'une variété proprement stupéfiante. La verderolle compense ainsi très largement par les qualités de sa voix la modestie de son plumage aux teintes brunâtres et beiges.

cd piste 40

Taille : 14 cm

Répartition géographique simplifiée : Europe moyenne (en France, à l'est et au nord)

Milieux fréquentés : prés marécageux ; en montagne, prairies à ombellifères ; localement, cultures

Période de présence : de mai à septembre

Degré d'abondance : localement assez commune

Postes de chant : végétation basse, arbustes, buissons

Période de chant : de mai à mi-juillet

Observation : assez facile à difficile

Particularité : imitatrice hors pair

Tourterelle des bois

Streptopelia turtur

Par les après-midi accablés de chaleur, la plupart des oiseaux se taisent, soit qu'ils vaquent aux occupations liées à la nidification, soit qu'ils attendent la fin vespérale de la fournaise pour donner de la voix. Pourtant, un chant retentit avec une belle constance. Un roucoulement prolongé, à la tonalité assez sourde, bien que parfaitement audible. La tourterelle des bois, africaine une bonne partie de l'année, salue à sa façon le beau temps et la chaleur. Son roucoulement peut passer pour monotone mais est l'une des pièces maîtresses de l'ambiance sonore estivale du bocage ou des bosquets et grosses haies perdus au milieu des champs.

De loin, le chant roucoulé de cette élégante tourterelle semble uniforme, enchaîné sans que l'oiseau ait besoin de reprendre sa respiration. De plus près, cependant, par exemple depuis un affût, on parvient à percevoir les brèves inspirations qui permettent au petit columbidé d'émettre un roucoulement prolongé, la gorge gonflée. Il est cependant vain de vouloir trop approcher la tourterelle. Inquiète, elle se tait. Si décidément l'intrus s'approche trop, la fuite s'impose. L'envol est brusque et l'oiseau file prestement avec des battements d'ailes saccadés, typiques de l'espèce. À distance suffisante, un crochet sec, qui permet d'apercevoir le collier de perles blanches terminant la queue, et la tourterelle s'enfonce dans le couvert salvateur de la haie touffue.

cd piste 41

Taille : 26 cm

Répartition géographique simplifiée : toute l'Europe sauf la Scandinavie

Milieux fréquentés : bois peu touffus, boqueteaux, campagne avec grosses haies

Période de présence : d'avril à septembre

Degré d'abondance : commune

Postes de chant : arbustes, grosses haies, arbres

Période de chant : d'avril à juillet

Observation : assez difficile à facile

Particularité : la femelle émet un chant analogue, moins soutenu

Troglodyte mignon

Troglodytes troglodytes

S'il fallait décerner la palme du meilleur rapport entre le poids et la puissance sonore, le troglodyte mignon la mériterait haut la main. Comment imaginer en effet, lorsque l'on ne connaît pas ce chanteur, qu'un tel volume puisse sortir d'un si petit gosier ? Ce passereau rondelet d'une dizaine de grammes, reconnaissable à sa petite queue presque toujours redressée à la verticale, est passé maître dans l'art de produire des décibels. Dans les régions suffisamment clémentes, il ne se tait jamais tout à fait en hiver mais, partout, c'est au printemps qu'il se fait entendre avec une belle constance. Son chant explosif d'une durée de quelques secondes respecte une même structure fondamentale mêlant trilles et répétitions de diverses notes. C'est ensuite une affaire d'humeur, d'invention, de broderies d'une émission à la suivante, d'un chanteur à l'autre.

Comme pour d'autres oiseaux, il s'agit pour le mâle de délimiter un territoire et d'entamer le processus de la reproduction. Toutefois, le troglodyte ne se contente pas d'attirer une seule femelle car il est polygame. L'insatiable passereau bâtit plusieurs ébauches de nids et fait ensuite la publicité de ces grosses boules de mousse sur le mode musical. Si une partenaire se laisse tenter par l'une des constructions amorcées, elle marque son intérêt en s'occupant de l'aménagement intérieur douillettement réalisé à l'aide de plumes, poils et brins de laine. C'est ce que l'on appelle la juste répartition des tâches…

cd piste 42

Taille : 10 cm

Répartition géographique simplifiée : toute l'Europe

Milieux fréquentés : bois, forêts, campagne avec haies, parcs, jardins (y compris en ville)

Période de présence : toute l'année

Degré d'abondance : très commun

Postes de chant : buissons, arbustes, arbres

Période de chant : presque toute l'année, surtout de février à juillet

Observation : facile à très facile

autres perchoirs

Alouette lulu

Lulula arborea

Pour apprécier le chant de l'alouette lulu à sa juste valeur, il ne faut pas hésiter à quitter son lit très tôt. Après avoir gagné la lande sèche dominée par quelques vieux pins alors que la lumière du soleil n'est encore qu'une promesse, il ne reste qu'à attendre.

Dans le silence du paysage qui s'éveille tout juste retentissent enfin les superbes phrases liquides, doucement descendantes, de la petite alouette. Elles proviennent parfois du faîte d'un arbre mais, plus souvent, elles tombent du ciel. Si l'éclairage n'est pas suffisant en raison de l'heure matinale, il est vain de vouloir repérer l'oiseau occupé à décrire un large circuit aérien. Mais même lorsque la lumière devient favorable, l'entreprise n'est pas aisée tant le chanteur évolue volontiers à bonne hauteur, au-delà d'une centaine de mètres. La meilleure solution pour observer cette alouette est de la localiser lorsqu'elle chante perchée au bout d'une branche morte.

Mais il importe finalement assez peu que l'on voie l'oiseau : son chant suffit à ravir celui qui a la chance de pouvoir l'écouter. Le rossignol plaît par sa fougue, le merle par sa suavité, l'alouette lulu, elle, séduit avant tout par l'extrême pureté de sa voix mais aussi par la variété qui préside à l'émission de ses motifs flûtés : du grand art.

cd piste 43

Taille : 14 cm

Répartition géographique simplifiée : toute l'Europe (manque dans la majorité des Îles britanniques et de la Scandinavie)

Milieux fréquentés : cultures ou landes mêlées de boisements clairs

Période de présence : toute l'année (au nord et à l'est, seulement en été)

Degré d'abondance : assez commune mais parfois localisée

Postes de chant : surtout en vol ; également, arbres, fils, poteaux

Période de chant : de janvier/février à août

Observation : assez difficile à facile

Particularité : peut chanter de nuit

Alouette des champs

Alauda arvensis

Le chant de l'alouette est l'un de ceux qu'il faut avoir entendus en pleine nature pour pouvoir comprendre la ferveur avec laquelle les poètes les ont célébrés. Les mélodies de l'alouette des champs seraient-elles un peu moins agréables, la mise en scène qui les accompagne suffirait, à elle seule, à les distinguer. Il faut en effet s'imaginer l'ascension de l'alouette, ailes vibrantes.

Elle quitte son domaine dépourvu de perchoirs satisfaisants pour gagner un poste de chant dominant : le ciel. Parvenue à plusieurs dizaines de mètres, elle fait oublier la modestie de son plumage de terre et de chaume en disparaissant presque. Il ne reste d'elle qu'un point, grain de beauté sur la joue d'un nuage de beau temps qui défile lentement. Mais de ce point au zénith déferlent les notes. La chanson de l'alouette, à la prodigieuse variété est aussi incroyablement prolongée. Durant plusieurs minutes parfois, le merveilleux enchaînement se poursuit sans trêve, au point que l'on se demande quand l'oiseau reprend son souffle. Roulades, sifflements, trilles, notes cristallines et imitations occasionnelles alternent en un concert que l'on écoute pantois. Comme si elle était à cours d'inspiration, la chanteuse aérienne se tait tout à coup et commence à perdre de l'altitude. Sa chute s'accélère comme elle approche du champ ou de la lande puis un brusque ralentissement lui permet de se poser en douceur, ailes écartées et palpitantes. Selon la nature de la végétation, elle disparaît du regard dans les cultures ou se laisse admirer un bref instant, perchée sur un maigre buisson ou un ballot de paille oublié.

cd piste 44

Taille : 17 cm

Répartition géographique simplifiée : toute l'Europe

Milieux fréquentés : campagne ouverte et landes

Période de présence : toute l'année (au nord et à l'est, seulement en été)

Degré d'abondance : très commune

Postes de chant : chante normalement en vol et, parfois, sur un perchoir bas, poteau ou buisson

Période de chant : surtout de mars à juillet

Observation : facile (mais repérage parfois délicat)

Particularité : quelques imitations

Ce n'est certes pas l'alouette
Qui, ce matin, me l'apprendra,
Elle qui fait des pirouettes
Au soleil et lui crie sa joie
D'être libre encore une fois.

Maurice Carême, L'Alouette, *Au clair de la lune*, Éditions ouvrières, 1977

Bruant fou

Emberiza cia

Le bruant fou mène une existence plutôt effacée dans les collines et les montagnes méridionales où il privilégie les pentes bénéficiant d'un ensoleillement généreux. Son plumage aux teintes automnales – feuilles mortes et ciel gris – lui permet en effet de se camoufler sans difficulté parmi les blocs rocheux environnés d'une végétation limitée à quelques buissons et arbustes.

Si l'on parvient cependant à repérer un mâle posté sur un point saillant de son territoire, on peut alors profiter à loisir du joli contraste entre le dessous cannelle et la gorge grise, ainsi que des délicats dessins noirs de la tête sur fond de cendre. La femelle est semblable mais ses teintes sont moins soutenues et les marques de la tête, moins apparentes.

Discret dans son comportement, le bruant fou l'est aussi lorsqu'il chante. Des variations existent d'un mâle à l'autre mais le schéma général est à peu près constant : deux ou trois notes introductives puis un bref babil pressé fait de trilles et de sons roulés. L'ensemble donne une courte phrase dansante, à la tonalité souvent agréablement pleine dans sa seconde partie, que l'on peut fort bien ne pas remarquer car elle n'est pas toujours très sonore.

cd piste 45

Taille : 16 cm

Répartition géographique simplifiée : Sud de l'Europe (en France, régions montagneuses)

Milieux fréquentés : versants montagneux rocheux et ensoleillés

Période de présence : toute l'année

Degré d'abondance : assez commun mais localisé

Postes de chant : rochers, arbustes, buissons

Période de chant : février/mars à juillet

Observation : assez facile

Cincle plongeur

Cinclus cinclus

Le cincle plongeur ne saurait laisser indifférent. Tout en lui est digne d'intérêt, voire surprenant. Son aspect, d'abord. Une silhouette rondelette à courte queue, un plumage chocolat sur lequel tranche une belle bavette d'un blanc pur. Son attitude, ensuite. Solidement campé sur une pierre émergée, il enchaîne les courbettes nerveuses avant de filer d'un vol évoquant un énorme insecte aux ailes vibrantes. Son comportement enfin, constitue le clou du spectacle. Comment ne pas être surpris en voyant cette boule de plumes sombre s'avancer dans l'eau cristalline et y disparaître entièrement !

Ce passereau qui joue au canard dispose de tout l'équipement pour se permettre cela. Plumage dense, glande à graisse très développée pour l'imperméabiliser, doigts robustes pour agripper avec force les galets du fond. Même en hiver, dans une eau glacée, le cincle continue à se prendre pour un sous-marin.

Le chant vient compléter le tableau de cet original. Sa tonalité pénétrante lui permet d'être audible malgré le fracas des chutes d'eau coupant les torrents de montagne. Chaque strophe fait se succéder sur un rythme rapide et durant une dizaine de secondes des sons variés, tantôt graves, tantôt aigus, plus ou moins agréables. L'ensemble peut curieusement faire songer aux sons modulés produits par un poste de radio à ondes courtes sur lequel on recherche en vain une fréquence...

cd piste 46

Taille : 17-20 cm

Répartition géographique simplifiée : presque toute l'Europe

Milieux fréquentés : torrents, cours d'eau peu profonds

Période de présence : toute l'année

Degré d'abondance : peu commun, localisé

Postes de chant : rochers, gros galets

Période de chant : toute l'année (sauf de juillet à septembre)

Observation : assez difficile

Particularité : chante aussi en vol ; le mâle et la femelle chantent

Étourneau sansonnet

Sturnus vulgaris

Avec lui on peut s'attendre à tout ! Un vrombissement de vélomoteur dans un arbre ? Une sonnette sur le faîte du toit ? Trois oiseaux chantant exactement au même endroit l'un après l'autre ? Le responsable de tout cela n'est autre que l'étourneau sansonnet. Cet artiste doué inclut toutes sortes d'imitations dans sa production vocale incroyablement variée. Bruits de la vie quotidienne – y compris ceux liés à la technologie la plus récente –, cris et bribes de chants d'autres espèces d'oiseaux, tout peut figurer au répertoire de l'oiseau noir que l'on confondrait avec le merle si sa voix ne levait aussitôt le doute. Chez le merle, tout est suavité et sons flûtés. L'étourneau, lorsqu'il n'imite pas, se contente de sons explosifs, rauques, grinçants, cliquetants qui n'ont décidément rien de mélodieux...

Quels que soient les sons qui sortent de son gosier, il les émet souvent dans une sorte de frénésie qui le pousse à agiter spasmodiquement les ailes. Il ressemble alors tout à fait à l'un de ces oiseaux mécaniques en vogue aux XVIIIe et XIXe siècles.

cd piste 47

Taille : 19-22 cm

Répartition géographique simplifiée : toute l'Europe

Milieux fréquentés : campagne, parcs, jardins, villes et villages

Période de présence : toute l'année

Degré d'abondance : très commun

Postes de chant : arbres, poteaux, bâtiments, fils aériens

Période de chant : presque toute l'année mais surtout au printemps

Observation : très facile

Particularité : bon imitateur

Guêpier d'Europe

Merops apiaster

Le guêpier d'Europe n'est pas à proprement parler un chanteur. Toutefois, sa voix est particulièrement agréable à entendre. L'oiseau « aigu » – chez lui, tout est pointu, les ailes, le bec et la queue – possède paradoxalement un cri souple, liquide, qui caresse l'oreille. Espèce sociable, en général observée en groupe de quelques individus évoluant ensemble, mais parfois en grandes bandes, le guêpier n'est pas avare de ses cris. Émis en vol, ces derniers servent à assurer la cohésion de la troupe, à informer les uns et les autres des activités et de l'humeur de chacun. L'ensemble des vocalisations donne un bel effet de chœur, d'autant plus réussi que les oiseaux sont nombreux. Bien que les cris ne soient pas particulièrement sonores, ils portent loin, en partie à cause de l'effet de groupe. Il n'est pas rare que des bandes en déplacement, notamment à l'occasion des migrations, soient détectées à l'oreille, alors même que l'œil a bien du mal à repérer les guêpiers évoluant haut dans le ciel.

Il faut d'ailleurs parfois se contenter de les écouter sans parvenir à les voir, ce qui est dommage quand on connaît la beauté singulière de cet oiseau chamarré à l'allure bien plus africaine qu'européenne.

cd piste 48

Taille : 25-29 cm

Répartition géographique simplifiée : Europe méridionale et orientale (en France, surtout dans le Midi mais peut se rencontrer un peu partout)

Milieux fréquentés : campagne ouverte avec quelques arbres, clairières, carrières de sable

Période de présence : de fin avril à début septembre

Degré d'abondance : assez commun au sud, plus localisé au nord de son aire

Poste de chant : s'exprime surtout en vol

Période de chant : coïncide avec la période de présence

Observation : facile

Hirondelle rustique

Hirundo rustica

Avril est déjà bien installé. Dans le Midi, les hirondelles le sont aussi, mais plus au nord, elles tardent encore un peu. Et puis, par une belle journée ensoleillée, un gazouillis se fait entendre, qui n'en finit pas. Une hirondelle rustique décrit un capricieux circuit au-dessus de la maison avant de se poser, sans cesser de chanter. Ses longs « filets » aux côtés de la queue confirment qu'il s'agit d'un mâle. Est-ce le même oiseau que l'année dernière ? On peut se plaire à le penser…

Toujours est-il que le retour des hirondelles est l'un des grands moments pour tout amateur d'oiseaux assez chanceux pour héberger sous son toit un ou plusieurs couples d'hirondelles rustiques. Le chant de l'espèce se fait entendre tout au long de sa présence sur le site de nidification. Chaque hirondelle a ses postes de chant favoris mais ne se prive pas de chanter en vol.

C'est une production qui brille surtout par sa volubilité et son caractère enjoué. Le babil précipité, agréable, est entrecoupé de trilles bourdonnants typiques. Très loquace et toujours sur le qui-vive, l'hirondelle rustique ne manque pas de signaler la présence de rapaces à grand renfort de cris dissyllabiques aigus. Non contente de crier avec vigueur, elle file droit sur l'intrus, le houspillant jusqu'à ce qu'il s'éloigne.

cd piste 49

Taille : 17-21 cm (plumes de la queue : 3 à 6,5 cm)

Répartition géographique simplifiée : toute l'Europe

Milieux fréquentés : campagne, villes (parfois) et villages

Période de présence : de mars à octobre

Degré d'abondance : très commune

Poste de chant : fils aériens, toits

Période de chant : peut chanter tout au long des mois de présence

Observation : très facile

Particularité : peut aussi chanter en vol

Que te ferais-je ? dis ! babillarde hirondelle ? [...]
Térée, impatient, veux-tu qu'avec mes doigts,
Je t'ôte cette langue et l'importune voix
Qui vient, dès le matin, du sommeil ennemie,
À mes songes heureux enlever mon amie ?

André Chénier, Contre l'hirondelle, *Bucoliques* (avant 1794),
Édition Becq de Fouquières, 1862.

Huppe fasciée

Upupa epops

Mars n'est pas installé depuis bien longtemps et déjà la huppe a repris possession de la partie méditerranéenne de l'Europe. Plus au nord, il faudra faire preuve de patience avant d'entendre, au cours d'une promenade matinale, le doux chant à la sonorité un peu étouffée. Le « oupoupou » qui a valu son nom latin à l'espèce, résonne surtout dans les jours et les semaines qui suivent son retour.

Il tend ensuite à se faire plus rare avant de disparaître tout à fait de l'ambiance sonore des régions fréquentées par l'espèce. S'il n'est guère difficile d'entendre le chant de la huppe, il n'est par contre pas toujours évident de la surprendre en train de l'émettre, à moins de bien connaître les habitudes d'un oiseau en particulier. En pleine campagne, la huppe est plutôt farouche. Alors qu'elle était invisible dans l'herbe, elle s'envole sans tarder, déployant de larges ailes barrées de noir et de blanc qui l'emportent dans un vol à la capricieuse souplesse.

Là où elle a choisi de vivre au contact de l'homme, elle se laisse observer un peu plus complaisamment tout en conservant une marge prudente. On peut alors parfois, au gré de ses émotions, la voir étaler en éventail les plumes qui ornent sa tête terminée d'un long bec arqué, précieux outil pour la quête des insectes enfouis dans le sol.

cd piste 50

Taille : 25-29 cm

Répartition géographique simplifiée : presque toute l'Europe, à l'exception des îles Britanniques et de la Scandinavie

Milieux fréquentés : campagne avec haies et boqueteaux, zones herbeuses

Période de présence : de mars/avril à septembre

Degré d'abondance : assez commune dans le sud, moins fréquente plus au nord

Postes de chant : piquets, tas de pierres, murets, arbustes, arbres

Période de chant : surtout en avril et mai

Observation : assez difficile

Monticole bleu (Merle bleu)

Monticola solitarius

Cap au sud. Le monticole (ou merle) bleu, pour être admiré, exige que l'on se trouve sous des latitudes méridionales. Il est ensuite possible de choisir entre l'intérieur des terres et le bord de la mer car l'espèce fréquente indifféremment ces deux types de milieu, pourvu qu'elle y trouve les grandes parois rocheuses qu'elle affectionne. Cette exigence garantit des observations dans des cadres somptueux, qu'il s'agisse, par exemple, de sites français, espagnols ou grecs.

Découvrir l'oiseau n'est pas toujours évident au milieu de la complexité graphique des falaises, même s'il aime occuper des postes dominants : corniches, pitons ou gros blocs rocheux. Une fois le monticole repéré, pouvoir profiter de la beauté subtile de son plumage bleu cendré nécessite la complicité du soleil tant l'oiseau paraît tout sombre lorsqu'il se tient à l'ombre. Bien que la voix du monticole bleu soit sonore, il est recommandé pour profiter pleinement de son chant, peu varié mais agréable à écouter, de choisir un site de gorges encaissées. Là, les jolies phrases à la tonalité vaguement mélancolique bénéficient d'une acoustique favorable qui les met en valeur.

cd piste 51

Taille : 22 cm

Répartition géographique simplifiée : Europe méditerranéenne

Milieux fréquentés : zones rocheuses, ruines, jusqu'à basse altitude

Période de présence : en général, toute l'année

Degré d'abondance : assez rare

Poste de chant : point dominant (corniche, escarpement…)

Période de chant : avril à juillet

Observation : assez difficile

Particularité : vol chanté occasionnel

Monticole de roche (Merle de roche)

Monticola saxatilis

Il est des oiseaux qui réunissent ces deux atouts que sont, à nos yeux, un beau plumage coloré et un chant musical. Le monticole (ou merle) de roche est l'un de ces privilégiés. Dans son univers à dominante minérale, plus ou moins mêlé de végétation, il tranche par son éclatante livrée tricolore. Par bonne lumière, le matin, c'est une vision qui peut arracher des cris d'admiration à ceux qui le découvrent comme à ceux qui le connaissent déjà mais sont tombés sous son charme.

Si l'on peut alors entendre le chant de ce bel oiseau, la séduction qu'il exerce atteint son apogée. Car le monticole a une voix pleine, chaude, dont il use au travers de phrases brèves, variées, où se glissent parfois des imitations. C'est en somme un curieux mélange entre la qualité de voix d'un merle et le rythme dansant d'une fauvette. Le monticole de roche apparaît déjà, on le voit, fort bien loti.

Pourtant, il dispose encore d'un attrait supplémentaire, son vol chanté. Lorsqu'il s'élève à quelques mètres, plumes blanches du dos ébouriffées, et évolue en ondulant, il émet un chant plus soutenu que celui qu'il lance posé. Du ciel vient alors un remarquable enchaînement mélodieux dont on voudrait qu'il ne prenne pas fin. Hélas ! le soliste aérien met bientôt un terme à sa prestation et gagne un perchoir en planant...

cd piste 52

Taille : 17-20 cm

Répartition géographique simplifiée : Europe méditerranéenne et centrale

Milieu fréquenté : régions montagneuses

Période de présence : d'avril à septembre

Degré d'abondance : peu commun

Postes de chant : corniches rocheuses, pitons rocheux...

Période de chant : d'avril à juin/juillet

Observation : assez difficile

Particularités : vol chanté, quelques imitations

Pipit des arbres

Anthus trivialis

Il est toujours agréable de retrouver le pipit des arbres au printemps. Sans lui, la lande ou le coteau calcaire piqués de quelques pins paraissent bien silencieux entre octobre et avril. Ce petit oiseau au plumage anodin – dont un examen plus minutieux révèle la délicatesse – occupe à lui seul une bonne part du paysage sonore des milieux où il s'installe à son retour d'Afrique.

Bien en vue au sommet d'un arbre ou d'un arbuste, il émet son joli chant sans ménager ses efforts. Au gré de l'inspiration, il lance des motifs faits de la répétition d'un son et rappelant les trilles émis par les canaris de cage, ou des sifflements musicaux prolongés, intervenant souvent comme une conclusion. L'agrément de ce chant suffirait à faire apprécier le pipit des arbres mais il ajoute une corde à son arc en pratiquant un vol chanté spectaculaire aux phases bien ritualisées. Après s'être fait entendre au bout d'une branche, il s'élève tout à coup silencieusement selon une trajectoire proche de la verticale, ailes vibrantes. Parvenu à une hauteur de quelques mètres, il commence à chanter puis, après avoir atteint l'apogée de sa course, amorce une descente oblique qui finit par le ramener à son point de départ ou sur un perchoir voisin. La descente, lente, ailes arquées en cloche, est accompagnée de sifflements purs, de longueur croissante. Même après avoir été observée à bien des reprises, cette prestation aérienne conserve un charme particulier.

cd piste 53

Taille : 15 cm

Répartition géographique simplifiée : presque toute l'Europe

Milieux fréquentés : bois, forêts, clairières, plantations ; apprécie les conifères

Période de présence : de mars/avril à octobre

Degré d'abondance : commun

Postes de chant : outre le chant aérien, arbres, arbustes

Période de chant : d'avril à juillet

Observation : facile

Rollier d'Europe

Coracias garrulus

Si le ramage du rollier était à l'égal de son plumage, ce serait à coup sûr l'un de nos plus merveilleux chanteurs. Seulement, si la nature l'a doté d'une livrée splendide, elle ne lui a accordé qu'une voix... de batracien ou, à la rigueur, de corbeau. On jurerait en effet entendre une grenouille lorsque ce si bel oiseau s'exprime. Une telle pauvreté est heureusement très largement compensée par la façon dont le rollier se comporte lorsqu'il « chante », car c'est en plein vol qu'il lance ses coassements ou croassements. Ses évolutions ont de quoi couper le souffle.

S'élevant à grande hauteur, il se lance dans des séries d'acrobaties d'une maîtrise et d'une souplesse remarquables. Pirouettes, piqués et ressources se succèdent, avant un piqué final, à grande vitesse, vers le sol. Toutes ces prouesses aériennes sur fond d'azur lumineux sont l'occasion d'admirer le secret du rollier : le superbe bleu violacé de l'avant de l'aile, masqué lorsque celle-ci est fermée. Le reste du plumage, à dominante bleue évoquant la turquoise et le lapis-lazuli, ne se révèle également qu'en plein vol. La beauté du tableau fait alors oublier la pauvreté du registre. Si l'on ajoute à cela la rareté de l'espèce en Europe, l'on accepte bien volontiers d'avoir l'oreille un peu heurtée.

Le document exceptionnel présenté en double page suivante montre la parade du rollier au moment où la femelle vient d'accepter l'insecte offert par son partenaire.

cd piste 54

Taille : 30 cm

Répartition géographique simplifiée : Europe méridionale et orientale (en France, arc méditerranéen)

Milieux fréquentés : campagne ouverte, sèche, avec arbres disséminés et bois clairs

Période de présence : de mai à août

Degré d'abondance : rare et localisé

Poste de chant : s'exprime vocalement en volant

Période de chant : surtout mai et juin

Observation : assez difficile

Rouge-queue noir

Phoenicurus ochruros

Ce petit amoureux des falaises et des éboulis rocheux a, au fil du temps, accepté de vivre à nos côtés. Il a ainsi étendu son domaine aux monuments et à leurs ruines, aux villages et, pour finir, aux villes elles-mêmes. Le pouvoir d'évocation jouant, le voir ou l'entendre au milieu de l'agitation citadine, c'est se transporter par la pensée dans un hameau de Vanoise ou au bord des Grands Causses.

Dans bien des régions, il disparaît complètement ou presque durant l'hiver, et son retour est l'un des premiers signes annonciateurs du printemps en marche. L'espèce est en effet l'une des plus précoces, précédant de plusieurs semaines la grande vague des migrateurs au long cours. Qu'il soit perché sur une corniche dominant une vallée ou posté sur une antenne de télévision, le rouge-queue noir lance son chant original dont la variabilité demeure modeste. D'ordinaire, il comprend un bref motif initial, un silence suivi d'un son évoquant un froissement de papier, du verre pilé ou le crissement de deux galets, puis un gazouillis sonore.

Nerveux, le rouge-queue change volontiers de poste de chant, s'interrompant parfois pour capturer au vol un insecte imprudent. Posé, il agite souvent sa queue orangée d'un tremblement bien typique.

cd piste 55

Taille : 14 cm

Répartition géographique simplifiée : presque toute l'Europe, sauf la Scandinavie

Milieux fréquentés : zones montagneuses, villes et villages, ruines

Période de présence : au sud et à l'ouest de son aire, presque toute l'année ; au nord et à l'est, de février/avril à octobre/novembre

Degré d'abondance : commun

Postes de chant : blocs rocheux, corniches, bâtiments

Période de chant : de mars/avril à juillet

Observation : très facile

Serin cini

Serinus serinus

Est-ce le bourdonnement d'un appareil électrique devenu fou ? Non, ce grésillement modulé, rapide, voire précipité, tombe du sommet d'un arbre et sort bien du gosier d'un oiseau. Comment des sons aussi forts et prolongés peuvent-ils être produits par une aussi petite boule de plumes ?

Infatigable, le serin cini, n'égale en rien son musical cousin détenu en cage, mais il le dépasse sans doute en matière d'endurance vocale. En outre, il possède une botte secrète dont il use volontiers. Quittant son perchoir, le voilà en effet qui, tout en continuant à chanter avec vigueur, se lance dans un circuit aérien apparemment sans plan précis. Durant quelques secondes, l'oiselet jaune acidulé se mue en un automate miniature aux battements d'ailes lents et saccadés. Lorsqu'il évolue ainsi, le cini ne peut guère passer inaperçu. C'est loin d'être le cas, par contre, quand il chante perché. Sa petite taille et son plumage strié le rendent assez difficile à repérer au milieu des branchages ou parmi les feuilles, en dépit de l'éclatant citron dont se pare sa poitrine.

Au total, même si le serin cini n'est pas un chanteur accompli, sa délicatesse et son comportement original suffisent à le rendre digne d'intérêt.

cd piste 56

Taille : 11 cm

Répartition géographique simplifiée : presque toute l'Europe, sauf les Îles britanniques et la Scandinavie

Milieux fréquentés : campagne, parcs, jardins, cimetières et vergers ; apprécie les conifères

Période de présence : à l'ouest et au sud de son aire, toute l'année ; au nord et à l'est, d'avril à octobre

Degré d'abondance : assez commun à commun

Postes de chant : en dehors du chant aérien, arbres, arbustes, bâtiments, fils aériens

Période de chant : presque toute l'année mais surtout d'avril à juillet

Observation : très facile

Particularité : vol chanté fréquent

Tarier pâtre

Saxicola torquata

Vêtu de son costume printanier de cérémonie, noir à faux col blanc et gilet orangé, le tarier pâtre s'est installé en bordure de la prairie où les vaches restent parfaitement indifférentes à son incessante activité. Perché tour à tour sur l'un des poteaux de la clôture, sur le fil barbelé ou sur l'une des hautes plantes épargnées par la dent du bétail, le tarier surveille son petit domaine. Aussitôt un alléchant insecte repéré, il pique sur sa proie qu'il capture en se laissant tomber au sol. Il a ensuite tôt fait de regagner un de ses postes de guet favoris. Sa femelle, au plumage plus terne, chasse activement pour son propre compte. La nidification est imminente et elle doit être en pleine forme, bien nourrie, pour supporter au mieux cette tâche harassante.

Plusieurs fois par jour, son compagnon se consacre au chant afin de rappeler à qui veut l'entendre qu'il est chez lui. Du haut d'un perchoir souvent élevé, bien en vue, il émet un petit babil aigrelet, pas désagréable mais pas non plus inoubliable. Là pourtant ne s'arrête pas sa façon de se faire remarquer. Quand l'envie lui en vient, il se lance dans une exhibition aérienne et musicale. Prenant son essor verticalement et parvenu à quelques mètres, il débite son chant tout en opérant des montées et des descentes saccadées. Au bout d'un moment, le ludion survolté juge que sa démonstration a assez duré et regagne un perchoir proche du sol.

cd piste 57

Taille : 12 cm

Répartition géographique simplifiée : presque toute l'Europe, sauf la Scandinavie et les pays baltes

Milieux fréquentés : campagne, ouverte ou avec quelques haies, friches herbeuses avec buissons épars, bord des routes

Période de présence : à l'ouest et au sud de son aire, toute l'année ou presque ; plus à l'est, de mars/avril à octobre/novembre

Degré d'abondance : commun à très commun

Postes de chant : grandes plantes, buissons, arbustes, poteaux, fils aériens

Période de chant : de février/mars à juillet

Observation : très facile

Particularité : bref vol chanté assez fréquent

Tarier des prés

Saxicola rubetra

Marqueté, damasquiné, ciselé : comment rendre au mieux l'impression qu'offre le dessus du plumage du tarier des prés, de la racine du bec à la naissance de la queue ? Les fins détails sombres, les menues mouchetures sont mises en valeur par la résille pâle des liserés de chaque petite plume. Mais ce n'est pas encore tout car le blanc du sourcil et de la moustache, allié à l'ocre de la poitrine peaufinent l'élégance de ce passereau à la posture dressée, toujours perché en évidence.

La voix ne dépare nullement l'ensemble. Elle manque certes de puissance mais pas de qualités. Le tarier des prés, au tempérament remuant, se montre un chanteur obstiné tant qu'il s'agit de rechercher une compagne et d'écarter les rivaux de ses arpents de prairie. C'est à cette période qu'il faut se hâter de profiter de ses prestations au cours desquelles il fait se succéder les courtes phrases sur un rythme soutenu. Aucune d'elles ne ressemble exactement aux autres. Le pot-pourri inventif fait alterner des notes sifflées, agréablement musicales, des sons plus rêches et des imitations du chant de diverses espèces, parfois très réussies.

Beaucoup moins souvent que le tarier pâtre, celui des prés, emporté par l'excitation du moment, peut se lancer dans un court vol chanté, porté par des battements d'ailes ralentis.

cd piste 58

Taille : 13 cm

Répartition géographique simplifiée : presque toute l'Europe

Milieux fréquentés : prés (surtout humides), alpages, friches herbeuses

Période de présence : d'avril à octobre

Degré d'abondance : peu commun à assez commun

Postes de chant : grandes plantes, buissons, arbustes, poteaux, fils aériens, arbres

Période de chant : avril à juillet

Observation : facile

Particularités : chante aussi en début et en fin de nuit ; imitations assez fréquentes ; vol chanté occasionnel

Tétras lyre

Lyrurus tetrix

Des sentiments mêlés, contradictoires, s'emparent du naturaliste privilégié lorsqu'il assiste, en montagne, à la parade du tétras lyre… La fascination, en premier lieu, devant tant de beauté. Esthétique des formes et des couleurs, agrément des roucoulements, étrangeté du spectacle et splendeur du cadre naturel, tout concourt à l'envoûtement, d'autant qu'il a fallu obtenir les indispensables autorisations et passer la fin de la nuit en altitude, allongé dans l'affût sommaire. Mais le plaisir a un goût amer quand on sait que cet oiseau splendide au comportement étrange est menacé dans le sud de son aire de répartition. Le tourisme « blanc » et son cortège de perturbations croissantes, hiver comme été, est en passe d'avoir raison de lui dans les Alpes – et la chasse au « petit coq de bruyère » n'arrange rien.

Pourtant, quel merveilleux patrimoine que cet oiseau aux parades étonnantes. Dès avant l'aube, les mâles se réunissent sur un espace dégagé, traditionnellement dévolu à cet usage. Leur queue en lyre redressée, exhibée, les ailes tombantes, ils vantent leurs qualités avec des allures compassées et de glougloutants roucoulements alternant avec des chuintements dignes de rapaces nocturnes. Attirée, une femelle rejoint le coq qu'elle juge le plus digne de la féconder. Les accouplements consommés, les tétras finissent par regagner les arbres protecteurs. L'arène semble soudain si vide que l'on pense avoir rêvé…

cd piste 59

Taille : 40 à 58 cm

Répartition géographique simplifiée : Nord de l'Europe et Alpes

Milieux fréquentés : clairières, marais et tourbières des régions montagneuses ; landes de plaine

Période de présence : toute l'année

Degré d'abondance : rare à peu commun ; localisé

Postes de chant : les « danses » se déroulent au sol ; peut chanter perché dans un arbre

Période de chant : de février/mars à juin

Observation : très difficile ; ne doit être menée que par des spécialistes respectueux

Tichodrome échelette

Tichodroma muraria

Le tichodrome échelette se mérite. Pour parvenir à l'observer dans son milieu naturel en période de reproduction, il faut accepter une marche en montagne, sac au dos, jumelles en bandoulière, et s'attendre à devoir patienter, peut-être en vain – à moins que l'on ne dispose d'informations précises sur la localisation de son territoire. Mais même dans ce cas de figure, l'attente peut être déçue et il faut bien se résigner à redescendre bredouille dans la vallée. Par contre, le jour où la chance sourit enfin, les regrets s'envolent aussitôt, remplacés par l'admiration béate.

Sur fond de paroi rocheuse plongée dans l'ombre, par endroits luisante d'eau infiltrée, le tichodrome volette tel un mouchoir rouge soumis au bon vouloir d'un vent capricieux. Soudain, il semble disparaître comme si l'ubac l'avait absorbé. Fermées, ses ailes masquent leurs plages carmin, rendant presque invisible l'oiseau grimpeur. Toutefois, des spasmes nerveux les entrouvrent bien vite et l'on peut à nouveau profiter de cette chaude couleur. La souplesse du vol, l'agilité de l'escalade et la beauté des larges ailes colorées placent très haut le tichodrome dans l'estime des observateurs. Ses qualités vocales, par contre, sont plus limitées. De courtes phrases aiguës, tantôt vibrations presque électriques, tantôt brefs sifflements, composent un chant assez rudimentaire que l'on se réjouit cependant d'entendre dans un cadre grandiose.

cd piste 60

Taille : 16 cm

Répartition géographique simplifiée : montagnes du Sud de l'Europe (en France, Alpes surtout, Pyrénées et Jura)

Milieux fréquentés : parois rocheuses

Période de présence : presque toute l'année ; perd de l'altitude en hiver

Degré d'abondance : assez rare, localisé

Poste de chant : parois rocheuses

Période de chant : avril à juin

Observation : difficile à très difficile

Tourterelle turque

Streptopelia decaocto

Voici moins d'un siècle, il fallait franchir le détroit du Bosphore pour pouvoir découvrir la tourterelle turque, d'origine asiatique, aujourd'hui présente dans presque toute l'Europe. La conquête massive s'est opérée sur un rythme assez soutenu, pour des raisons demeurées obscures, sans doute liées à des facteurs génétiques ayant favorisé un comportement pionnier et les facultés d'adaptation nécessaires pour le mettre en œuvre.

Vivant surtout au contact de l'homme, la tourterelle turque a presque partout été bien acceptée, probablement grâce au capital de sympathie dont bénéficient colombes et tourterelles, sans doute aussi en partie grâce à sa ressemblance frappante avec la tourterelle rieuse, largement détenue en captivité. Elle a ainsi pu prospérer à travers le continent européen sans rencontrer de grands obstacles. Et voilà comment le chant de cette gracieuse voyageuse retentit à présent d'Athènes à Londres et de Stockholm à Madrid. Ce roucoulement est très facile à mémoriser tant la tourterelle turque le répète avec conviction – au risque de le rendre vaguement lancinant… Souvent assez placide, elle se montre bien plus démonstrative en période nuptiale (ce qui peut correspondre à l'année entière dans certaines régions), s'élevant à la verticale à grands renfort de claquements d'ailes, puis se laissant redescendre en vol plané, tout en poussant un curieux vrombissement nasillard.

cd piste 61

Taille : 31-34 cm

Répartition géographique simplifiée : presque toute l'Europe

Milieux fréquentés : parcs, jardins, cimetières, villages, villes

Période de présence : toute l'année

Degré d'abondance : commune

Postes de chant : bâtiments, poteaux, fils aériens, arbres, haies

Période de chant : presque toute l'année, mais surtout de mars à août

Observation : très facile

Pigeons des forêts tourterelles
Roucoulent en si naturel

Jacques Charpentreau, Les Pigeons, *La Ville enchantée*, L'École, 1976.

Traquet motteux Traquet oreillard

Oenanthe oenanthe, Oenanthe hispanica

Entre ces deux traquets, le cousinage est évident. Mêmes ailes sombres, dessous blanc identique, queue à dessin blanc et noir analogue, tête dessinée de noir, avec un bandeau chez l'un (et parfois aussi chez l'oreillard), avec un masque chez l'autre. La posture dressée, la queue battante et une certaine nervosité sont également des caractères communs. Peut-être le traquet oreillard, le méridional aux tons plus chauds, de miel, de cannelle et de sable détient-il d'une courte tête la palme de la beauté, mais c'est affaire subjective... Au printemps, les mâles aux couleurs avivées sont tous deux splendides.

Leur parenté, déjà évoquée, se trouve renforcée lorsqu'ils chantent. Leurs productions, d'une manière générale, sont de très courtes phrases comprenant souvent des sons grinçants. Chez le motteux, le chant, haché, est fait de sons étranglés avec quelques bribes plus musicales. Chez l'oreillard, la composante gazouillée donne au chant une tonalité un peu plus musicale. Motteux et oreillard se lancent l'un comme l'autre dans des vols chantés, remarquables démonstrations d'exubérance.

cd pistes 62 (Traquet motteux) et 63 (Traquet oreillard)

Taille : 13,5 cm-16,5 cm

Répartition géographique simplifiée : traquet motteux, l'Europe ; traquet oreillard, Sud de l'Europe

Milieux fréquentés : traquet motteux, zones ouvertes herbeuses et pierreuses, landes ; traquet oreillard, zones rocheuses à buissons et arbustes épars

Période de présence : de mars/avril à septembre/octobre

Degré d'abondance : traquet motteux, commun à très commun ; traquet oreillard, peu commun, localisé

Postes de chant : murets, rochers, poteaux, fils aériens ; arbustes et arbres (surtout pour l'oreillard)

Période de chant : de mars à mai/juin

Observation : assez facile à facile

Particularités : vol chanté assez fréquent. L'oreillard peut être un remarquable imitateur.

Traquet rieur

Oenanthe leucura

Un observateur européen désireux de découvrir cet oiseau d'un noir profond de nuit sans lune, pouvait autrefois se contenter d'aller dans le Roussillon, au pied des Pyrénées orientales. Il lui faut à présent franchir la frontière car l'espèce n'est pas parvenue à se maintenir en France, où sa rareté avait contribué à la rendre quelque peu mythique. C'est donc sur les falaises de la Costa Brava ou sur les escarpements de la Costa del Sol, que l'on pourra rencontrer le traquet rieur, ou encore dans les nombreuses gorges qui entaillent parfois profondément les plateaux du centre de l'Espagne.

Sous la citadelle d'Alicante, ou ailleurs, sa taille respectable et son plumage noir peuvent le faire passer pour un merle, surtout si, vu de dessous et masqué en partie par une corniche, le blanc de l'arrière du corps et d'une partie de la queue reste invisible. Toutefois, dès l'envol, la confusion s'efface et l'aspect bicolore évoque alors un bonbon menthe-réglisse… La sobre beauté de son aspect est complétée par le comportement du traquet rieur. Un vol décidé, des hochements mesurés de la queue et un caractère farouche lui confèrent une allure attrayante. Le chant, composé de brefs gazouillis un peu grinçants, évoque une émission vocale de fauvette et est agréable à entendre, surtout si les caractéristiques acoustiques du site lui donnent une ampleur bienvenue.

cd piste 64

Taille : 17 cm

Répartition géographique simplifiée : en Europe, seulement en Espagne

Milieux fréquentés : pentes rocheuses à végétation clairsemée

Période de présence : toute l'année

Degré d'abondance : peu commun, localisé

Postes de chant : rochers, escarpements, corniches, buissons, arbustes

Période de chant : de mars à mai/juin

Observation : assez facile

Particularité : vol chanté papillonnant

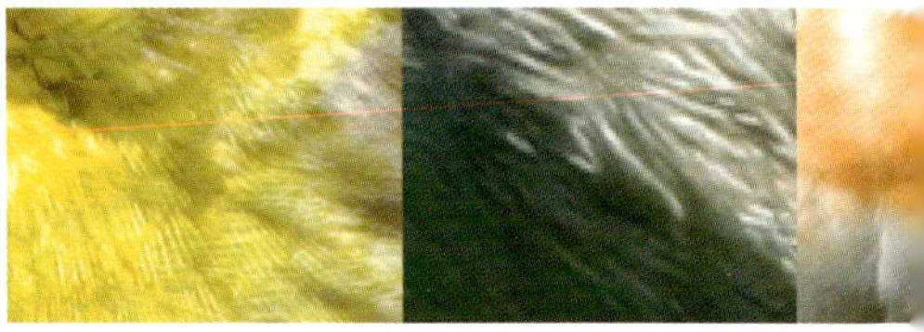

Annexes

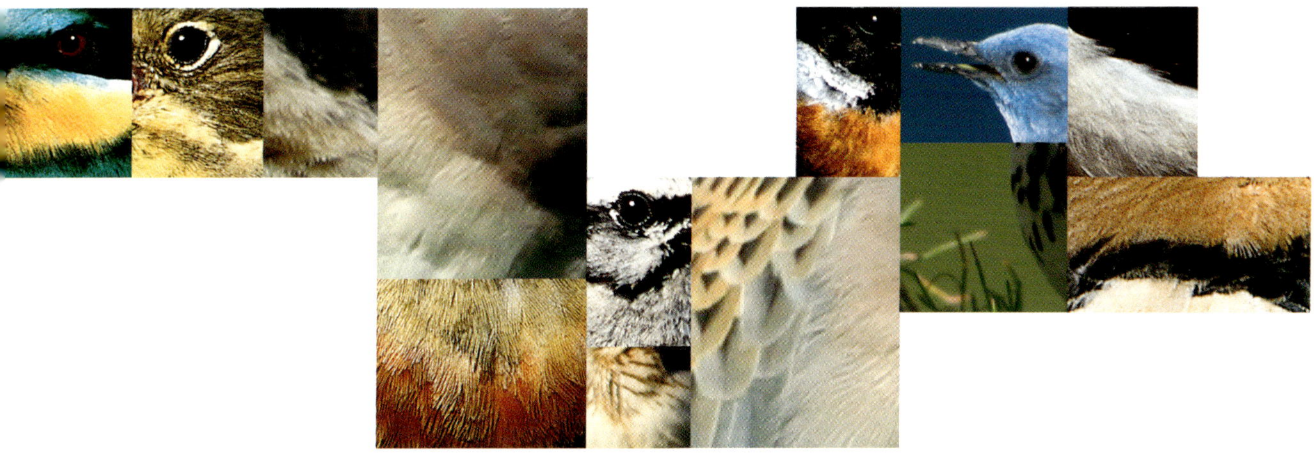

Les prises de vue

Alain Jouffray

Techniques de prises de vue

Plusieurs techniques ont été utilisées pour réaliser les photos de ce livre, toutes prises en milieu naturel avec des oiseaux sauvages.

L'approche. Elle consiste, au hasard des rencontres (ce qu'on appelle la « billebaude »), ou dans des lieux connus et repérés, à approcher les animaux en profitant de la configuration du terrain. Je l'ai assez peu utilisée, et seulement dans des cas particuliers, comme pour la photo d'oiseaux en vol, ou quand la légèreté de l'équipement s'avère indispensable. Dans ces cas, on se contente d'un objectif léger et éventuellement d'un camouflage limité au filet.

L'affût. C'est la technique principale, consistant à se dissimuler le mieux possible dans le paysage grâce à une cachette. J'utilise deux types d'affûts.

L'affût mobile. De l'extérieur on aperçoit un cube d'un mètre de côté, très rapide à installer, et qui peut être déplacé facilement quand on est à l'intérieur (notamment pour améliorer le cadrage des photos). Ne prenant pas de photos d'espèces sensibles au nid, je n'utilise pas les affûts fixes pré-installés avant la nidification et que l'on laisse en place jusqu'au départ des jeunes.

La voiture. C'est un affût mobile auquel beaucoup d'oiseaux sont habitués et qu'ils n'assimilent pas à l'homme. Cela nécessite un dispositif spécial pour fixer le téléobjectif sur la vitre, et bien sûr un filet de camouflage.

La repasse. Ce procédé permet d'attirer les oiseaux chanteurs près de mon affût en leur faisant entendre le chant de leur espèce, simulant ainsi un concurrent qui viendrait sur leur territoire.

Conditions de prises de vue

La météo. Très sensible à la beauté de la couleur des oiseaux, je ne réalise des prises de vue qu'en présence du soleil qui la met en valeur. Dans ce domaine, la région de Montpellier – où je prends beaucoup de mes photos – est un atout non négligeable.
Le vent, assez fréquent dans le Languedoc, est en revanche un facteur limitant : plus personne – pas plus les oiseaux que nous ! – n'arrive à localiser les chants, ni même parfois à les entendre…

La connaissance des espèces et du terrain. Que ce soit à l'approche, ou pour choisir l'emplacement d'un affût, rien ne doit se faire au hasard. Il faut certes connaître la biologie des espèces que l'on cherche, mais aussi observer au préalable, de loin, les individus que l'on souhaite photographier, pour repérer leurs comportements et habitudes. Pour les oiseaux chanteurs qui m'intéressent, c'est la recherche des points hauts (perchoirs) utilisés pour le chant, qui est capitale. Ceci permet d'avoir une idée du territoire de l'individu.

Précautions à prendre pour la repasse. Cette technique, si elle n'est pas aussi risquée que la photo au nid, peut toutefois de perturber les oiseaux. Elle est donc à utiliser avec modération. Si l'oiseau ne répond pas dans la première minute, il est inutile d'insister. Certains même, que l'on a localisés auparavant, se taisent et s'éloignent : il ne faut surtout pas récidiver. On peut avoir affaire, dans ce cas, à un mâle qui ne s'est pas encore fixé sur un territoire, et on risque de l'en chasser artificiellement. Parfois, l'oiseau vient tout de suite, observe l'affût, puis s'en va. Là aussi, inutile d'insister : il a compris que ce n'était qu'un leurre. Il est de même vain de revenir les jours suivants : l'individu ne réagira plus de la saison. D'autres, au contraire, s'approchent et se montrent aussitôt très coopératifs. Paradoxalement, il ne faut pas abuser de leur crédulité au risque de les fatiguer, mais plutôt savoir interrompre la repasse.

Autres techniques de prises de vue

La digiscopie. Avec les compacts numériques sont apparus de nouveaux outils de prise de vue : l'assemblage d'une longue-vue et d'un compact numérique permet de faire des photos bénéficiant d'un grossissement beaucoup plus important qu'avec un reflex classique. Avec les appareils numériques qui ont des capteurs de taille variable, on est obligé de raisonner en focale équivalente 24 x 36. Avec un 600 mm et un reflex Canon 300D, on obtient

une focale de 600 x 1,6 soit 960 mm (grossissement de 19,2). En digiscopie, on peut atteindre des focales de 2 000 à 4 000 mm (grossissement de 40 à 80) : pour le calculer, vous multipliez le grossissement de votre longue-vue par la focale équivalente de votre appareil 24 x 36.

On voit donc tout l'intérêt de cette technique qui autorise les mêmes cadrages en étant environ quatre fois plus loin, ce qui permet de diminuer d'autant le dérangement des oiseaux. Pour ce qui est des oiseaux chanteurs, cette technique est tout à fait adaptable à ceux qui se montrent sur un perchoir. Pour ceux qui chantent au milieu d'un buisson et qu'il faut inciter à se montrer, elle n'évitera pas d'utiliser la repasse, et dans ce cas la mobilité du sujet (par exemple, les roitelets, voir photo page 42) sera difficilement compatible avec la digiscopie qui nécessite un certain temps pour viser le sujet et faire la mise au point. Quant à la qualité des photos obtenues, si le piqué n'est pas encore tout à fait au niveau de la photographie traditionnelle, cette technique va très certainement encore s'améliorer et permettra d'obtenir des photos très convenables qui pourront être utilisées jusqu'au format 13 x 18, voire A4. Je rappelle son grand intérêt pour des espèces farouches ou fragiles.

Radiocommande. Dans le cas d'espèces farouches, on peut éviter l'installation d'un affût et le remplacer par un appareil photo muni d'un petit téléobjectif, fixé sur un pied et radiocommandé. Le photographe, à une centaine de mètres de là, contrôle la visée dans un oculaire de type caméscope, dirige l'objectif sur 30° en azimut et 180° en rotation et déclenche avec une radiocommande. Ceci nécessite d'avoir repéré un site précis où vient se percher régulièrement l'oiseau. Un tel matériel peut être construit par un électronicien. Mais un fabricant le propose actuellement dans le commerce (adresses p. 158).

Traitement des images

La photographie n'a pas pour but de restituer la réalité, mais d'essayer de rendre par l'outil photographique ce que le photographe a vu et ressenti sur le terrain, comme un peintre utilise sa palette et ses pinceaux. C'est pourquoi il m'a toujours paru légitime, à partir de l'enregistrement qu'a réalisé l'appareil, de le corriger, de recadrer, d'adapter les contrastes, la densité… Autrefois, au laboratoire, on utilisait différentes techniques sophistiquées de masquage. Maintenant le laboratoire numérique, c'est-à-dire l'ordinateur avec un logiciel de traitement d'image, permet de réaliser tous ces travaux beaucoup plus facilement. Ceci s'applique aux photos numériques, mais aussi à nos bonnes vieilles diapositives que l'on peut scanner puis traiter de la même façon.

Il ne s'agit pas, en ce qui me concerne, de « truquer » les images. Aucune des photos de ce livre n'a été truquée : par exemple aucune photo d'oiseau n'a été déplacée du milieu où elle a été prise, aucun fond n'a été placé artificiellement derrière l'oiseau.

Précisions sur les photographies

Presque toutes les photos de ce livre ont été prises à l'affût (sauf deux à l'approche et deux au vol). Les objectifs utilisés étaient des 600 mm (ou des 400 mm pour les photos à l'approche et au vol). En 1992, je suis passé de Nikon à Canon en raison de la qualité de l'autofocus. Depuis 2002, j'utilise des boîtiers numériques qui présentent le gros avantage d'offrir gratuitement un multiplicateur de focale de coefficient 1,6.

Les photos des tétras lyres ont été réalisées avec l'autorisation du parc national du Mercantour.

DANS LES ARBRES

16
Accenteur mouchet
L'Écot
Savoie (73)
16 juillet 2003

18
Chardonneret élégant
Gorges de la Nesque
Vaucluse (84)
29 avril 2003

20
Fauvette à tête noire
Montpellier
Hérault (34)
12 avril 2003

22
Grimpereau des jardins
Montpellier
Hérault (34)
11 mars 2000

22
Grimpereau des bois
Autrans
Isère (38)
5 mars 1993

26
Grive musicienne
Montpellier
Hérault (34)
16 février 2003

28
Loriot d'Europe
Montbazin
Hérault (34)
16 juin 1996

30
Merle noir
Autrans
Isère (38)
2 janvier 1998

32
Mésange bleue
Lattes
Hérault (34)
12 janvier 1994

34
Mésange charbonnière
Autrans
Isère (38)
23 février 2003

36
Pinson des arbres
Autrans
Isère (38)
31 mars 2003

38
Pouillot véloce
L'Isle Crémieu
Isère (38)
17 mai 2004

38
Pouillot fitis
Nogent-sur-Vernisson
Loiret (45)
7 mai 2004

40
Pouillot de Bonelli
Termignon
Savoie (73)
8 juin 2003

42
Roitelet huppé
Le Boréon
Alpes-Maritimes (06)
30 avril 2002

42
Roitelet à triple bandeau
Autrans
Isère (38)
30 avril 1996

44
Rouge-gorge familier
Montpellier
Hérault (34)
11 octobre 2003

48
Rouge-queue à front blanc
Montpellier
Hérault (34)
8 mai 2003

50
Sittelle torchepot
Chartreuse de Valbonne
Gard (30)
1er avril 2003

52
Verdier d'Europe
Autrans
Isère (38)
5 mars 1984

DANS LES BUISSONS

56
Bruant jaune
Autrans
Isère (38)
8 août 2002

58
Bruant ortolan
Arboras
Hérault (34)
2 mai 1997

60
Bruant proyer
Guzargues
Hérault (34)
27 avril 2003

62
Bruant zizi
Montbazin
Hérault (34)
30 mai 2003

64
Cisticole des joncs
Portiragnes
Hérault (34)
11 mai 2003

66
Fauvette grisette
L'Isle Crémieu
Isère (38)
17 mai 2004

68
Fauvette mélanocéphale
Montpellier
Hérault (34)
15 mars 1997

70
Fauvette passerinette
Massif de la Gardiole
Hérault (34)
14 avril 1991

72
Fauvette pitchou
Saint-Jean-de-Védas
Hérault (34)
1er juin 1991

74
Gorgebleue à miroir
Île de Ré
Charente-Maritime (17)
22 mai 1982

76
Hypolais polyglotte
Guzargues
Hérault (34)
20 mai 2003

78
Linotte mélodieuse
Portiragnes
Hérault (34)
12 mai 2002

80
Pie-grièche écorcheur
Autrans
Isère (38)
5 août 2003

80
Pie-grièche à tête rousse Montbazin
Hérault (34)
2 juillet 2002

82
Rossignol philomèle
Montpellier
Hérault (34)
17 avril 1993

86
Rousserolle effarvatte
Forêt de la Reine
Meurthe-et-Moselle (54)
19 mai 2002

88
Rousserolle turdoïde
Portiragnes
Hérault (34)
11 mai 2003

90
Rousserolle verderolle
L'Écot
Savoie (73)
7 juin 2003

92
Tourterelle des bois
Montbazin
Hérault (34)
7 juillet 2003

94
Troglodyte mignon
Palavas-les-Flots
Hérault (34)
30 janvier 1993

AUTRES PERCHOIRS

98
Alouette lulu
Arboras
Hérault (34)
25 avril 2004

100
Alouette des champs
Col de Larche
Alpes-de-H^{te}-Pr. (04)
20 juin 2003

102
Bruant fou
Extremadure
Espagne
1er mai 1991

104
Cincle plongeur
Gorges d'Engins
Isère (38)
20 février 2004

106
Étourneau sansonnet
Montpellier
Hérault (34)
1er février 2003

108
Guêpier d'Europe
Portiragnes
Hérault (34)
10 juillet 2001

110
Hirondelle rustique
Portiragnes
Hérault (34)
2 mai 2003

112
Huppe fasciée
Portiragnes
Hérault (34)
12 mai 2002

114
Monticole bleu
Banyuls
Pyrénées-O^{les} (66)
3 mai 2003

116
Monticole de roche
Arboras
Hérault (34)
15 mai 1993

118
Pipit des arbres
Col de Larche
Alpes-de-H^{te}-Pr. (04)
19 juin 2003

120
Rollier d'Europe
Saint-Gely-du-Fesc
Hérault (34)
5 mai 2002

124
Rouge-queue noir
Montpellier
Hérault (34)
12 avril 2003

126
Serin cini
Autrans
Isère (38)
29 juillet 2002

128
Tarier pâtre
Guérande
Loire-Atlantique (44)
5 juin 1984

130
Tarier des prés
L'Orgère
Savoie (73)
9 juin 2003

132
Tétras lyre
Parc du Mercantour
(06) et (04)
30 avril 2002

136
Tichodrome
Gorges d'Engins
Isère (38)
17 juillet 1988

138
Tourterelle turque
Île de Ré
Charente-Maritime (17)
21 août 2003

140
Traquet motteux
Col de Larche
Alpes-de-H^{te}-Pr. (04)
21 juin 2003

140
Traquet oreillard
Arboras
Hérault (34)
1er juillet 1994

142
Traquet rieur
Matmata
Tunisie
12 mars 2003

La prise de sons

Fernand Deroussen

L'écoute demande beaucoup d'attention. Mieux vaut rester en poste fixe, respirer plutôt par la bouche, tranquillement, car les parois nasales proches du système auditif entraînent à chaque respiration des perturbations sonores, éviter les vêtements bruyants; on peut aussi grâce à ses deux mains placées en coupe derrière les oreilles amplifier l'écoute.

Le principal ennemi de la prise de son est le moteur sous toutes ses formes : avions (éviter les couloirs aériens : carte disponible mais changeante), voitures, trains et même tracteurs, sans oublier les tronçonneuses. Donc, il faut savoir attendre le bon moment ou trouver les lieux tranquilles.
L'enregistrement permet de fixer un chant entendu pour le plaisir et de le restituer à volonté, ainsi que de constituer une base d'informations utile à l'identification des espèces.

Attention ! vous intervenez durant la période de reproduction : l'approche doit être discrète. Évitez le recours à la « repasse » : du point de vue du preneur de sons, mieux vaut un chant lointain mais naturel qu'un chant provoqué, court et quelque peu artificiel.

Trois techniques d'enregistrement

L'affût. Utilisation de longs câbles. Ce procédé de contrôle à distance exige de la patience.

Le piège à sons. On installe un matériel compact sur un site repéré et l'on revient en fin d'enregistrement. Vous voyant partir, l'oiseau reprend son activité normale avec des comportements naturels réservant parfois des surprises. Inconvénients : météo, écoute ultérieure longue et fastidieuse, pas de contrôle technique du système.

Le reportage. Plutôt réservé à la parabole (voir plus loin) ; mêle balade et approche; enregistrements immédiats.

Page de droite :
fauvette des jardins
(chant n° 4 sur le CD)

Les enregistreurs

Les magnétophones à bande et à cassette analogiques sont dépassés : place au numérique, mais attention ! L'enregistreur est là pour acquérir l'information provenant du micro et doit pouvoir enregistrer les signaux parfois aigus qu'émettent les oiseaux. Il doit restituer une bande passante de 20 Hz à 20KHz.

Deux formats de baladeurs ont été utilisés depuis dix ans : le DAT (Digital Audio Tape) et le Minidisc. Le DAT est abandonné par les constructeurs : pièces détachées et cassettes DAT manqueront bientôt… Le Minidisc, abordable, a encore de l'avenir : c'est un très bon enregistreur pour les oiseaux. Les nouveaux formats – informatiques : disques durs enregistrables et baladeurs avec cartes-mémoire – sont appelés à un grand succès.

Une précision : on n'utilise jamais de MP3 ou de système compressé pour enregistrer le chant des oiseaux. Il est donc indispensable d'acquérir un magnétophone ou un baladeur en format non compressé (Wave ou PCM) ; cette exigence incontournable vous guidera pour choisir parmi les éventuels futurs systèmes.

Les microphones

Le microphone est le premier lien avec le chant de l'oiseau, sa qualité est primordiale et l'essentiel du budget doit lui être consacré. Il est impossible d'améliorer un mauvais signal sonore grâce à une chaine hifi, un baladeur ou un ordinateur. De plus, le chant de l'oiseau, en raison de sa vitesse d'exécution et de la complexité de son signal, demande un matériel qui puisse supporter de tels changements.

Le micro nu. Seul ou en couple pour restituer la stéréophonie, il est utilisé en affût au bout d'un câble pouvant atteindre 100 m. Difficile à mettre en œuvre – repérage, aléas météorologiques, attente, longueur du câble –, c'est pourtant la garantie d'un son de qualité, naturel, sans pollution sonore.

Le micro-canon. Restitution naturelle agréable mais proximité risquée dans le cas d'oiseaux nicheurs. Ce n'est pas un amplificateur de son : il capte le signal provenant de face et abaisse tous les sons provenant des côtés ou de l'arrière.

La parabole. Véritable « téléobjectif » sonore, elle restitue le chant d'un oiseau éloigné grâce à une réelle amplification. Le signal sonore frappe le fond de la coupole, rebondit et se concentre (effet parabolique) sur la capsule du microphone disposé à l'envers.
Dans le cas des oiseaux, le signal est parfaitement restitué avec parfois quelques intermodulations et distorsions.
Les bruits de manipulation et les insectes qui tapent sur la coupole sont de petits inconvénients. Un filet recouvrant la parabole permet de faire glisser le vent.

Autres matériels

Un casque servant à contrôler la dynamique et la qualité de l'enregistrement ; des câbles de rechange (en avoir toujours un d'avance) ; des bonnettes antivent, indispensables pour recouvrir les micros nus.

Bibliographie

Bossus, A. et Charron, F.,
Guide des chants d'oiseaux d'Europe occidentale. Delachaux et Niestlé
ISBN 2-603-01276-2 Paris, 2003.
Le guide de référence d'apprentissage au chant des oiseaux (avec 2 CD).

Elliott, L., *Music of the birds*
Houghton Mifflin Company
ISBN 0-618-00697-4
Boston, New York, 1999 (avec un CD)

Sample, G., *Bird songs & calls of Britain and Northern Europe*. Collins Field guide
ISBN 0-00-220037-6 London, 1996
(avec 2 CD)

Discographie

Catalogue L'Oreille Verte

Catalogue Sittelle

La revue Sonatura, revue sonore trimestrielle par abonnement dédiée aux sons de la nature et à l'enregistrement.
Président : Fernand Deroussen
Association loi 1901.
24, rue de Paris
94220 Charenton-le-Pont
www.sonatura.com
e-mail : info@sonatura.com

Quelques adresses

Jama Électronique, matériel spécialisé pour la photographie animalière
22, rue de la Fraternité
12100 Millau
05 65 60 76 01
www.jama.fr

Photo&Nature
10, rue Parmentier
06100 Nice
04 93 98 24 36
www.photo-nature.fr

Scoop, la boutique du chasseur de sons
30, rue David d'Angers
75019 Paris

Le Microphone
18, rue Victor-Massé
75009 Paris

Paraboles Telinga
http://www.ceba.fr

Index alphabétique

Source d'émerveillement et de plaisir, les oiseaux sont aussi et avant tout des êtres vivants, fragiles et souvent menacés. Leurs chants nous réjouissent et nous émeuvent. Mais pour que la tourterelle et le pinson, le rossignol et la mésange continuent à jeter leurs notes au fil des saisons, il convient de les respecter et de préserver l'environnement dans lequel ils vivent.

Partenaire de cet ouvrage, la **Ligue pour la Protection des Oiseaux** s'est donné pour mission la protection des oiseaux et des écosystèmes dont ils dépendent et, en particulier, la faune et la flore qui y sont associées. La LPO agit au quotidien en France et à l'étranger en faveur de la biodiversité.

LPO La Corderie Royale – BP 90263 – 17305 ROCHEFORT CEDEX
Tél. (+33) 05.46.82.12.34 – Fax (+33) 05.46.83.95.86 – www.lpo.fr

Responsable éditoriale Odile Perrard
avec la collaboration de Virginie Freyder
Responsable artistique Sabine Houplain
Conception de la maquette et mise en page Dune Lunel aka Modzilla!
Fabrication Florent Roger et Marc Chalmin
Suivi de fabrication du CD Hervé Millancourt / L'Oreille Verte
Relecture correction Dominique Choffel

Photogravure : APS Chromostyle
Achevé d'imprimer en France par Mame Imprimeurs à Tours
Dépôt légal : 56097, avril 2005
ISBN : 2.85120.612.5
65 4101 5-01